POLITICAL CRIMINALITY

Volume 136, Sage Library of Social Research

RECENT VOLUMES IN
SAGE LIBRARY OF SOCIAL RESEARCH

POLITICAL CRIMINALITY

The Defiance and Defense of Authority

Austin T. Turk

Volume 136
SAGE LIBRARY OF
SOCIAL RESEARCH

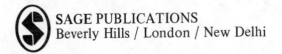

SAGE PUBLICATIONS
Beverly Hills / London / New Delhi

To

Ruth-Ellen Marie Jacqueline Grimes

For information address:

SAGE Publications, Inc.
275 South Beverly Drive
Beverly Hills, California 90212

SAGE Publications India Pvt. Ltd.
C-236 Defence Colony
New Delhi 110 024, India

SAGE Publications Ltd
28 Banner Street
London EC1Y 8QE, England

Printed in the United States of America

Library of Congress Cataloging in Publication Data

Main entry under title:

Turk, Austin T., 1924-
    Political criminality.

    (Sage library of social research; v. 136)
    (Includes bibliographical references and index.
    1. Political crimes and offenses. 2. Social
control. 3. Police—Political aspects. I. Title
II. Series.
HV6254.T87   1982   364.1'31   81-18531
ISBN 0-8039-1772-4   AACR2
ISBN 0-8039-1773-2 (pbk.)

FIRST PRINTING

pd
12-20-83

CONTENTS

PREFACE

Along with many other people, social scientists and their students have in recent years become increasingly aware that an adequate understanding of lawbreaking necessarily includes understanding how it is related to the creation, interpretation, and enforcement of laws. While surely no one would seriously argue that there is no offensive *behavior* in the absence of legal labeling, many have come to see that there is no *criminality* of behavior unless an individual's actual, imputed, or potential actions involve him in trouble with officials empowered to define and handle lawbreaking. Furthermore, many have become aware that the creation and use of laws directing and authorizing the exercise of such power have fundamentally political origins, aims, and effects. These basic insights regarding the definitional nature of criminality and the political nature of legality are especially crucial for understanding political criminality.

The defiance and defense of legal authority in modern states is the stuff of everyday news; but one quickly finds that relatively little systematic research has yet been done by social scientists on either political criminality or political policing, much less on their intimate linkage. To be sure, considerable attention has been given to revolutions, riots, and other forms of collective "domestic" violence, usually from a control or counterinsurgency perspective. However, such work has nearly always neglected the more routine aspects of political criminality and policing in settings characterized as "normal" or "stable" rather than "explosive" or "in turmoil." This volume is designed not only to introduce the reader to the study of political criminality and policing, but to emphasize the point that they are intrinsic to the process of conflict by which the ongoing political organization of social life is accomplished.

Apart from those who refuse to accept the definitional nature of criminality and the political nature of legality, some who accept the implied relativity of criminality and legality as a general principle find it hard to maintain the principle when it comes to political criminality and policing. Angered or frightened by what they may perceive as treachery, subversion, or terrorism on the one hand, or as oppression, exploitation, or corruption on the other, they may suspend the principle in order to express in morally absolute tones either their approval of those who defy the power of the state and their condemnation of "crimes of government against the people," or their approval of those exercising the power of the state and their condemnation of "rebels, anarchists, and terrorists." Granted that there are times when the expression of moral indignation or political faith is honorable and necessary, neither effective defiance nor effective defense of legal authority is likely without knowledge biased as little as possible by one's preferences and aversions. Accordingly, this book is intended to promote the scientific investigation of political criminality and policing, rather than partisan commitment to one or the other.

Many friends, colleagues, and students have been interested in my effort to understand the behavioral and definitional realities of political criminality. Whether agreeing or disagreeing, their reactions and comments have contributed greatly to the analytical rigor and empirical anchoring of my postulates, generalizations, and speculations. William Chambliss, David Greenberg, Gary Marx, Richard Moran, Richard Quinney, Edward Sagarin, Clifford Shearing, James F. Short, Jr., and Philip Stenning deserve special recognition for their efforts to help me avoid errors and distortions. I am grateful to Marvin Wolfgang and his colleagues and students of the Center for Studies in

Criminology and Criminal Law, University of Pennsylvania, for providing me with a stimulating and congenial environment in which to complete this book. The needed year of freedom from my regular academic duties was made possible by a sabbatical research grant from the University of Toronto and a research leave fellowship awarded by the Social Sciences and Humanities Research Council of Canada.

CHAPTER 1

INTRODUCTION

Conflict cannot be excluded from social life.
. . . "Peace" is nothing more than a change in
the form of the conflict or in the antagonists
or in the objects of the conflict, or finally
in the chances of selection.
                    Max Weber (1949: 27)

Both reactionaries and revolutionaries have dreamed of a human society in which everyone is profoundly concerned with the happiness and welfare of everyone else. No one coerces or exploits anyone else, and all know freedom, love, and the joy of life. Relationships are freely created and totally open. There are no real conflicts; whatever misunderstandings may arise are soon resolved by mutual enlightenment. Goodness, truth, and beauty are the same for everyone because they are commonly understood and appreciated. Life is unclouded by any basis for distrusting, fearing, or hurting any other person.

That is the dream. Without it there is little hope for anything more than the "nasty, brutish, and short" life of Hobbes's bleak vision of the "war of every man against every man." Lacking the dream of a perfect society, people settle for whatever particular constellation of miseries they find themselves in by becoming merely competitors, sycophants, or parasites. For those who cannot endure the idea that social Darwinism is all life can offer, there are the consolations of magic, other-worldly religious fatalism—and madness.

Social reality is, of course, neither the utopian dream nor the bleak vision, but a fascinating composite of both—of "dreams"

11

and "realities," "dreamers" and "realists." The great majority of people both dream and try to get along as best they can. For the most part, we dream a little and settle a lot. Neither our selfishness and ruthlessness nor our altruism and compassion are total and consistent. In practice, we may hope vaguely for a better world for everyone, while behaving so as to make sure that we and ours will survive and prosper regardless of what may happen to others. Somewhere beyond the Hobbesian war and despair, but short of the dream society, lies real social life—where the tension between the war and the dream is expressed in that fundamental dimension of human relatedness which is the process of political organization.

The Process of Political Organization

The political organization of social life results from and is characterized by conflicts (often more implicit than explicit) among different individuals or groups of people trying to improve and ensure their life chances—that is, the likelihood that *they,* at least, will have the means and opportunities to realize their respective visions of the good life. Although conflicts between individuals sometimes play a significant part in instigating or aggravating wider conflicts, inter*personal* conflicts as such appear to be essentially irrelevant for understanding the systemic nature of inter*group* conflicts (Rapoport, 1974: 133-173). Therefore, for present purposes we may safely limit our attention to conflicts among people grouped together in some degree, whether by circumstances, their own inclinations and preferences, or the labeling behavior of other people.

Such groupings (anything from couples, families, tribes, or communities to churches, corporations, social classes, or nations) may arise from any perceived or imputed difference among human beings; and the conflicts among and within them may vary greatly in the extent to which they are directly and overtly linked to the material life chances of the people involved. Clearly the most consequential groupings are those defined by differences in the material resources available to members, and most directly involved in implicit and explicit conflicts over the terms of allocation. The fewer material resources available, the less chance of obtaining and enjoying life's goods, whatever they may be. Except, perhaps, for mystics genuinely indifferent to personal and intellectual survival, even persons whose primary concerns are nonmaterial—religious salvation, esthetic expression, scientific comprehension, or whatever—need material resources to sustain and further their enterprises. Every human effort and experience costs something, requires some expenditure of energy. This implies that any given distribution or projected redistribution of resources can be expected to facilitate certain enterprises, impede some, and preclude others.

For instance, the capitalist world system (Wallerstein, 1976; Gunder Frank, 1967) promotes the growth of multinational corporate power above all other concerns—including the development of Third World national and regional economies and, especially to the point, alternatives to Western world views and lifestyles. As financial strategies, changing production technologies, and/or shifting markets dictate the channeling of resources away from some areas and enterprises to others, the life chances of the people involved improve or deteriorate in nonmaterial as well as material terms. While it has long been understood that rapid and, especially, uneven economic development is incompatible with many traditional beliefs and ways of life (Spicer, 1952; Mead, 1955; Lerner, 1958; Finkle and Gable, 1966), it is even clearer—from the histories of colonized and exploited peoples everywhere—that impoverishment corrodes and ultimately destroys the faiths, moralities, sensibilities, and knowledge by and for which people live.

Individuals may, of course, be unaware of participating in conflictual intergroup relationships, may value intangible goods far more than material resources, and/or may be unconcerned about the implications of their activities for the distributing of life chances. Sufficiently insulated from contradicting and threatening experiences, they may never realize that in a finite world of distinctions between "them" and "us," simply to be alive is to be involved in intergroup struggles over the means and terms of collective existence. Mergers and alliances are forever changing the alignments, and overwhelmingly supportive and trusting relationships are possible—at least among individuals. Nevertheless, material resources are not infinite, and there are human limits to empathy and commitment (though we seldom love enough to reach them). Recognition of these constraints leads to the sociological postulate that any social relationship has a conflictual, or "competitive," dimension (Simmel, 1955: 15; Collins, 1975: 60, 89), and the theory that the most fundamental empirical sources and implications of the conflict lie in the distribution and redistribution of material life chances (Marx and Engels, 1962: 362-364, 368-369; Weber, 1968: 38-40; Dahrendorf, 1979).

While any social relationship is by definition organized in some sense or other, to organice it *politically* is to construct and enforce explicit or implicit rules for making and implementing decisions about how the relationship is to be lived. The relative political power of a party in a social relationship is, then, definable as the degree to which that party is able to control the procedures for deciding what is to be done. From a couple deciding whether or not to marry to a nation deciding whether or not to go to war, the party whose arguments, promises, threats, or other manipulative actions disproportionately influence the eventual decision may be said to have demonstrated the greater political power.

Having power in a social relationship means having some relative control over the resources available to persons in that relationship. *Using* power means demonstrating that control by altering the range of relative attractiveness of behavioral options open to others in the relationship. Though the measurement of power continues to be a horrendous problem for social scientists, for analytical purposes five forms or dimensions of power may be distinguished in terms of five kinds of resource control:

(1) control of the means of direct physical violence, or *war* or *police* power;
(2) control of the production, allocation, and/or use of material resources, or *economic* power;
(3) control of decision-making processes, or *political* power;
(4) control of definitions of and access to knowledge, beliefs, and values, or *ideological* power; and
(5) control of human attention and living time, or *diversionary* power (Turk, 1976).

Depending on the nature of the relationship, people do not necessarily know or care how much power they have, and may be unaware of using any power in relating to one another. Either intimacy or distance may preclude awareness or concern. People in love are wise not to dwell on the fact that they have and use tremendous power—especially diversionary and ideological—to shape and sustain their relationship. At the other extreme, social class relationships and legal authority are most secure when few people know or concern themselves with the mechanisms by which power is allocated and mobilized in the absence of direct interaction and open confrontation (Baldus, 1975).

The concept of political organization differs from the more general one of social organization in that it focuses attention upon the manipulative devices by which people try to forestall or resolve conflicts with "them" on terms favorable to "us"— including all devices from the most subtle and gentle to the most obvious and cruel, and all forms of dominance and control from the most democratic to the most autocratic. Clearly, the process of political organization can be observed in any social relationship, any grouping from a friendship to an industry to a league of nations. However, insofar as a superordinate position within a territory is achieved by some grouping or alliance of groupings, it appears (as Machiavelli so well understood) that both the achievement and the maintenance of such a position depend upon the effective use of the full range of manipulative techniques, culminating in the formal control mechanisms of the polity, or state, with their main locus in the authorization (prototypically in the criminal law) and organization (prototypically in the police and army) of the means of violence.

The Political Organization of Societies

A fully elaborated conflict analysis of a given society would identify many isomorphisms between the processes by which the polity and the less inclusive or overriding social groupings in it are created, sustained, and changed or destroyed. A full analysis would also trace the functional or contradictory relationships between the polity and subpolity levels of political organization. Moreover, a complete analysis would extend to the geopolitical and other features of the social and natural environments in which the society is embedded, and by which the theoretical or legal autonomy of the polity is made empirically relative. The objective in this small volume is far more modest: to provide a general introductory analysis of what is viewed as the key to understanding the process of political organization at the societal or polity level, that is, the relationship between political criminality and political policing.

To begin, whatever else is or might be true of politically organized societies, or polities, the historical reality is that they are hierarchical. The emergent distribution of power among the various groupings involved in the process of organization is unequal. At least in relative terms, some are winners and some are losers. Moreover, as Jesus, Marx, and many other social analysts have observed, the initially advantaged are better able than the initially disadvantaged to improve and ensure their life chances by extending their control of resources—usually at the expense of the disadvantaged. "For to him who has will more be given; and from him who has not, even what he has will be taken away" (Mark 4:24 RSV). That is, emergent power differences tend to become established ones, a process implying the stabilization and probable widening of initial differences in life chances—that is, the creation of a stratification system.

As the structuring of power becomes increasingly explicit, a new and basic differentiation in terms of unequal power appears that between *authorities* and *subjects*. Authorities are those who make and try to implement decisions affecting the polity as a whole; subjects are those who are affected by, but do not themselves make, such strategic decisions (Turk, 1969: 32-33; Dahrendorf, 1959: 290-295).

To be sure, the analytical distinction between authorities and subjects requires much care in its use, minimally because of (1) the divisions of labor and power, and the differences of perception and interest, among different kinds and levels of officials; (2) the frequent discrepancies between public, formal, official, or apparent power and private, informal, unofficial, and real power; (3) the variable power of subjects, especially as variations in their power are related to variations in specific issues and concerns; and (4) the complexities of determining the nature and effects of (especially "meaningful") political participation (see Miliband, 1969: 131-159). For example, the extent to which the ordinary police—as opposed to the Gestapo—of Nazi Germany were "authorities" in regard to the making and implementation of the "final solution" is clearly an empirical question, the answer to which varies from place to place and time to time (Peterson, 1969: 125-148, 268; see also Delarue, 1964: 27-166). Nonetheless, the essential point stands: that decisions affecting the life chances of all members of a polity are made by some, not all, members.

The transforming of power into authority is a process that is always problematic and never finished, and is therefore reversible. Elsewhere, in discussing the nature of legal order, I have characterized the process in "ideal type" terms as historical movement toward realization of the following conditions: military dominance, established jurisdiction, institutionalized policing, demographic continuity, and ideological hegemony (Turk, 1972a: 173-175).

MILITARY DOMINANCE

The most elementary form of the struggle for survival and control is resolved by the military ascendance of one party, including coalitions, over all others in the arena. At this level of conflict the arena is always territorial, whatever other features it may have. Who shall occupy the land, who has sole or prior claim to its resources—these are the questions answered by the demonstration of military superiority. Once achieved, military dominance is used to eliminate, as far as possible, the remaining military potential of the conquered. Monopoly of the means of collective violence on any militarily significant scale removes the possibility of reversing the military decision.

It was not merely indifference to the everyday lives of everyday people that led historians for so long to write almost as though waging and surviving warfare were the main things that went on in former societies, and as if the most important figures were always those who led people into and out of wars. Nor was it simply a taste for "blood and iron" that led thinkers from Polybius and Ibn Khaldun to Gumplowicz, Ratzenhofer, and Oppenheimer to emphasize military conquest in their evolutionary theories of the *polis* and state (for a brief review of these theories, see Becker and Barnes, 1952: 702-730). Excepting perhaps a few extremely tiny and isolated tribes in Borneo and elsewhere, the people of every known society have had to meet the threat of intergroup violence to their collective survival. Andreski (1968) has provided impressive comparative and historical evidence for the thesis that societies failing to develop adequate institutions for controlling and mobilizing the means of violence will probably succumb to internal war, conquest, or both.

No society, however, has managed to eliminate completely the possibility of violent challenge. Apart from the continuing dangers of conventional wars and nuclear threats, collective violence repeatedly erupts not only where regimes are militarily weak and politically shaky (such as India and throughout east-central Africa), but also in nations (such as the United States and China) characterized by the most awesome concentrations of military and political power the world has yet seen. Even so tightly monitored and regimented a polity as the Soviet Union has a long history of sometimes violent Ukrainian, Georgian, Moslem, and other ethnic-nationalist resistance to Russification and Politburo directives (Thaden, 1971: 356, 470-472, 506-510, 572-573; Massell, 1968).

To the extent that stability in military terms is in fact established in an area, it at least becomes possible to define the arena within which the political organization of social life can occur. This is the point at which the idea of "jurisdiction" begins to acquire social reality as a constraint upon human mobility and interaction.

ESTABLISHED JURISDICTION

Establishing jurisdiction is a matter of successfully asserting the territorial and social boundaries of the polity. Egress and ingress are controlled; neither insiders nor outsiders can operate with impunity within the area marked off by the claims and definitions of the locally dominant. Their normative expectations and demands become unavoidable contingencies—"the law"—for anyone inhabiting or entering the area. Having the power, incipient or established authorities can claim the right to control, or at least monitor, social life within "their" land, and to present themselves as the embodiment (or, somewhat less pretentiously, as the leadership) of the people who live there.

The ability of authorities to create and maintain political boundaries depends, before all else, upon acceptance of those boundaries by external and militarily significant parties, most notably the authorities of contiguous polities. In its crudest expression, the drawing of boundaries is a function of the logistical limits of military conquest. The determinant is who can keep the strongest force operative at the greatest distance from the centers of supply and administration. Given an equivalent level of military technology, improvements in transportation and communications facilities favor bigger over smaller polities (Andreski, 1968: 79), with a corresponding weakening of the jurisdictional claims of the authorities of smaller polities.

Bigness alone, however, is not sufficient. More important is the efficiency of military organization, largely determined by the degree to which military dominance has been achieved within the polity. Success both in defending and in expanding polity boundaries has been associated with the creation of an army subservient only to the authorities, an overwhelming force of their own "and not the armed force of aristocratic or feudal retainers" (Eisenstadt, 1969: 130).

Though hardly superseded, the military factor in defining jurisdictional boundaries has been augmented over centuries of interpolity contacts by the development of international law. Authorities have found it usually and increasingly more advantageous to deal with (or try to subvert) one another than to engage in open violations of the only generally accepted "preemptory norm" of international law (overriding even treaties): the basic rule against aggression (Akehurst, 1970: 60-61). Economic interdependence, mutual fear, recurring common problems (such as controlling access to coastal waters and to air space, dealing with fugitives and exiles, validating claims to newly discovered territories and resources), and the advantages of predictability over uncertainty have strongly encouraged authorities to conform to the rules of international relations. As long as the long-term advantages of conformity are believed to outweigh the short-term advantages of deviance, international law and custom constitute an ideological resource of enormous significance in defining and confirming jurisdiction.

Because jurisdictional boundaries are functions of both the social realities of military power and the cultural realities of international law, they shift with changes in the balance of power. The total relative power of a polity is a complex blend of the various kinds of resources which authorities control and can mobilize. Military and economic resources are the most obvious and empirically the most decisive, but to some extent military and economic power may be offset by political realities created under international law. Thus, the authorities of such a powerful nation as the United States may eventually find it more expedient to recognize Cuban jurisdictional boundaries than to try another Bay of Pigs invasion. Even then, the invasion was unsuccessful mainly because the rule against aggression at least kept the Americans from sending in regular forces to help the "Cuban exiles seeking to regain their homeland"—who were, of course, trained and equipped by the CIA.

Military and economic inequalities inevitably produce some discrepancies between the officially recognized and the actual limits of effective control defining a polity. To handle problems arising from such discrepancies, the concept of "spheres of influence" has frequently been invoked as a justification for actions otherwise prohibited by the rules of international relations. The notion is simply that the authorities of a formidable polity consider their interests best served by forbidding other authorities to "interfere" in the affairs of the affected area, while claiming that right for themselves. A classic example is the Monroe Doctrine, under which American governments have frequently intervened more (for example, in the Nicaraguan, Dominican, and numerous other invasions) and less (in the overthrow of Allende's elected government in Chile) directly in Latin America. Another instance is the Soviet Union's use of the concept to excuse the bloody 1968 invasion of Czechoslovakia.

That a self-proclaimed "sphere of influence" is a legally and logically poor justification is almost beside the point: its value lies only in signalling that a more or less demonstrable *factual* condition must be accepted if war is to be avoided. In the absence of any justification at all, other authorities could not as readily estimate the potential threat such aggressions pose to their own interests. Boundaries may be established by "tacit bargaining" (Schelling, 1960: 53-80), but the more explicitly settled they are, the freer authorities will be to develop an effective structure of internal control.

INSTITUTIONALIZED POLICING

As military dominance and jurisdiction are achieved, authorities consolidate their position by instituting a system in which internal control is accomplished by the process of policing instead of the more costly and less efficient one of military occupation. *Occupation* is characterized by maximal social distance between controllers and controlled ("no fraternization"), primary reliance upon the threat and use of deadly violence by large units trained for war, only a rudimentary monitoring of the social life of the subject population, and minimal concern with justifying domination to the dominated. In contrast, *policing* is characterized by minimal social distance, primary reliance upon techniques of "coercive persuasion" employed by individuals or small units trained to minimize the use of violence, extensive and intensive monitoring, and a major concern with legitimation. Occupation confirms power; policing transforms power into authority.

In its earliest development, policing is scarcely more than the not always successful use of military force to quell particularly troublesome instances of collective resistance to impositions such as enslavement, conscription, and taxation. As recently as two centuries ago in England, policing the smugglers of Sussex amounted for many years to little more than sporadic ineffectual forays by military detachments sent to assist the beleaguered customs officials (Winslow, in Hay et al., 1975: 119-166). Sometimes the expeditions ended in tragedy, but frequently they ended in comedy—the soldiers bought off or drunk under the table by the smugglers, or else abandoning the tax battles after exchanging a few token shots to earn their shillings.

Even after police forces are differentiated from the military, authorities may view them only as more finely calibrated and flexible instruments of controlled violence. "It has been a recent development which has seen the police as an appendage of the law rather than as an extension of the violence potential of the state" (Manning, 1977: 40). Not until Sir Robert Peel finally persuaded Parliament in 1829 to authorize creation of the London Metropolitan Police was the idea firmly established that the objective of policing is not to terrorize people, but to tranquilize them. Thereafter, and notably during the halcyon days of British imperial grandeur in the late nineteenth century and early twentieth century, the London police became the nearest approximation to the ideal force—policing instead of occupying the land, and encouraging the populace to identify with the polity and to accept the decisions of their rulers as wise and just. Instead of just a coercive military, economic, and political order, the ideal polity comes to be also a *legal* order— that is, one sustained regularly by the pressure of ideological consensus instead of the threat of violence.

Ensuring that a police force does in fact police rather than attempt to occupy an area is a constant problem for authorities, who may themselves have no clear understanding of the nature and aims of policing. Even Peel seems to have had no ideologically consistent conception beyond a conviction, shared by many, that something had to be done about the abysmal quality of policing in the major governmental and commercial center that London had become (Manning, 1977: 74-81). His genius was that he saw with remarkable clarity what it would take to have efficient policing, and was politically and administratively skilled enough to sell and implement his ideas with considerable success. Peel's key insight was that the less explicit the threat of violence and the more explicit the concern for public safety, the more effective policing is likely to be.

The trick is to keep the threat credible without tarnishing the image of an organization whose official *raison d'être* is "to serve and protect" (motto of the Toronto police). To this end, authorities must be able to count upon the police to distinguish among "situations where coercion is needed, situations where police action is unnecessary (given limits upon the resources which can be invested in policing), and situations where coercion is self-defeating in that the net result of the police effort is to increase, rather than decrease, the need for coercion" (Turk, 1972a: 174).

Policing is inherently a difficult process to keep under administrative control, because to do their job police officers routinely have to be widely dispersed, alone or in very small groups, and given considerable discretion in judging when to threaten or use what degree of violence (Bordua and Reiss, 1966; Bittner, 1970: 36-47). Occupationally constrained to "take charge" (assert their authority) and "handle situations" with efficiency and dispatch, police officers are subject to the temptation to rely excessively upon their privileged access to the means of violence. Peel's solution was to recruit patient, imposing men who were strongly encouraged to rely upon courteous though firm admonition and example unless grievously provoked, and who then were to subdue the recalcitrant subject with as little injury as possible. To further induce them to accept this policy, the "bobbies" were armed only with stout clubs—which helped to reassure the populace and encourage offenders themselves to forgo deadly violence in contending with the police.

The limits of authorities' control within a polity are marked by their ability through institutionalized policing to define, detect, and punish criminality—including both preexisting (such as murder, rape, theft) and specially invented (treason, poaching, tax evasion) types of social deviance which are thereby made "official business." Effective control is demonstrated to the extent that there is little to detect and punish. Policing is the mechanism by which authorities, whether or not they realize it, establish the framework and gain the time needed for the development and operation of even more subtle and powerful modes of political socialization.

DEMOGRAPHIC CONTINUITY

An often neglected factor in analyzing the formation and characteristics of polities is that of sheer durability. Durability is, of course, a *consequence* of the process of political organization; the point here is that it is also a *condition* necessary for the process to occur. It may take years, perhaps centuries, for military dominance to be achieved, jurisdictional boundaries to be established, and the transition from occupation to policing to be made to any significant degree. For those years or centuries to be available, the population of a polity must survive as a demographic entity. *The* people must continue even if *some* people do not, falling as military, policing, or economic casualties.

Demographic continuity is a function of population size and composition, as well as the size and technologically available natural resources of the jurisdictional area. Given at least an agrarian economic base, the larger the population, the longer the polity is likely to survive (compare Lenski, 1966: 195). Large populations can more readily sustain casualties, and especially are more likely than smaller ones to have functionally equivalent replacements available. If, for example, skilled crafts-men such as tool makers, medical practitioners, or military leaders are lost in a particular disaster, a large population will probably have "reserves" who happened to be elsewhere. In addition, the larger the population, the greater the rate at which equivalents and potential replacements are produced and—mainly because of administrative needs and economic exi-gencies—dispersed.

Finally, the greater social differentiation that tends to charac-terize large populations provides more alternative organizational pathways through which innovations and adaptations can be generated to repair or correct for breakdowns in the social structure. Larger units generally have many more kinds of emergency services and back-up systems, which can be mobil-ized as needed. "Repairing" is exemplified in the provision of alternative organizations able both to handle specialized tasks beyond the expertise of local officials and people and to relieve them of the "great overload of decision and administrative work" (Barton, 1970: 284). "Correcting for" may take the form of deciding (perhaps by applying the principle of triage) which stricken communities, beleaguered frontier posts, or the like will be helped and which abandoned to their fate.

Population composition refers here to the age and sex distri-bution characterizing a population. A younger population is obviously more vigorous and hardy than an older one. Not of least importance, it can sustain a higher "military participation ratio" (Andreski, 1968: 33); that is, a greater proportion of the population can be mobilized for military purposes. This is made possible not only by the greater ability of younger persons to withstand the physical and, perhaps, mental stresses of warfare, but also by—all else equal—the greater productivity of younger workers. Thus, the military participation ratio is closely linked to the dependency ratio—the ratio of productive people to those dependent upon them. The sex composition of a population is important not only because men tend to be stronger for work and warfare, but also because the higher the proportion of younger women, the greater the capacity of the population to reproduce itself at a rate exceeding the survival minimum—that is, to produce (from the perspective of grand strategists) workers, soldiers, and breeders faster than they are lost.

The extent of a polity's jurisdiction (not strictly conterminous with its officially designated territory, the reader will recall) is correlated with the extent of natural resources available within it. Larger areas are more likely than smaller ones to contain everything from sufficient water and arable land to essential mineral deposits. A polity whose jurisdictional boundaries are too truncated is unlikely to last as long as one with wide boundaries. Exceptions such as Switzerland and the small principalities of Europe are more apparent than real, existing mainly thanks to "accidents" of nature, of military technology and objectives in crucial eras, and of geopolitics. Therefore, unless their boundaries are erased by conquest or more or less superseded by political compromises with economic and/or military realities, small polities can be expected to war over territory, as in Africa now, and to be eventually forced to merge or be swallowed up as conquests, satellites, or economic dependencies by larger states. The various outcomes are illustrated in the incorporation of Latvia and Estonia into the Soviet Union, the formation of the European Economic Community, and the imposition of *Pax Romana* and the later *Pax Britannica* over sizable parts of the earth. In a novel reversal of the usual process of erasing or superseding previously meaningful boundaries, the Republic of South Africa has recently been "divested" of a fairly large territory granted formal independence in late 1976 as the Transkei Republic—the boundaries of which are effectively superseded at the outset (Carter et al., 1967; SAIRR, 1977: 228-246).

The primary significance of demographic continuity is that the longer the polity endures, the more likely are military dominance, jurisdictional boundaries, and policing to constitute a controlled learning environment in which the inescapable reality of "the power structure" itself is the prime lesson to be learned. In particular, after two or more generations presumably no one is left who directly experienced the early struggles to decide the terms on which the process of political organization would begin.

> Later generations grow up with the limits and under the conditions set by the outcome of their ancestors' struggle to answer the power question. They start learning their places, acquiring identities, statuses, roles, from birth in a system whose main features are already set by the terms of the power settlement. The very idea that things were different and could be different becomes more and more just an idea, having no grounding in the actual experience of living people. It becomes, because of the increasing detachment of such ideas from the experiences of real people in real life, more and more difficult even for people to think about their situation in terms other than those set by a culture part of whose bedrock is the explanation and justification of the power structure [Turk, 1972a: 174].

IDEOLOGICAL HEGEMONY

At its ultimate reach, the process of political organization culminates in control over feelings and thoughts as well as actions. Not only are there no challenges to the structure of authority, it does not even occur to people that there is anything to question. Authorities and subjects, respectively, act out their interdependence in terms of social norms of dominance and of deference (Turk, 1969: 40-50), buttressed by a cultural consensus that the polity is a manifestation of nature's order. In the minds of the people, social life as it *is* becomes social life as it *ought* to be.

Such a model of the universal embracing of structured inequality has never been fully realized; but it has often been approximated to an extent reassuring to those who crave social order above all else, and chilling for those who value human freedom. Following Tocqueville, Bendix (1964: 41-42) has described the patrimonial-feudal authority structure of medieval Europe as one in which, to an enormous degree, "aristocratic masters and their servants feel strongly identified with each other . . . think of each other as an inferior or superior extension of themselves." Though "selfish willfulness on one side and

manipulating subservience on the other" were an obvious part
of the reality, even such "abuses and aberrations" were still
within the terms of a "finished rhetoric of manners and motives . . . which for centuries was based on the structure of
medieval political life."

What came afterward has not been all that different, if one
emphasizes general historical parallels rather than specific
historical shifts. Since the end of the *ancien régime* in the
eighteenth century, the "false consciousness" of urban and rural
proletariats has frustrated revolutionaries everywhere. Complementing proletarian diffidence, even the most ruthless capital-
ists have easily come to believe in their superiority (demonstrated, of course, by their power) as sufficient justification for
running everybody's business for their own ever-growing power
and profit. Detailed examples of the process by which capital-
ists may eventually metamorphose into aristocrats are found in
Collier and Horowitz (1976) on "the Rockefellers," Newman
(1975) on "the Canadian establishment," and Sampson's (1971)
"new anatomy" of British elitism.

A similar parallel appears in a kind of "revolutionary" inver-
sion of the capitalist hegemony. From the perspective of those
trying to save the world for the capitalist version of democracy,
the "enslaved peoples" behind various Iron and Bamboo Cur-
tains have been frustratingly unresponsive to exhortations from
"the Free World," and Third World peoples have obtusely
persisted in their resistance to enlightenment about the benefits
of neocolonial life. In turn complementing such *un*proletarian
"false consciousness," triumphant revolutionaries and their
successors—notably in the Soviet Union and China—have taken
their ascendancy to be the mark of their superior understanding
of "what is to be done" to move lesser mortals along the road
to collectivized perfection. Thus, "Communist Parties direct
and check up on all the work of the organs of state power and
administration, correct any shortcomings in their activity and
help state organs to mobilize the working people for the active
fulfillment of the tasks of socialist construction" (Chkhikvadze,
1969: 85).

Political socialization is far more than deliberate indoctrination. In Sigel's (1965: 4) words, it is

a learning process which begins very early and is most influenced by the same agents or forces which influence all social behavior: first and foremost, the family; then socially relevant groups or institutions, such as school, church, and social class; and finally—last but not least—society at large and the political culture it fosters. . . . Much of this learning is incidental to other experiences; . . . it is acquired in a subtle, nondeliberate way, often in a context which seems totally void of political stimuli yet is often rife with political consequences.

Whatever teaches people that order is always better than disorder, that consensus is always preferable to conflict, that governance is the prerogative of some and obedience the duty of others, that authority goes with power, helps to deaden concern about inequalities in the distribution of life chances, and about the institutions that maintain those inequalities. As many dissident intellectuals have learned, "radical answers cannot be given to students without radical questions" (Michalowski, 1977: 70).

Authorities are not, of course, indifferent to the possibility of increasing by propaganda and censorship the effectiveness of political socialization. In Chapter 4, information control as a major function of political policing is examined in some detail. For now, we may simply observe that *totalitarianism*—defined as state control over all sectors of social life—is not an attribute of only some polities, but is instead a variable feature of all polities. Pro-Marxist university professors are certainly more likely to be found in the North American and Western European democracies than are anti-Marxist ones in the Eastern European, Soviet, and Chinese socialist states. Nonetheless, the freedoms of speech, association, and petition continue (as will be seen in subsequent chapters) to be only partially and fitfully available where they are most loudly proclaimed. In practice, "national security" turns all such freedoms into contingent privileges rather than inalienable rights.

Irrespective of the particular blend of inadvertent and deliberate political socialization through which it is attained, a high degree of ideological hegemony is the strongest support upon which political authority can rest. The stronger the consensual base, the more resources can be diverted from internal control

to deal with natural and social environmental problems. Ideological power thus amplifies other forms of power in a kind of
feedback process: as military, economic, and political power
facilitate the creation of ideological resources, so does ideological power increase the available amounts and facilitate the
mobilization of more tangible resources. Bonded together by
the conviction that authority is "of, by, and for the people," a
politically organized population can perform prodigious feats—
whether of construction or destruction. Without that bond,
authorities may have great difficulty in even mobilizing the
polity against a despised and dreaded invader (for example, the
terrible experience of the Soviet people under Stalin's dictatorship when the German army attacked in 1941).

To summarize, given that an initial *power* structure has
resulted from struggles to maximize life chances, it becomes an
authority structure (a "legal" order) to the degree that the
people involved begin assuming the inevitability of the unequal
distribution of resources, and therefore of life chances. Whether
they believe in, much less agree on, the justice of their inegalitarian relationship is a quite different matter. In the real world,
as distinct from the realm of legal and political philosophies,
"legitimation" has meant acceptance of "the given order,"
regardless of why it is accepted.

Legitimation and Political Crime

The concept of *legitimation* has traditionally been taken to
mean not only that people accept the power structure in which
they live, but also that it is *right* for them to do so. Grounded in
some variant of natural law theory, "ideologies of agreement"
(Shklar, 1964: 88-110) have been developed to explain why
people should defer to authority *qua* authority even when
particular figures or acts are disapproved. The key notion is
that, now or ultimately, the interests of authorities and subjects
are identical. Given that common ideological premise, specific
justifications for accepting the power structure as an authority
structure may vary greatly in emphasis and complexity. Following Weber's (1968: 212-216) familiar analysis, the major kinds
of justification, or "types of legitimate domination," may be

distinguished according to whether the justifications rest primarily upon *charismatic, rational,* or *traditional* grounds.

Charismatic legitimacy rests upon the belief that authority figures have unique sources of insight and power, derived either from their innate extrahumanness or from their having control of the symbols of office, such as a golden stool or an oval office. Legends of royalty everywhere emphasize the tests and signs by which "royalness" is "found" in a perhaps improbable individual (such as a young shepherd or a kidnapped princeling), or else "acquired" by a surpassing feat (such as drawing a magic sword from a rock or killing the current ruler). Modern equivalents of the royal legends tend to stress the unique "genius for leadership" of authority figures and/or "the charisma of the office." To such varied notables as Churchill, Gandhi, and Lenin is imputed an awesome personal capacity to determine collective destinies, to know what people should do and to get them to do it. Supporting personal charisma (or, in the case of less imposing figures, substituting for it) is the belief that insight and ability somehow inhere in a position or structure of authority—either by human design (the genius then perhaps being imputed to "the founding fathers") or supernatural intervention (such as the doctrine of Papal infallibility). A related idea is that even relatively mediocre individuals may be inspired or constrained by role expectations so that they rise to appropriate levels of performance ("some men have greatness thrust upon them").

Rational legitimacy is conferred by the belief that authority is structured and exercised according to accepted factual premises and logical principles. It is assumed that authorities act upon the basis of adequate objective knowledge rationally applied to particular situations. A reinforcing assumption is that authorities have greater knowledge and powers of reason than do subjects. Insofar as scientific and technical expertise are harnessed to the purposes of authorities, and most people are left ill-educated and ill-informed, the assumption may be empirically confirmed. Probably nothing promotes rational legitimacy more than the mystique of "the law"—that institutional complex of formulas, agencies, and procedures which serve, among other functions, to impress upon the uninitiated the feeling that extraordinary intellect and arcane knowledge are required to exercise political authority—at least at the higher levels.

Traditional legitimacy is founded in the belief that contemporary authorities are maintaining the ways found, through the experiences of preceding generations, to be the best. The closer the adherence to established norms, the better off everyone presumably will be. Security is equated with stability. However miserable the conditions of social life, people cling to their conviction that political changes can only bring worse. If no institutional solution to the problem of succession—of replacing deceased, retired, or failed incumbents—has been developed, then people may be genuinely terrified by the news that "the King is dead," until the continuity of political order is assured by the proclamation of "long live the King." Where authority depends much upon traditional legitimacy, innovations must be construed as applications or extensions of custom to particular cases. Thus, successful authorities tend to be those most adept at substantively camouflaging new ideas and practices in the familiar forms of old ones (and at seeing to it that unduly restrictive old ways are conveniently forgotten).

All three types of justifications may be found blended in varying proportions to constitute the ideological reflection of the structure of power. People may, for instance, accept and approve a bicameral legislature because of (1) the personal and/or office charisma of some legislators, (2) conviction that bicameralism is a technically superior organizational principle facilitating rational decision making, and (3) belief that the two-class division of legislators is a precious legacy of ancestral enlightenment. In any case, the specifics of ideological consensus are far less significant than the fact of its accomplishment. The crucial element in legitimacy is that power is transformed into authority insofar as people learn to live with it—that is, either to exercise it if they have it or to defer to it if they do not have it (even if they defer only for tactical reasons stemming from fear or opportunism). For them, both the more and the less powerful, to accept and believe in the power distribution without question or even reflection would constitute the ultimate outcome of the learning process by which the structural reality of power generates the cultural reality of authority.

Apart from the question of whether people view their power relationships as inevitable and/or just, it has often been theorized that no social relationship is likely to persist unless the parties involved are getting at least something out of it. It has, for instance, been argued that social interaction is possible only where there is some basis in mutual gratification (Parsons, 1951: 5-7, 9, 11-13). Such a proposition would seem to underlie the popular view that increasing misery must sooner or later result in a revolutionary explosion, as the mutuality of gratification drops below some critical minimum. Perhaps rather surprisingly, the Marxian expectation that exploitation and immiseration of the proletariat will (given certain facilitating conditions) generate class consciousness and class struggle apparently rests upon a similar line of reasoning. Against such reasoning, however,

> it seems more realistic to assume that large masses of people, and especially peasants, simply accept the social system under which they live without concern about any balance of benefits and pains, certainly without the least thought of whether a better one might be possible, unless and until something happens to threaten and destroy their daily routine. Hence it is quite possible for them to accept a society of whose working they are no more than victims [Moore, 1967: 204].

While it does seem that exploitative relationships can indeed be maintained almost indefinitely, there is probably a limit to how much a dominant class can appropriate the fruits of their subjects' labor without "something happening to threaten and destroy the daily routine" of peasant or proletarian life. The more severe the exploitation, the more likely it is that acceptance of their lot by the exploited will depend more upon their being periodically and inescapably subjected to violent and ideological coercive persuasion than upon any dull lack of awareness and concern.

In any case, even though the degree of exploitation, as well as the degree of authority and the difference in power, may vary greatly among polities (with corresponding variation in the extent to which they rest directly and routinely upon coercion rather than consensus), all contemporary polities, at least, are characterized by the use of formal control mechanisms to promote acceptance of and identification with the structures and personages of authority, and to suppress at least the most insistent of those who resist. Challenges to authority are expected, do occur, and are met by the more or less routine mobilization of the agencies of control.

As long as people subject to a polity's jurisdiction believe— correctly or erroneously—that their life chances are reasonably improved, tolerably maintained, or at least largely unaffected by the actions of the polity's authorities, challenges to authority will most probably be limited to "conventional crimes"— that is, officially prohibited deviations from such norms as those dealing with nonpolitical personal and property violence, sexual expression, responsible or "normal" role behavior, and the misappropriation or misuse of property (Turk, 1969: 80-90). When, however, all or some subjects believe—correctly or erroneously—that their life chances are excessively threatened or reduced by the actions (or inactions) of the authorities, they may challenge the authorities more directly and fundamentally by spontaneous or calculated, organized or unorganized dissent, evasion, disobedience, or violence. Such direct challenges to authority will at some point—depending upon the seriousness of the challenge as perceived and interpreted by the authorities—become intolerable enough to them to be either openly or "operationally" defined as *political crimes.*

Where the definition of challenges as political crimes is relatively open, the authorities will invoke laws expressly prohibiting various forms of resistance. Less openly, the definitional process may involve the invocation of laws, but is characterized by more or less covert police operations rather than formally legal procedures. In either case, identifying events and persons as politically criminal is (as will become evident in subsequent discussions) a complex process in which the congruence of perceptual and objective realities is highly problematic— as are the consequences of the process for the polity.

Some analysts, such as Sagarin (1973) and Quinney (1975: 147-161), have argued strongly for including illegal acts of political repression in the concept of political criminality and, therefore, for defining the instigators and perpetrators of such acts as another category of political criminal. However, no matter how heinous such acts may be, calling them political crimes confuses political criminality with political policing or with conventional politics, and therefore obscures the structured relationship between authorities and subjects. There is also the considerable danger that an empirical criterion (what the authorities do) will be abandoned for a nonempirical one (our application of our own interpretations of law).

Even though authorities may indeed act illegally and authoritative personages may be criminalized by others, the crucial question is whether these events have any direct significance for the basic struggle over authority itself. Where they do, we are looking at political resistance and policing. Where they do not, the concepts of "conventional politics" and "factionalism" seem to be more appropriate. The ambiguities we encounter are a function of the complex structures of authority that characterize modern polities.

Summary

Neither the dream of earthly paradise nor the apparition of earthly hell adequately characterizes social reality. Instead, in real social life there is a constant tension between utopianism and realism. That tension is expressed in the process of political organization, set in motion and sustained by conflicts among people trying to secure their chances of living the good life as they understand it. Whether they realize it or not, people are inevitably involved in intergroup struggles over who shall have what resources in a finite world.

Given ultimately limited material resources and the human impossibility of loving everyone equally, distinctions between "them" and "us" become the bases for collective decisions on whose claims are to have priority. Such decisions are not easily reached, nor are they ever final. The process by which social differences are made criteria for social stratification is that of political organization—the ongoing creation through conflict of explicit or implicit rules for allocating resources, and therefore for deciding who shall have greater and who lesser chances in life.

Political organization inevitably favors the parties with the greater initial power, who predictably will try to use their advantage to consolidate their disproportionate control of the available resources. Because there is never total certainty that security has been achieved, there is a very strong (possibly inexorable in intergroup relations) tendency for the aim of consolidation to become the practice of increase—toward absolute, rather than relative, control of violence, economic, political, ideological, and diversionary resources. Of course, people may neither know nor care about the power aspect of a particular relationship; and both very intimate and very distant relationships are most secure when relative power is of no concern.

The key to understanding the process of political organization at the societal level is to analyze the relationship between political criminality and political policing. A polity is characterized by the emerging hierarchical differentiation of authorities and subjects. Intrinsic to that differentiation is the transformation of power into authority, a problematic and reversible movement toward the establishment of military dominance, jurisdictional boundaries, institutionalized policing, demographic continuity, and ideological hegemony. To the degree that people learn to live with one another in terms of the complementary social norms of dominance and of deference, and to believe the charismatic, rational, and/or traditional justifications legitimating their unequal life chances, the power structure that is the polity is also an authority structure. Insofar as the complete and final authority structure is not and cannot be realized, political policing is relied upon to define and control intolerable resistance to political socialization. Political criminality becomes understandable as a socially defined reality, produced by conflict between people who claim to be authorities and people who resist or may resist being their subjects.

CHAPTER 2

POLITICAL CRIMES AND
LEGAL DEFINITIONS

It is part of the function of "Law" to give
recognition to ideals representing the exact
opposite of established conduct. Most of its
complications arise from the necessity of
pretending to do one thing, while actually
doing another.
Thurman Arnold (1962: 34)

Legal systems, including both "law talk" and "law in action"
(Stone, 1966: 44-47, 62-71, 728-734), do not exist apart from
the process of political organization. They originate in truces
and other accommodations among conflicting parties, and are
developed in the course of efforts by both authorities and
subjects to reduce the costs and risks of social conflict. To
authorities, a legal system is desirable as long as they believe
that it facilitates their acquisition and exercise of power, while
protecting and justifying the good life which power enables
them to enjoy. To subjects, the desirability of a legal system
depends mainly upon its perceived effectiveness in restraining
the authorities from at least the grosser forms of exploitation,
thus giving the relatively powerless some hope of a tolerable and
perhaps better life. In spite of their opposing class perspectives,
both authorities and subjects are likely to agree on the need for
a legal system (with reservations on both sides about the one
they actually have), minimally in order to reduce force, fraud,
and uncertainty in interpersonal relations.

A legal system articulates the ways in which social life is constrained by the polity: what is proscribed, prescribed, or permitted in what circumstances. Most importantly, mechanisms are established for deciding who is authorized to do what. Ambiguities or disputes in regard to the validity of presumed rights and obligations are resolved by officials whose own claims and decisions are supported ultimately by the organized violence of the polity. Even though the threat of violence is often well hidden in the complexities of officialdom, bureaucrats and judges can expect police support if needed, as the police can count upon military help if resistance is more than they can handle.

For a polity to have a legal system, it must have survived long enough for policing to be fairly well institutionalized and for a significant degree of ideological hegemony *ergo* consensus to exist. Legal systems vary in the degree to which official decisions are expected to be mutually consistent, especially with preceding ones in similar cases. At one extreme is "khadi justice" (closely analogous to "people's justice"), in which officials apply their personal wisdom to deciding each case ad hoc, without having to specify the principles and reasoning that led to the decision. "Code," or "civil law" systems approximate the opposite pole: Each decision is theoretically mandated by a logically consistent statement of all the postulates, definitions, substantive norms, and procedural rules that constitute the framework of official action. "Common law" systems retain something of the "khadi" focus upon the case at hand, but each decision is in principle (*stare decisis*) demonstrably consistent with relevant preceding ones. "Socialist law" systems are code systems explicitly subordinated to the political judgments of the highest echelon of authorities: the ruling party.

The legal system of a specific polity may, of course, contain features of any or all of the types mentioned, as well as idiosyncracies produced by the history and current circumstances of the polity. In each instance, the nature of the legal system is defined by the direct and indirect cumulative effects of official decisions, both those verbalized and those merely implied by the impact of actions by officials. Diversity and idiosyncracy should not, however, be exaggerated. Though there clearly are some significant differences among legal systems, especially in the "law talk" component, there is also much evidence of consequential and increasing similarities— especially in the "law in action" component (Friedman, 1975: 220-221; Merryman, 1969).

Whatever its particular characteristics, the legal system of any modern polity will incorporate both "command" and "field" control mechanisms:

> In contract to the bluntness and directness of laws in the form of commands, laws designed to manipulate fields are likely to approach their goals indirectly. They are not intended to command each individual to follow a precisely prescribed path, but rather aim at an aggregate or systemic response. They are designed to control the *rate* of an activity by altering the costs of engaging in it [Feeley, 1976: 511].

For example, political dissent may be suppressed by officially forbidding it or by making it very difficult for dissidents to travel, organize public meetings, publish statements, find employment, and so on. Of course, the most effective kind of field control of dissent, as of other behavior, is that imposed by the political environment itself, insofar as people are continuously socialized to think and behave in terms of politically tolerable beliefs and values.

Conventional Laws and Political Offensiveness

Virtually every formula provided in a legal system, civil as well as criminal laws, may serve to discourage the questioning of authority. Compulsory education laws, for example, may help to protect children from being overworked, and may even stimulate a more inquiring attitude about their society. But such laws have also meant the subjection of people to years of more and less subtle pressures to learn palatable answers to whatever questions they might have. In every modern polity the schools have been expected to equip people with needed work skills, or else simply to "keep them off the streets" if there is a labor surplus (in the sense of not enough "jobs" for which people will be paid, not that there is ever any real lack of work needing to be done). In either case, "loyalty" is supposed to accompany literacy. If a subject's productive capacity is unneeded, and therefore undeveloped or shelved, she or he can at least be a "good citizen" who quietly accepts the fate which "life" has somehow mysteriously decreed—or at least be patiently trusting while the authorities study "the problem."

Not everyone, of course, is patient and trusting enough. Those who make sufficient fuss will eventually be defined as political offenders in a sociologically meaningful sense, if not necessarily in a legal sense. Their class, race, age, or other identifying characteristics become stigmata—the marks of a "dangerous class" of people. Accordingly, they will as a class receive disproportionate police surveillance, and will have higher rates of trouble with the police. Individuals within the dangerous class, as well as sympathizers from outside it, who are especially articulate or active in challenging the authorities will be punished in some way.

If the authorities decide it is better not to define a challenge explicitly as a political one, they may punish the offender more indirectly (such as with inordinate delay in the processing of passport applications, frequent tax audits, manipulation of credit information) and/or more directly. Direct punishment may vary from routine police harassment (differing only in degree or specificity from the usual pattern of interaction between police and dangerous classes) to formal arrest and adjudication for ordinarily nonpolitical, conventional offenses of which the individual may or may not be guilty. The point is that conventional crime definitions may be used to justify the coercive treatment of persons whose most significant attribute in the eyes of the authorities is their resistance to political authority.

Conventional crime laws have been used politically wherever subjects have struggled against the terms of their subjection—

economic, racial, or political, as these appear in various complex blends. Additionally, in a gray area between conventional crime laws and explicit political crime laws, specialized bodies of law have been created defining the accepted "etiquettes" of labor relations, race relations, and conventional politics. Every arena of struggle has provided many illustrations of the use of both kinds of conventional laws, criminal and specialized.

Labor history is filled with instances in which either conventional crime laws or specially invented laws have been invoked to justify the rejection of demands for a less inequitable allocation of economic resources and deprivations. Attempts by workers "peaceably to assemble" and organize in order to question their share of goods and services, or the disproportionate costs of technological change or warfare, have been variously construed as conspiracies to commit crime (including that of "syndicalism," or organizing), incitement to riot, creating a public disturbance, trespassing, restraint of trade, price fixing, or any other offense label that happened to be handy. Union organizers and leaders have often found themselves being charged with, and often convicted of, offenses ranging from vagrancy, trespassing, or spitting on the sidewalk to arson, assault, or murder.

It has been stated that the "United States has had the bloodiest and most violent labor history of any industrial nation in the world" (Taft and Ross, 1969: 221). Certainly the conflict over whether and how workers might organize has been intense and the casualties many, though consolidation appears to have outweighed expansion in trade union strategies of recent decades. One of the key battles for the right to unionize was the General Motors "sit-down" strike of 1936-37, when the United Automobile Workers of America occupied and picketed factories in Flint, Michigan, and elsewhere in defiance of company threats and reprisals, court orders, police and military force, and vigilantism by foremen and others hostile to unionization. In the course of the strike, workers and organizers were variously charged with "kidnapping GM plant guards, malicious destruction of property while rioting, felonious assault, and criminal syndicalism" (Fine, 1969: 240); trespass and inciting to riot (p. 272); contempt of court for violating an injunction against trespassing and picketing (pp. 292-293); "rout and riot" and malicious trespass (p. 316). Local judges and police uniformly supported the company against the strikers, inhibiting by every available means (including condoning violent attacks upon unionists) their efforts to assert their rights of assembly, speech, combination, petition, and even self-defense.

"Big Bill" Haywood, a miner and official of the Industrial Workers of the World (the "Wobblies"), experienced the full gamut of legalized punishment for his militant activities on behalf of "industrial justice" (Haywood, 1929); he ultimately died in exile in the Soviet Union. In one celebrated case, he and two fellow workers were attacked on the street in Denver by several deputies. As the deputies were pistol-whipping them on the sidewalk, Haywood shot the leader—who happened to be a police captain's nephew. Haywood was charged with "assault with intent to commit murder" and jailed. Apparently because the attack was so flagrant, and the assailant was not fatally wounded, "Big Bill" was soon released after being treated for his own injuries. Upon being told by the doctor that all three bullets had fortunately hit the assailant's arm in front of his chest, which had probably saved the man's life, tough Bill's pragmatic conclusion was: "I'm sorry I hurt him so badly, but from now on I'll carry a stronger shooting gun" (Haywood, 1929: 145).

The GM strike and Haywood's shoot-out are part of a history beginning in the resistance of English rural workers to the programs by which the dominant classes further enriched themselves at the expense of the subjugated: the Industrial Revolution. Immiseration and death for the many was the price of the centuries of "development" and "progress" that brought affluence to the few, and prepared the ground for modern capitalism and, eventually, state socialism. As the people found repeatedly that their petitions for the recognition of ancient legal rights were useless, their traditional claims upon the land's resources were asserted and defended in ways recognized in the newly created or reinterpreted offenses for which great numbers of them were penalized, such as hunting deer, "poaching" rabbits and fish, cutting trees, damaging fish ponds or rabbit warrens, writing anonymous threatening letters, taking anything from wrecked ships ("wrecking"), trading in defiance of the new customs laws ("smuggling"), and burning the houses, barns, and ricks of oppressive landholders (Hay et al., 1975).

In 1723 and as extended in the next several years, the Black Act made absolutely clear the determination of the masters to crush the resistance to their self-serving ideas about the proper organization of society. The death penalty was eventually pre-scribed for over 200 offenses, including those mentioned above, as well as that which gave the Act its title: "blacking" one's face as disguise while raiding the gentry's property (as the "Waltham Blacks" did in Berkshire and Hampshire). As a law aimed explicitly at violent and nonviolent property offenses, the Black Act provided a virtual model for the later elaboration of polit-ical crime laws. Trials could be held anywhere; prosecution witnesses could be held and threatened; the community where the offense occurred would be fined if the offender was not caught and convicted within six months; offenders who did not surrender within forty days after being accused could be executed without a trial; and so on (Thompson, 1976: 270-277). In time the Black Act and other laws did their part in, as the Communist Manifesto of Marx and Engels put it so insensitively, rescuing the people "from the idiocy of rural life" (noted in Pearson, 1978: 134). From the eighteenth century on, the lesson has been driven home for the laboring classes every-where:

> [The] connections between property, power and authority are close and crucial. The criminal law [is] critically important in maintaining bonds of obedience and deference, in legitimizing the status quo, in constantly recreating the structure of authority which [arises] from property and in turn [protects] its interests [Hay, 1975: 25].

It is, moreover, increasingly evident that the civil law—from taxes and tenancy to debt and divorce—is at least equally important in performing precisely the same functions. The "law of the poor" teaches that owners, creditors, employers, and officials are more consequential than renters, debtors, employees, and clients, even of welfare agencies (ten Broek, 1966; Carlin et al., 1966).

In an overlapping arena of conflict, resistance by racial minorities to exploitative, degrading, and even genocidal treatment has typically been met with legal repression given an extra impetus by racist beliefs and fears. The term "racism" has referred ordinarily to black-white stereotyping, in which behaviorally significant genetic differences are imputed on the basis of externally observed physical attributes. It should, however, be recognized that racist views have historically been elements in the ideology of class domination. Whether in their indigenous or colonial variants, the English upper classes, for instance, have never found it difficult to believe in the "bestial," or at least irremediably mediocre, "nature" not only of the abominable Irish, but also of their own less privileged fellow Englishmen (or Canadians, or Americans, or whatever).

Dehumanizing less advantaged others seems to make it easier for the more advantaged to bear the burdens of power and privilege. Where the line between authorities and subjects has been drawn in color, a cycle has been set in motion by which the effects of political and economic repression upon subordinate racial groups are taken to be effects of their racial characteristics. The marks of oppression become the justification for further repression under laws designed to protect the dominant "civilized" color groups from the sometimes ungratefully rebellious subordinate "uncivilized" ones.

Legalized racism has been developed most explicitly and extensively in the United States and in the formerly British nations of southern Africa. With unremarkable similarity, both the American and the South African legal systems have provided rationales and devices for imposing "white" rule over African and other generally darker peoples, and for demanding that the superiority of "white" cultural and economic interests be politically asserted and guaranteed. "White supremacy" or "baaskap," the principle has been articulated in laws intended to control nearly every facet and dimension of "nonwhite" behavior. Interaction between "whites" or "Europeans" and "Negroes," "nonwhites," or "non-Europeans" has been strictly regulated in a constant effort to restrict such interaction to the servicing of the dominant group's needs and desires.

There have always been some Africans, Native North Americans, Asians, Latinos, and other representatives of "inferior races" who have resisted the presumption, often violently. Many others have succumbed to the pressure to be "good niggers," and come to see (and often hate) themselves as little more than adjuncts, extensions, or imitations of their masters. Most have sought merely to survive, as honorably as they could, hoping that a better deal for themselves or their descendants would somehow be forthcoming "someday." All, irrespective of their reaction to it, have been painfully taught the reality of their condition: that the law is intended to prevent that "someday" from ever coming.

American blacks have fought and endured legal slavery, the post-Civil War "black codes," segregation laws, and the hidden legal supports for "institutional racism." With some provisions for judicial review when penalties were especially severe, slavery was maintained largely by the granting of vast discretionary powers to masters, officials, specially licensed patrols, and, indeed, virtually anyone deemed white who encountered an unsupervised "Negro." It was an offense to teach slaves reading, writing, or any other skill not expressly required for the service of the owner, and, of course, an offense for a slave to seek such instruction. The black codes passed in several Southern states in the years 1865-1867 continued the pattern: The former slaves were to be kept under control so as to meet the labor requirements of their former masters (Myrdal, 1944: 228).

Legally, the black codes ended with passage of the Thirteenth, Fourteenth, and Fifteenth Amendments to the American Constitution. But many of the practices they had articulated and authorized persisted in the daily practice of "the Southern way of life," and were eventually given legal restatement and extension from about the 1880s in "Jim Crow" laws meant to restore white supremacy. Blacks were forced by the tenancy and vagrancy laws to stay indefinitely at work on their employers' and creditors' farms ("debt peonage"), and were excluded from many occupations which had been open to them—some of which, such as hairdressing (for whites), had in fact been traditionally reserved for them. Woodward (1957: 7-8) found that

> in bulk and detail as well as in effectiveness of enforcement the segregation codes were comparable with the black codes of the old regime, though the laxity that mitigated the harshness of the black codes was replaced by a rigidity that was more typical of the segregation code. That code lent the sanction of law to a racial ostracism that extended to churches and schools, to housing and jobs, to eating and drinking. Whether by law or by custom, that ostracism eventually extended to virtually all forms of public transportation, to sports and recreations, to hospitals, orphanages, prisons, and asylums, and ultimately to funeral homes, morgues, and cemeteries.

Organized rebellion against racist oppression culminated in the civil-rights movement of the 1950s and 1960s, for which a legal beachhead had been carved out over many years of legal efforts by the NAACP (National Association for the Advancement of Colored People) and other agencies. The years of legal struggle resulted finally in the U.S. Supreme Court's 1954 decision that "separate but equal" was no longer an acceptable rationale for racial discrimination. As the following decade brought more formal than substantive changes in the structure of inequality, blacks and white sympathizers began to challenge the system more directly by such tactics as "sit-ins" and boycotts. Muse (1969) dates the beginning of "the American Negro revolution" from the 1963 nonviolent "march on Washington" of about 170,000 blacks and 30,000 whites, who were insisting upon an end "now" to all forms of discrimination and oppression.

During the years since, civil-rights demonstrators and voter-registration workers have been harassed, hosed, bitten, beaten, arrested (and sometimes convicted), jailed, tortured, sexually assaulted, and murdered. (Many other blacks and whites suffered the same for no reason other than that they happened to be available and vulnerable as surrogate targets for racist rage.) The legal justifications for such treatment have been endless: disorderly conduct, disturbing the peace, loitering, vagrancy, parading without a permit, trespassing, destroying and defacing public property, curfew violation, obstructing an officer, assaulting an officer, resisting arrest, and contempt of court. Students who participated in the voter-registration campaign reported being arrested (1) for traffic violations such as either "speeding," by driving one mile per hour over the speed limit, or "creating a traffic hazard," by driving a few miles per hour under the limit; (2) for "indecent exposure," for wearing shorts and halter top in ninety-degree heat; and (3) for "public intoxication," for holding an open beer can and inadvertently stepping on a sidewalk in front of a voter-registration office (personal conversations).

Just how bizarre the legalisms could be is illustrated in the MacMurray College case, in which a group of ten students on a 1960 field-study trip through the Deep South were arrested, along with their professor, his wife, and nine local blacks with whom they were having lunch in a "Negro" restaurant in Montgomery, Alabama. Some time after being jailed they were informed that the charge was "disturbing the peace." The Judge of the City Recorder's Court found them guilty on the argument that

for whites to eat with negroes was so offensive to southern customs that a breach of the peace might have been committed by whites if they had learned of this behavior, and that the defendants were therefore clearly guilty of "conduct calculated to provoke a breach of the peace" [Durr, 1965: 50].

The verdict was affirmed by the Alabama Circuit Court, but was ultimately reversed by the U.S. Circuit Court of Appeals, which held that the arrests were illegal as a matter of law (Nesmith v. Alford, 318 F. 2d 110, 5th cir. 1963). The U.S. Supreme Court refused to hear an appeal by the State of Alabama, after which the cases finally ended with the Alabama officials having to pay all court costs and Professor Nesmith's expenses.

While specifically racist laws and, to a considerable extent, racist use of conventional crime and civil laws have been successfully challenged in the United States, the South African dominant whites have elaborated and continue to impose a vast structure of laws explicitly designed to curb African, Coloured, and Asian demands for economic and political freedom. Assembly, education, employment, housing, recreation, residence, taxation, travel, and virtually every other aspect of social life is minutely regulated under an endless stream of legislation, executive proclamations, and administrative judgments. Some relaxation of "petty *apartheid*" (petty segregation laws, such as those prescribing separate post office entrances and counters for nonwhites, designating park benches by race, and the like) has been accomplished for political reasons; but the basic legal framework for controlling nonwhites, particularly Africans, remains in place, as does the pattern of discrimination and intimidation in the enforcement of conventional crime laws.

A major current emphasis in the legal control of Africans is to force them into accepting "citizenship" in the pseudo-independent states being created in an attempt to divert African political aspirations without relinquishing control of their labor—which is indispensable to the South African economy. In 1976 over 250,000 African men and women were arrested under "pass laws" aimed at restricting travel, residence, and employment opportunities: curfew regulations, controls over the entry of foreign Africans into urban areas, laws regarding the registration and production of documents, and the Bantu (Urban Areas) Consolidation Act. Penalties for such offenses were greatly increased despite the recommendation of the government's own Viljoen Commission that the pass laws be decriminalized if in fact they were at all necessary. Africans who forfeit their legal claims as South Africans by becoming citizens of the new substates are to be rewarded by the exchange of their "reference books" for "travel documents" containing much the same information. Even though they remain subject to "influx control" and other laws of South

Africa, such citizens are to be given preference in employment, housing, and other matters. Meanwhile, Xhosa-speaking Africans with no ties to the Transkei Republic (the first "independent" substate) were being pressured to apply for Transkei citizenship before being granted work-seekers' permits, passports, and other essential documents, while the police were arresting hundreds of Africans—mostly for pass law violations—in mammoth "cleaning up operations" (South African Institute of Race Relations, 1978: 384-391).

The classic racist imputations of genetic inferiority and superiority have been officially excised from it, but the ideology of apartheid continues to sustain white supremacy as strongly as ever. Modernized apartheid is designed to achieve the same objectives as the ostensibly discarded policy of *baaskap*—that is, economic exploitation and political subjugation of nonwhites, especially Africans. The difference lies in the substitution of more indirect methods closely analogous to the old British colonial system of indirect rule (compare Adam, 1971: 45-46). Regardless of the distinctions, there is still no evidence that the rulers of South Africa are able or willing to lessen their reliance upon coercive legalism and military force in dealing with nonwhites' resistance to both cultural or attitudinal racism and institutional racism (Turk, 1972a, 1977).

Closely related to class and racial struggles has been the long effort to expand the rights of individuals to believe whatever they please, to seek knowledge and happiness as they see fit, to disseminate their views as effectively as they can, and to seek by democratic means to control the polity. "Civil liberties" and "human rights" have been the main rubrics under which people have struggled for spiritual, intellectual, political, sexual, and other personal freedoms. Although the ideology of individual liberty has often run counter to the ideologies of class and racial solidarity, in specific cases the quest for the personal emancipation of human beings has generally coincided with that for their collective emancipation. This is to be expected, since class and racial attributes furnish a major part of the arsenal of stigmata that dominant respectables (by their own criteria) use to identify others as deviant.

Individuality is a threat to any polity, for it implies a potential for questioning the necessity of differences in life chances. Persons who have strong senses of their own unique worth do not readily grant the claims of others to superiority warranting greater privileges and powers. Similarly, persons with religious or other commitments transcending the ideological parameters of polity membership cannot be fully trusted to remain "loyal and obedient servants"; they may interpret some demand by the authorities to be morally *ultra vires* (for example, the refusal of Jehovah's Witnesses to be conscripted for military service). And persons who, as bohemians, beatniks, hippies, freaks, or simply the disreputable, fail to conform to conventional esthetic and ethical norms suggest by their existence the possibility of defying conventional political norms as well. As Gurr (1976: 183) makes the point, the "fundamental precondition for public order is congruence between the cultural values of the ordinary members of a society and the operating codes of order and opportunity maintained by political elites."

In every known society there has been a distinction between the "normal" range of individual variability and the "abnormality" of observed or imputed characteristics outside that range. There has been continuing tension between the reality of behavioral or relational incapacity and the interpretive process by which people have applied their standards of abnormality. Deviations from conventional norms of political belief and action have often been more expediently treated by authorities as symptomatic of personal abnormality rather than as expressions of resistance to real oppression. Rarely has the diagnosis in political cases been as candid as in that of Viktor Feinberg: "You are suffering from a dissident way of thinking" (U.S. Senate, 1972: 139).

The connection between the development of the Anglo-American law of criminal insanity and the concern for political order has always been close. That connection has generally been interpreted as one of juridical interposition of restraints upon governmental punitiveness toward those who denigrate or defy constituted authorities. "Sovereigns have always found the exemption of the insane from punishment a difficult doctrine to swallow when their personal safety or honour has been involved" (Walker, 1968: 183). The story is, however, hardly one of enlightened reason triumphant over callous autocracy.

The process of creating and refining the law of insanity has reflected the long struggle by the bourgeoisie to bring the British monarchy and aristocracy under parliamentary control while at the same time keeping the rural and urban working classes in their traditional subjugation. High-handed execution of anyone threatening royal prerogatives has been curtailed by legislation requiring due process under the common law. Nevertheless, the special concern for protecting the structures and therefore the symbols of authority led, after Hadfield's attempted assassination of George III, to the Act of 1800, which provided for a "special verdict" of acquittal on the grounds of insanity. Persons so acquitted were to be held in strict custody at the Crown's pleasure. The act was retroactive (to dispose of Hadfield), and also provided for the indefinite detention of persons whom the courts deemed (without having to consider medical evidence) too deranged to be released irrespective of any legal defenses otherwise available to them (Walker, 1968: 78-80).

In 1843, Daniel M'Naughton, intending to kill Prime Minister Sir Robert Peel, mistakenly shot Peel's private secretary, Edward Drummond. M'Naughton was subsequently found "not guilty on the grounds of insanity" and thereupon incarcerated "to await the Crown's pleasure." He waited until he died in 1864, shortly after being transferred to the new Broadmoor facility for the criminally insane. Such "leniency," as many saw it, led Queen Victoria (who herself was the target of at least seven attacks during her reign) to complain in a letter to Peel; and the House of Lords summoned all fifteen of the common law judges to questioning about the insanity defense. Their collective answers became known as the famous M'Naughton Rules: that the accused is entitled to the "special verdict" if because of mental disease (rather than merely ignorance, error, or deviant opinions) she or he is either unaware of what she or he is doing, or that it is wrong (Walker, 1968: 90-102; Moran, 1977).

Since then, "the fact that M'Naughton's crime was a political crime has been ignored" (Moran, 1977: 9). It has been assumed that M'Naughton was obviously insane because he killed the wrong man and was deluded in thinking himself persecuted. Moran, in contrast, has found strong evidence that M'Naughton was a very active participant in working-class politics and that he was indeed a target of harassment because of his activism. Sir Robert Peel, Tory Prime Minister and creator of the London Metropolitan Police, came to be perceived by M'Naughton as a key figure—as he certainly was—in promoting economic policies which "public opinion and the majority of newspapers" considered disastrous for the working classes. Having for some days observed Drummond going in and out of Peel's offices, M'Naughton not unreasonably concluded that the unfortunate secretary was Peel. Ignoring such questions as how the apparently unemployed M'Naughton could have acquired the enormous sum of 745 pounds (which bought him the best defense available), the court soon arrived at a verdict which

> served to discredit Daniel M'Naughton and the political ideas he represented by interpreting his act as the product of a diseased mind. The widespread political problems that the Tory government was experiencing throughout Britain were reduced to a personal problem plaguing Daniel M'Naughton. By regarding [M'Naughton as a lunatic] the court indicated that the explanation for this behavior would have to be sought in medical or psychiatric terms instead of political terms [Moran, 1977: 22-23; see also Moran, 1981].

British precedent has been closely followed in American practice. Politically troublesome or threatening individuals have frequently been neutralized by being treated as mental incompetents rather than as authentic political resisters. The standard official and public view is that there is of course no "physical oppression" in a democracy, therefore serious—especially violent—individual or collective political resistance is symptomatic of mental disorder. A typical conclusion:

> All those who have assassinated or attempted to assassinate Presidents of the United States (with the possible exception of the

Puerto Rican nationalist attempt upon President Truman) have been mentally disturbed persons who did not kill to advance any rational political plan [Kirkham et al., 1969: 62].

Thomas Szasz, himself a psychiatrist, has vigorously condemned the readiness with which many psychiatrists have facilitated American governmental suppression of political dissidents such as the poet Ezra Pound (Szasz, 1963: 199-207) and the general Edwin Walker (Szasz, 1965: 178-225). Accused of treasonous broadcasts from Rome during World War II, Pound was not allowed to defend his claim that his motives were patriotic. Despite ample evidence that Pound, then 59 years old, had capably managed his personal and professional life until then and was quite prepared to assist in his own defense, he was institutionalized after a questionable trial resulting in a verdict of "unsound mind." He was kept in St. Elizabeths Hospital, Washington, D.C., from 1945 to 1958, when upon petition he was released as "incurably insane, but not dangerous." Pound resumed his eccentric "hyperactive, flamboyant, at times bizarre" lifestyle, declaring upon his return to Italy that "all America is an insane asylum!"

Ironically, General Walker commanded the federal troops who maintained order during the 1957 school desegregation crisis in Little Rock, Arkansas. Having resigned from the Army in 1961, the following year he went to Mississippi, where federal troops were again being used—this time to enforce the court order compelling the University of Mississippi to admit a black student, James Meredith. Walker's explicit opposition to the "anti-Christ conspirators of the Supreme Court" and his presence at the scene of the night's rioting led to his arrest on an assortment of charges, ranging from "assaulting, resisting, or impeding" federal marshals to "inciting, assisting, and engaging in insurrection against the authority of the United States." Instead of being tried, Walker was quickly sent to the Medical Center for Federal Prisoners at Springfield, Missouri, even before the federal district court was asked to order his psychiatric examination. When a habeas corpus petition was filed, the government made no attempt to justify Walker's confinement at

Springfield. Walker was released on $50,000 bond with the stipulation that he would report within five days for examination at the Southwest Medical Center in Dallas, Texas. Walker was subsequently found competent to stand trial, but the prosecution failed to obtain an indictment and the case was dismissed. Szasz (1965: 225) concludes that the "strategic purpose" of such psychiatric diversion is always "to prevent the subject from playing a particular role." By invoking the imagery of psychological incapacity, authorities can avoid or safely defer legal confrontations on politically embarrassing or dangerous substantive issues.

The foregoing illustrations from the arenas of class, racial, and civil-libertarian struggles merely suggest the range of ways in which conventional legal formulas and processes can be used by authorities to inhibit political challenge. Linkages between such conventional legal controls and the special measures now to be discussed are extremely complex, and tend to be hidden less by the lack of evidence than by the lack of perspective. The ultimate politicality of all deviance and control is made harder to see when the definition of political criminality is legalistically restricted to the words of political crime laws. We shall look at such words and their uses, but without forgetting that they are only the most visible part of the "law talk" used to justify political policing—where the distinction between conventional and political legal control becomes increasingly blurred.

Political Crime Laws

In spite of the rubbery utility of conventional laws, the creation of laws aimed more explicitly at intolerable challengers and resisters has apparently everywhere accompanied the process of political organization, most markedly since the emergence of the modern nation-state. Among the distinguishing features of such laws are their explicit politicality, their exceptional vagueness, and their greater permissiveness with respect to enforcement decisions and activities.

(1) Legal norms defining political offenses (such as treason, sedition, subversion, or disloyalty) are publicly justified as

defenses of the polity and its governmental structure, and assert or imply the primacy of collective or ruling group interests over subcollectivity or individual interests.

To be sure, under objective and occasionally subjective pressures to take liberal, humanistic, and democratic values into account, the proponents and users of such laws play down the extent to which they are aimed at defending incumbent regimes and ruling group interests, and stress rather the protection of the (real or putative) interests of the people as a whole against the (again, real or putative) threats of foreign aggressions and machinations, alien ways and ideologies, dangerous internal political and intellectual aberrations, or—in the case of revolutionary regimes—counterrevolutionary activities, tendencies, and vestiges.

Whatever the political realities, authorities at least since Napoleon have nearly always paid lip service to the idea that they act on behalf of "the people's" true interests—as will supposedly become clear in the long run even if it seems not so in the short run. In this connection, the institutions of law have been presented as the chief means by which the true interests of the people are to be fairly determined and realized. The consensual rather than the coercive foundations and functions of law have been emphasized, even to the point of defining law as an impartial facility for equitably resolving the conflicts, misunderstandings, and problems of social living. In a truly remarkable achievement of social engineering, the cumulative efforts of superb Machiavellians, brilliant scholastics, and sincere peacemakers have created and sold the powerful mystique of law as a people's (even all mankind's) collective wisdom.

However, the mystique of law alone does not account for its relative effectiveness as a means of social control. For many, perhaps sometimes most, of a polity's subjects, the politicality of legality is further obscured by the fact that the law does provide numerous protections and services (a point usually missed or minimized by radical activists; an exception is Tigar, 1971: 330-331). Furthermore, it is also obscured by the fact that those for whom the law is more an oppressive presence than a protector and servant generally find it difficult to articulate and communicate widely and effectively their consciousness of oppression. As long as these conditions hold, both the respectably advantaged and the oppressed tend increasingly to feel the presence and workings of legal control as inevitable, and ultimately as intrinsic, features of social life. In this way the legal mystique is ostensibly validated by experience.

Both mystique and validating experience are, more than anywhere else in law, directly challenged by the existence of laws defining political crimes. In providing for the criminalization of political opponents, authorities come closest to an explicit acknowledgement of the fact that legal conceptions, agencies, and processes are (instead of facilities available and beneficial to all interested parties) ultimately partisan weapons used as needed to eliminate or neutralize those who will not or cannot play the game of interests-in-conflict by the more or less discriminatory rules of conventional politics.

(2) Legal norms defining political offenses are exceptionally vague, except insofar as political significance is asserted or recognized with respect to any act or attribute ordinarily defined as conventionally criminal.

Even then, the processes by which political significance is determined remain opaque even in comparison with the usual routines for interpreting and classifying social deviance. Moreover, even ordinarily legal activities or attributes may be made politically offensive by forbidding politically intolerable persons from engaging in or possessing them. "Probably the most striking and incontestable characteristic of the political crime concept is its elusiveness" (Allen, 1974: 26).

It is, of course, easy to find examples of vaguely defined political offenses in the laws of the most notorious of police states (such as Nazi Germany or Stalinist Russia), in which the essential element of offensiveness is simply that the authorities may punish "dangers to the state" and "enemies of the people." One of the most straightforward examples of such law is the Meiji Japanese Peace Preservation Law of 1887, which authorized the police (who had secret instructions to kill any resisters) to remove anyone living within seven miles (covering nearly all opposition spokesmen) of the imperial palace whom they thought to be "scheming something detrimental to public tranquility" (Moore, 1967: 294). A contemporary example is South Africa's blanket prohibition as "communism" of, among other things, "any doctrine or scheme ... which aims at bringing about any political, industrial, social or economic change within the Republic by the promotion of disturbance or disorder" (quoted in Matthews, 1972: 97). However, it turns out to be just as easy to find historical and contemporary examples in the laws of such liberal democratic states as Sweden, West Germany, and the United States.

In 1972, the Swedish government proposed special antiterrorist legislation which was widely condemned for its vague definitions, broad criteria of dangerousness, and loose standards of proof (Elwin, 1977). A "presumptive terrorist" would be any foreigner claimed by the Security Police to belong to or work for "an organization or group which can be expected to use violence, threat, or coercion." Presumptive terrorists could be denied entry to Sweden and were subject to arrest and to deportation; along with their Swedish contacts, they would also be liable to searches of person and residence, mail checks, and wiretapping. The "dangerousness" of an individual would be determined not necessarily by past or expected acts, but by membership or "openly expressed solidarity" with a suspect organization. Subsequently, the law was passed, and applied in several instances. Under fire, the government in 1975 replaced the special law (which had to be renewed annually) with essentially the same law made a part of the Foreigners' Code—and thus permanent. Regardless of semantic alterations, the law still left it up to the Security Police to decide when there was a "risk" of terrorist acts by a person or organization.

Also in 1972, the West German federal and eleven state governments jointly announced in Hamburg an official policy of *Berufsverbot* (job ban) to purge the civil service—which includes academics of every level—of persons whose loyalty is questionable (Mankoff and Jacobs, 1977; Oppenheimer, 1978). Such persons may be denied appointments or, if already in the service, tenured status; they may be disciplined in various ways and, in some cases, fired. Article 18 of the 1949 Constitution says that anyone who abuses the "basic rights" of a free citizen "to combat the free basic democratic order, shall forfeit those basic rights." Criminal laws based upon this article severely limit the rights of even journalistic and academic criticism and dissent. Article 33 goes on to constrain civil servants to support *actively* the "free and democratic foundations of the society." As specified in Principle 1 of the "Hamburg decrees," the only persons who are acceptable are those "who can at all times guarantee support for the free basic democratic order," actively and beyond doubt demonstrating that support "by his total behavior" both in and out of office. Belonging or having belonged to suspect organizations, being in any way connected with suspect individuals, past or current leftist political activities, including even signing election petitions and writing letters to newspapers, being critical of policies or officials—any such deviations have been enough for punitive actions to be taken against students, academics, attorneys, doctors, social workers, a tenured police officer, and even a locomotive engineer (Oppenheimer, 1978).

Probably the most internally contradictory legal system of all liberal democracies has been that of the United States, in which the strong cultural emphasis upon political freedom has been joined with a vast intolerance of actual political diversity. Since its founding, the American polity has been characterized by struggle between those who took the noble words seriously and those who used them merely as "useful fictions."

The American Constitution—with its deliberately restrictive definition of "treason" (Hurst, 1971: 3-7)—was to the Federalist authorities of the day obviously inadequate as a basis for defending their political and economic interests against the Jeffersonian Republicans. The high-handedness of the French Directorate in dealing with the American emissaries (sent to resolve the American-French conflicts precipitated by the larger struggle between France and Britain) gave the Federalists their opening. The Alien and Sedition Acts of 1798 were rammed through Congress with minimum concessions to either the Jeffersonians or the Constitution (Smith, 1956: 3-155).

There was, of course, relatively little opposition to the Alien Enemies Law—still the basis for wartime American treatment of resident nationals of enemy countries. Although certain particularly repulsive proposals (such as subjecting enemy aliens to retaliation for severities against American nationals) were offered and debated, the final product was a basically reasonable measure for emergency use in time of war.

More sweeping measures, however, placed stricter limitations upon the naturalization of immigrants, gave the executive broad discretionary powers to define and deport "dangerous" aliens in peace or war, and made it punishable as "sedition" for anyone to "combine or conspire together with intent to oppose any measure or measures of the government of the United States, which are or shall be directed by proper authority, or to impede the operation of any law of the United States, or to intimidate or prevent any person holding a place or office in or under the government of the United States, from undertaking, performing or executing his trust or duty" (Smith, 1956: 435-442).

Even though the Alien and Sedition Acts—excepting the new naturalization law and the Alien Enemies Act—expired by the end of John Adams's presidential term, this early American departure from the limitations set by the Constitution did establish precedent for the later expression in law of the authoritarian perspective which had been reflected in these acts. In the name of "national security," and invoking the constitutional guarantees to the states of "a republican form of government" and protection against invasion and domestic violence, the Congress has enacted measures such as the Espionage Act (1917), the Sedition Act (1918), the Smith Act (1940), the McCarran Act (1950), and the Communist Control Act (1954). Similar, and often even more sweeping, laws (such as those against "criminal syndicalism") have been enacted by state legislatures and by local governments.

The wartime Espionage Act of 1917 provided criminal penalties for aiding the enemy by various forms of espionage or sabotage, interfering with military operations by subverting military discipline or obstructing recruiting, interfering in any of several ways with the foreign relations or commerce of the United States, or attempting or conspiring to commit any offense under the Act. Postal service was denied to any communication, publication, "or thing, of any kind" that violated any provision of the Act. In 1918 the Espionage Act was amended by the Sedition Act, which made punishable interfering with the war effort by making or conveying "false reports or false statements" about military affairs or economic investments; using "disloyal, profane, scurrilous, or abusive language" regarding the American government, constitution, military forces, flag, or the army or navy uniforms; urging, inciting, or advocating any curtailment of production of anything necessary to the war effort; willfully advocating, teaching, defending, or suggesting anything prohibited by the Act; or "by word or act" supporting or favoring "the cause of any country with which the United States is at war or [opposing] the cause of the United States therein."

Title I of the Smith Act of 1940 and subsequent anticommunist legislation reasserted the early Federalist approach by outlawing radical political opposition regardless of whether the nation is legally at war. Not only did Title I penalize anyone who should "knowingly or willfully advocate, abet, advise, or teach the duty, necessity, desirability, or propriety" of revolutionary violence or political assassination aimed at overthrowing "any govenment in the United States," it also made punishable anyone who organized, helped to organize, or belonged to any group promoting such policies. In accord with the 1798 precedents, Titles II and III enacted more stringent provisions regarding the exclusion, registration, and deportation of aliens.

Part of the Internal Security Act of 1950, the Subversive Activities Control (McCarran) Act required registration of "Communist-action" and "Communist-front" organizations with the Attorney General, and created the Subversive Activities Control Board to facilitate implementation of the Act. In addition to requiring disclosure of the organization's officers, funds, structure, printing facilities, and (for communist-action organizations) membership lists, the Act also required individual members of communist-action organizations to register personally if their names were not on submitted membership lists. A communist-action organization was defined as one "substantially directed, dominated, or controlled" by the international communist movement, and whose objectives were to use any necessary means to overthrow the existing American government in order to establish a totalitarian dictatorship subservient to the Soviet Union. A communist-front organization was one substantially controlled by a communist-action organization and used primarily to aid a communist-action organization, a communist foreign government, or the world communist movement.

In the Communist Control Act of 1954, Congress declared open war upon the Communist Party, creating an insoluble legal problem by simultaneously depriving the Party or its successors of all "rights, privileges, and immunities attendant upon legal bodies" while maintaining its legal existence for the purposes of the Internal Security Act of 1950 (*Yale Law Journal,* 1955). Besides outlawing the Communist Party, the Act generated further ambiguities by asserting that the provisions of the Internal Security Act of 1950 apply to any knowing and willful members of the Communist Party or of any other organization whose objective is to overthrow American government by force, and by extending the provisions of the McCarran Act to "Communist-infiltrated" organizations (that is, those controlled by communists or their allies).

Some of the offenses indicated in the above examples of political crimes also exemplify the transformation of conventional crimes into political ones. For example, homicide may be defined as assassination; obstructing justice or interfering with a police officer may become treason; disorderly conduct in the form of excessively vivid or ill-timed profanity may be sedition; arson or vandalism may be interpreted as sabotage. Examples of the turning of ordinarily legal activities and attributes into political crimes are also seen, especially in the anticommunist laws. For example, public opposition to governmental war policies, analysis of the conditions under which a people may legally use violence against "their" government, membership (or past membership) in then-legal organizations, and operating a business such as a print shop or newspaper may all be interpreted as constituting one or more of such political crimes as treason, sedition, espionage, or subversion. Even these vague rubrics have often been supplemented by still more nebulous ones (for example, conspiracy, on which see Epstein, 1971: especially pages 75-101) in the course of generating procedural rules for detecting and penalizing political criminals.

(3) Legal norms defining political offensiveness provide for the relaxation or abrogation of usual legal restraints upon the processes of creating, interpreting, and—especially—enforcing legal norms.

Legal control agents are given greater discretionary powers in dealing with suspected or known violations of such laws. For instance, in Canada the ordinarily wide powers of arrest, search, and seizure granted the police are extended for the Royal Canadian Mounted Police by "writs of assistance," and under the provisions of the War Measures Act politically troublesome or suspect persons can be (and were in 1970) detained without charge or bail for up to three weeks (Grosman, 1972). In particular, the extraordinary nature of many of the tasks of political policing is very likely to be recognized in the creation of special enforcement staffs—security police, special prosecutors, political prisons, and even separate judicial or quasi-judicial officers and facilities.

Not only is it inherently difficult to specify the meanings of such terms as treason, sedition, and subversion, it is generally in the interest of authorities to leave themselves as much discretion as possible in dealing with intolerable political opposition. Implementation of political crime laws begins with the premise that the overriding objective is to destroy or at least neutralize intolerable opposition, and no legal restraint upon enforcement policies and practices is allowed to inhibit political policing to the point where such opposition has a serious chance of bringing about the destruction or radical transformation of the structure of power. Apparent exceptions, such as the Weimar Republic's hesitant responses to Nazism, are far more attributable to weakness, miscalculation, the tendency for insecure rulers to be more sympathetic to rightist than to leftist revolutions, or cooptive tactics by economic elites attempting to ride with instead of against the winds of political change than to any legalistic or idealistic commitment to the rule of law.

In this connection, Ingraham and Tokoro (1969) have pointed out that the nineteenth-century liberalization in Western Europe (excepting England) of legal doctrine regarding the definition and punishment of political crimes occurred only where (and as long as) "the dualism or pluralism of morality is well recognized"—thus accepting the possibility that a regime can be morally and honorably defied—and in polities

(1) in which the dominant political philosophy was liberalism, (2) where the state's claim to legitimacy was infirm and relativistic, (3) where there was a clear division between the concept of the state (as merely representative of those interests in society politically in the ascendant) and the society as a whole, and (4) where the government's or the state bureaucracy's conception of itself was not as the representative of all the people of the society, but rather as the *custodian* or *protector* of a constitutional order which ensured the institutions constituting the source of its political and economic power.

They go on to note that such a lenient view was associated with the political activities of dissident members of the ruling class (errant "sons" or "brothers") who were more or less temporarily out of power, and that the doctrine has declined with the spread of mass democratic political participation in the twentieth century. In regard to the specific concerns of their article, they thus account for the recent decline of the doctrine in Japan and its never having been accepted in the United States.

Even though political policing is not necessarily limited by legal procedural norms, it is to some extent constrained by them as at least official legitimations and guidelines, as well as factors to be taken into account in calculating the consequences of enforcement decisions. Therefore, the extent to which departures from the ordinary legal inhibitions upon enforcement activities are prescribed or permitted is a clue, at least, to the authorities' degree of concern about such usual procedural restraints and about the relative differences between legal orders and police states.

South Africa's laws provide many examples of the curtailment, neutralization, or abrogation of procedural norms usually
or formerly directing and limiting enforcement activities. For
example, in 1965 the Police Act was amended to permit any
member of the force, regardless of rank, to "search without
warrant any person, premises, other place, vehicle, vessel or
aircraft, or any receptacle of whatever nature, at any place in
the Republic within a distance of one mile of any border
between the Republic and any foreign State or territory and
seize anything found by him upon such person or upon or at or
in such premises," and so on, in performing the legal functions
of preserving the internal security of the Republic, maintaining
law and order, investigating any offense or alleged offense, or
preventing crime. In addition, under various statutes, judicial
decisions, proclamations, and regulations, persons suspected of
engaging in, contemplating, or knowing something about such
crimes as sabotage and terrorism—both very broadly construed
(see Matthews, 1972: 164-177)—may be legally detained incommunicado, indefinitely, and without being charged before
a court with any offense, may be spied upon and restricted as
the police (notably the security police) see fit, and may be
convicted on the basis of entrapment, self-incrimination,
coerced testimony, the statements of unknown and unexamin-
able witnesses, failure to *disprove* allegations and charges, or
many kinds of inferential or other evidence whether obtained
legally or illegally. While the South African legal system is
outstanding in the degree to which explicit and detailed attention has been given to the removal of restraints upon political
(and increasingly upon more ordinary) policing, the authorities
of many polities have, in practice, if not always as explicitly,
gone as far in shedding the restrictive formulas of whatever may
be the local variant of "the rule of law."

In the United States the reduction or elimination of ordinary
legal restraints in dealing with political criminality has been
accomplished partly by direct legislation and judicial decision,
but largely and more effectively by the creation and operation
of special investigative and quasi-judicial bodies (such as the
House Un-American Activities Committee and the Subversive

Activities Control Board), as well as various counterinsurgency "intelligence" agencies and programs. Some of the extraordinary measures which have been authorized by the Congress, and generally supported by the courts, are: revocation of naturalized citizenship; preventive detention; restriction of the right to travel, both outside and within the country; limitation of the right to seek and hold employment, governmental and nongovernmental; electronic and nonelectronic surveillance on a "possibly relevant" instead of a "probable cause" basis; compulsory disclosure of self-incriminating evidence; and denial of access to trial courts. It should be noted that such legislation has typically undergone some delimitation in the judicial process, and has in rare cases ultimately been found unconstitutional (for example, the registration provisions of the Internal Security Act and its creation of the Subversive Activities Control Board—after nearly twenty years of legal appeals).

Where special legislative and administrative bodies have been established, their procedures have been modeled only very loosely after those of the ordinary legal process, so that the ordinary inhibitions (such as rules of evidence, prior discovery, specific charges, and personal accountability) have little or no effect. The legislative investigating committee ("that legalized atrocity," as Walter Lippman called it fifty years ago) has received particularly severe criticisms because of many historically notable examples of cavalier disregard for legal and ethical principles. Legal analysts and civil libertarians, and, on occasion, the Supreme Court, have been especially unhappy with the development of the technique of punishing political dissidents by unproven accusations (made safe for the accuser by legislative immunity) and publicity adding up to "character assassination" (Pritchett, 1958: 31-47). "McCarthyism" was not invented by the one-time senator from Wisconsin (see Theoharis, 1971), nor did it end with his eventual condemnation—precipitated by his failure to heed the advice of experienced red-baiters such as Richard Nixon (Harper, 1969: 128) and to distinguish politically appropriate targets such as leftist intellectuals from inappropriate ones such as military leaders.

Politicality, vagueness, and permissiveness in the legal definition of political criminality are especially apparent in the
growing preoccupation with "terrorism." (Exactly one year
after the 1976 bibliography of 103 items on terrorism, the
American Law Enforcement Assistance Administration issued a
second edition listing 168 items.) Analysts such as Yonah
Alexander, editor of a new (fall 1977) research publication,
Terrorism: An International Journal, have noted that there is
"state terrorism" as well as revolutionary terrorism; but nearly
all of their attention is being given to the latter.

Even when the concern is exclusively with revolutionary
terrorism, conceptual confusion is rampant. For example,
participants in a 1973 conference held in Italy attempted
unconvincingly to distinguish between "indiscriminate terror
tactics" and "legitimate rebellion." Violent acts by persons
"engaging in wars of national liberation [are] lawful [when
they are not] committed indiscriminately, disproportionately
and contain an international element or are against interna-
tionally protected targets" (Bassiouni, 1975: xii). The editor of
the conference proceedings himself offered the concept of
"purely political crimes": any violations on behalf of freedom
of thought, expression, and belief, association, and religious
practice "if they do not incite to violence" (Bassiouni, 1975:
407-408). The general state of legal and scholarly thought on
terrorism is reflected in the conclusion of a recent examination
of relevant Canadian law, that "the term has acquired an extensive meaning that tends to embrace all acts of which one does
not approve and in which some element of either horror or
threat independent of the act itself is involved" (Green, 1976:
4). As South African law makes plain, terrorism does not even
have to be restricted to violent acts; there one is a terrorist if
one does anything, inside or outside the Republic, considered
even likely "to embarrass the administration of the affairs of
the State" (quoted in Matthews, 1972: 170).

Summary

The legal system of a modern polity includes both "law talk"
and "law in action" components used by the authorities to

control the subject population both directly (command controls) and indirectly (field controls). Both kinds of controls serve to discourage resistance to the political will of the authorities. If the level of discontent and questioning of authoritative decisions becomes unacceptable, conventional civil and criminal laws, as well as political crime laws, may be used to justify and facilitate suppression of opposition. What alternatives or combinations will be employed depends upon the not necessarily synchronized judgments of various official and, often, unofficial authorities regarding the balancing of potential costs and benefits.

Whether the basis for resistance has been class exploitation, racism, or the denial of personal freedoms, legal controls have always been used to counter efforts to bring about any really drastic changes in the established structures of power and privilege. In addition to the general arsenal of legal controls, bodies of law have been developed to deal with such specialized problems as keeping labor relations, race relations, and political activism within safely conventional bounds. Centuries of workers' resistance to expropriation of their lands and exploitation of their labor have led to relatively sophisticated legal devices by which class conflict may be managed without being resolved. Officially repudiated almost everywhere today, programs of racial domination have been articulated most fully in the legal systems of the United States—until recent years—and of the Republic of South Africa. Demands for civil rights, including the right of political dissent, have been legally resisted in an ingenious variety of ways, perhaps most chillingly by treating the politically contrary as mental incompetents.

Laws explicitly defining political criminality are distinguished by their politicality, vagueness, and permissiveness regarding enforcement procedures. Though the ideology of modern legal systems is democratic, this mystique is belied by the promulgation of laws overtly designed to facilitate the suppression of political opposition. Vagueness in defining the elements of such crimes as treason and sedition permits the insecurities and ambitions of authorities to override juridical reasoning in deciding their meaning in specific instances. Those assigned the task of political policing are given extraordinary leeway to find the most efficient means, the ultimate aim being preservation of the authority structure irrespective of legal constraints. The currently most fashionable term for revolutionary politics, "terrorism," epitomizes the conceptual arbitrariness of legal definitions of political criminality.

CHAPTER 3

THE CRIMINALITY OF
POLITICAL CRIMINALS

What is a rebel? A man who says no . . .
        Albert Camus (1956: 13)

In his brilliant treatise on rebelliousness, Camus (1956) assumes the identifiability and authenticity of *l'homme revolté,* and immediately proceeds to explore with critical sympathy the historical styles and rationales of revolutionary expression. Camus's work is indispensable as an introduction to the psycho-philosophical springs and dilemmas of individual and collective revolution. But it is the identifiability and authenticity of particular rebels, not the philosophy of rebelliousness, that constitute the crucial problems for activists and analysts in the world of political struggle. Whether seeking allies, enemies, or simply the truth, the prime task is to specify in predictively useful ways the locus and nature of political offenders and offensiveness. The pressing questions are: *Who* is the rebel who says no? *Which* of the people are, or are likely to become, rebels who insist on their right to draw the limits beyond which authorities are not to go? *Whose* inclination is to resist the given order instead of deferring to it? *How* committed are the resistant? *What* forms does or will their resistance take?

How such questions are to be answered depends upon finding criteria by which to define rebellious people and rebellious behavior. The methodological problem is that of specifying what rebels must actually do or be to authenticate their claims to be such, or else to validate authorities' labeling of them as rebels.

Identifying a political criminal as "anyone who commits X" is obviously inadequate when the slippery nature of political crime laws leaves the meanings of both "X" and "commits" so open to manipulation. We know that political crimes are offenses attributed to persons defined by the authorities as politically intolerable. What we do not know is whether and when there is an adequate factual basis for such attributions, even where judicial decisions or police practices have established some working definitions of otherwise impossibly vague legalisms. Therefore, to characterize political criminals it is necessary to learn what we can about persons who have clashed with authorities, whether or not deliberately and whether or not they have been legally designated as political criminals.

Aside from relatively objective studies, many propositions about political offenders and offensiveness have been advanced by writers who themselves were active in political conflicts. Such "participant observations" obviously cannot be taken at face value, but they do provide inside, firsthand evidence to supplement the generally more indirect and inferential research of outsiders. However, insider materials on political criminality must be treated with special caution because of the unusual concern of participants in struggle (compared with those in other situations) with promoting appropriately biased impressions. ("We" are noble and wise; "they" are cruel and benighted.) Because the effort to bias observations and conclusions is so intense and deliberate—and is extended as far as possible to affect objective research as well—the first step in locating and characterizing political criminals is to understand and be alert to the tactical significance of stereotyping in conflicts over political authority. After considering the role of stereotyping, we attempt in this chapter to specify (1) the social characteristics of political resisters, (2) links between social characteristics of resisters and modes of political resistance, and (3) relationships between combinations of resisters and resistance, on the one hand, and variations in the control effort, on the other.

Stereotyping in Political Struggles

People never can know everything about one another, so all social interaction proceeds on the basis of perceptions grounded in less-than-perfect information. Direct and vicarious experiences with one another, other people, and other situations generate the criteria by which distinctions are drawn, expectations formed, and judgments reached. Applied more or less unconsciously, these criteria give significance ("social reality") to exterior attributes (such as physical features, articles of clothing, body movements, speech patterns, or objects in possession or use) by imputing their links to interior ones (such as genetic make-up, emotional state, mental capacity, behavioral predispositions, or moral character). To the degree that initial judgments of significance are maintained irrespective of the presence of disconfirming or the absence of confirming evidence, selective perception becomes stereotyping.

Stereotyping furnishes both a reflection and a means of political conflict. Opponents are more sensitive to their respective faults than to their respective virtues. The more intense the struggle, the more negatively will salient, identifying characteristics of the opponent be evaluated. At the extreme, the process of stereotyping eventuates in dehumanization: The enemy is judged to be so inhumanly evil or contemptible that anything may be done to "it" without subjectively compromising one's own humanity and sense of morality. (One does not torture a young boy, but "interrogates a terrorist," just as one does not murder a father of young boys, but "offs a pig.")

The negative stereotyping of one's enemies is matched by the positive stereotyping of oneself and one's allies. Within the camp, the common struggle promotes appreciation of one's fellows. Formerly unfavorable judgments tend to be revised so as to downplay or ignore defects, or even redefine them as virtues. Thus, a brutal killer may be perceptually transformed into "a good man to be with in a tight spot," or an ignorant zealot into "a dedicated patriot and loyal comrade." There are, of course, limits: The subjective tendency to overappreciate supporters and allies may be overridden by evidence of dangerous ineptness or undependability, or by tactical decisions requiring sacrifices or purges.

Not surprisingly, then, intolerable dissidents tend to be unfavorably stereotyped by their enemies and favorably stereotyped by themselves and their friends. Very little relatively nonpoliticized (that is, "objective") evidence is available. In addition to the growing number of studies of "rioters" and of student activists and demonstrators, there are some historical studies of revolutionists and biographical studies of assorted dissidents and champions against injustices, supplemented by a growing literature on contemporary terrorists.

Common to both "subjective" and "objective" characterizations is a noteworthy lack of concern with whether the individuals or groups being characterized have been found innocent or guilty of lawbreaking. This may be taken as another bit of evidence pointing to the fluidity, if not the irrelevance, of legalistic distinctions when authority-subject conflicts involve or imply political challenge rather than merely conventional crime. That conventional offenses and political acts may overlap is recognized; but everyone understands that this is not really the point—which is, in a word, the *politicality* far more than the *criminality* of the challenge.

Characterizations of political criminals by officials and respectables emphasize the moral and/or intellectual deficiencies of anyone challenging, or even relatively indifferent to, the structures and personages of authority. The inadequate socialization and consequent intellectual disabilities of political criminals may be asserted, while even those few who are recognized to be genuine in their moral convictions may still be depicted as tragic objects to be pitied rather than admired (unless, of course, they were eventually vindicated by history as winners).

A major recent statement of this view has been offered by Schafer (1974), whose conception of the political criminal (as apparently of all criminals) is that of a person who has not been adequately socialized to comprehend fully the moral principles and realities of the social order into which he or she has entered. Because of the limitations on his or her knowledge and reasoning produced by inadequate moral education, or "saturation," in terms of the prevailing morality, the political criminal "is more open to the influence of emotional forces" and has a "broader freedom of will" (Schafer, 1974: 111). The lack of emotional control and intellectual discipline makes it likely that the individual will, upon encountering the normative requirements of "his social group" personified in a sovereign authority, develop "anxiety, anger, hostility, or other emotions over the threat to the worth of his self, his morality, and his society, as he views them" (p. 112). Unable to grasp the formulations and resolutions of moral issues with which he or she is presented, the political criminal seems likely to be confirmed and reinforced in his or her antagonism and psychic distress by "the threat of being punished by criminal law, or better, the element of sanction in the definition of morality" (p. 112).

Not being either "necessarily ignorant" (p. 113) or "necessarily mentally sick" (p. 139), the political criminal may, as a genuine or "convictional" offender, construct out of his or her "inner torment" (p. 154) an altruistic-communal image of a better social order that "mirrors the hopes of all those common people who are likewise inadequately socialized to the moral command, but who somehow do not reach the degree of inner conflict that can lead to the action-prompting emotional dilemma" (p. 150). Alternatively, of course, the political offender may be merely "pseudoconvictional," an opportunistic and egoistic law-violator no different from "conventional criminals" (pp. 145-146, 154-158).

In similar vein, Hacker (1978) has offered psychiatric conjectures about the kinds of people who practice "terror" and "terrorism"—his terms for "the manufacture and spread of fear" by the powerful and the "so-far powerless, the would-be powerful," respectively. Seeking to control by frightening, "terrorists from above and below" employ "carefully staged and choreographed" displays "to intimidate their audience into submission or rebellion, paralysis or violent action, all presumably for the benefit of the terrorized" (Hacker, 1978: xi). After recognizing that most violent acts are committed by "so-called normal people" and criticizing the use of "psychiatric jargon . . . for aggressive denunciation" (p. xiv), Hacker somewhat inconsistently goes on to distinguish three types of terrorists: "the crazy, the criminal, and the crusading (the most typical variety)" (p. 8).

Though noting that these types are rarely encountered in pure form, Hacker (1978: 13-19) goes on to list the distinctive attributes of each type, both "from below" and "from above." The flavor of his characterizations is indicated by the following excerpts from his extensive chart:

Crazy	Criminal	Crusading
predominantly inward-directed aggression, intrapunitive, suicidal	predominantly outward-directed aggression, extrapunitive, homicidal	intrapunitive and extrapunitive, suicidal and homicidal
unstable, immature, often distractible and inept individuals with weak ego and overt behavior disturbances	detached, often dehumanized individuals, often unstable and inept but also often with seemingly intact ego and without overt behavioral disturbances	fanatical individuals, often with seemingly intact ego, without overt behavior disturbances
unpredictable, vascillating, hesitating	predictable, mostly determined, ruthless	predictively unpredictable, determined, ruthless

Hacker's summary portrait of the really political offender, the "crusading terrorist," is that of a pseudo-social fanatic blindly entrusting conscience, identity, resources, hopes, and life itself to a group cause, the rationale for which is often unrealistic and usually understandable only to sympathizers. The slant in this psychiatrist's perspective is that psychopathic terrorists "from below" seem to be the rule among those who resist political authority, while their opposite numbers "from above" are exceptional psychotics such as Idi Amin of Uganda and the Greek Cypriot strong man Nicholas Sampson. Repeatedly decrying any resort to violence as barbaric and futile, Hacker (1978: 262-285) yet implicitly accepts in his policy recommendations the inevitability on occasion of last-resort governmental violence to stop terrorism from below (if "negotiation" fails), but offers no policy advice on when and how terrorism from above might be nonviolently, much less violently, resisted.

Such ostensibly sympathetic and patronizing images of political criminals are more often presented by scholars than by legal officials, who are inclined to deliver more forthright denunciations of political criminals as neurotics, psychopaths, fools, self-serving hypocrites, or the treacherous agents of foreign powers. The late J. Edgar Hoover provided some classic examples in his many publications, speeches, and official reports and statements as he characterized those involved in various "extremist" associations. For instance, he characterized the Students for a Democratic Society in the following typically vivid terms:

[They are] embittered, vociferous revolutionaries who have ignited many campus insurrections [and] have nothing but contempt for this country's laws. [Their extremism is] all the more dangerous because it emanates from a group of young people (many of whom are highly trained academically) whose bitterness against their country is so intense that many of them want blindly to destroy without much (if any) thought as to what is to emerge from this destruction. Their ill will is guided more by whim than plan, more by cynical pessimism than hope for a better future, more by the spiteful revenge of the frustrated than by dedication to a noble cause. A type of youthful barbarism seems to have taken hold of this . . . extremely small minority of our college generation. [Characterized by] a shallow intellectualism, a lack of knowledge, and an arrogant self-righteousness ... they have been captured by an antiquated totalitarian system known as Marxism-Leninism [Hoover, 1969].

Against the demeaning or hostile imagery promulgated by the establishmentarians, the opposition of course offer images of themselves as the true patriots, the moral and even the intellectual elite, or the really creative and spiritually free members of society. Political offenders tend to be depicted sympathetically as essentially altruistic and noncriminal public nonconformers, who are driven only by repression to define themselves as criminals against the state and to engage in criminal acts as political tactics (see Clinard and Quinney, 1973: 159-164). The emphasis is upon the nobility and authenticity of the political criminal, as opposed to the oppressor's unprincipled greed, cruelty, and hypocrisy. The revolutionary is generous where the oppressor is niggardly, helpful and polite where the oppressor is exploitative and rude, and so on through a litany of virtues against vices. Not only does nobility inhere in political criminality, but its tactical necessity is often emphasized, as in Guevara's (1969: 45-46) fairly detailed prescriptions to the effect that

> the guerrilla fighter, as a person conscious of a role in the vanguard of the people, must have a moral conduct that shows him to be a true priest of the reform to which he aspires. To the stoicism imposed by the difficult conditions of warfare should be added an austerity born of rigid self-control that will prevent a single excess, a single slip, whatever the circumstances. The guerrilla soldier should be an ascetic, ... a sort of guiding angel [always helping the peasants] technically, economically, morally and culturally.

Marighella ("the Guevara of urban warfare") offers a similar portrayal in his *Minimanual of the Urban Guerrilla* (reprinted in Mallin, 1971: 70-115):

> A definition of the urban guerrilla ... A political revolutionary and an ardent patriot, he is a fighter for his country's liberation, a friend

of the people and of freedom. . . . Today to be an assailant or a terrorist is a quality that ennobles any honorable man because it is an act worthy of a revolutionary engaged in armed struggle against the shameful military dictatorship and its monstrosities. . . . The urban guerrilla is characterized by his bravery and decisive nature. He must be a good tactician and a good shot. . . . The moral superiority is what sustains the urban guerrilla [who] must possess initiative, mobility, and flexibility, as well as versatility and a command of any situation [Mallin, 1971: 71-73].

The positive and negative stereotyping of political resisters does not result merely from an understandable regard for "us" as against an understandable hostility toward those perceived to be our enemies. More important appears to be the crucial significance of ideological power resources in the struggle over political authority. Regardless of whether the labels reflect the genuine beliefs of those who wield them, they are weaponry in the effort to manipulate what people know and feel about the political organization of their lives. Apart from their value as morale-boosters for activists, the greater value of the labels lies in their impact upon the general population—those who are not immediately involved but who are potential members or allies of either the establishment or the opposition forces.

The manipulation of perceptual realities is the key to success in revolutionary and counterrevolutionary politics (Turk, 1972b: 16-17, 59-61). The political offender, to the extent that she or he is aware and purposeful, seeks to destroy the assumptions about what "is" and "ought to be" upon which the authority of rulers largely and finally depends. This not only increases the material costs of control, but also eventually destroys or reduces the capacity of rulers to use the organized violence of police and military forces (much less the instrumentalities of conventional politics and law) to resist challenge and suppress resistance. A case in point is the loss of credibility and power experienced by the Shah of Iran.

Authorities, on the other hand, try to deal with challenges to their authority—that is, their rightfulness and their presumed effectiveness—by counterpropaganda designed to protect the structure of beliefs, ignorance, and force upon which the polity rests. In short, the confrontation of positive and negative stereotypes of political criminals is a product and a part of what is fundamentally a "battle for minds."

As observed in the introductory chapter, the transformation of power into authority is accomplished by conditioning the great majority of people to accept power relationships as real, inevitable, unavoidable, and perhaps even right. The longer a polity endures, the more accustomed people become to thinking and living in ways supportive of the status quo. Authorities try to maintain their ideological hegemony as the best long-term insurance against threats to their structural dominance, though never relinquishing violence as the best short-term insurance. (The point is developed in the following chapter on the nature and functions of political policing.) Revolutionaries, in seeking to destroy all habitual understandings and beliefs about the social order, make it as difficult as possible for established sources and channels of information and exhortation to function. The more severe their conflict, the more both authorities and revolutionaries use stereotyping, not only to make themselves look good and their opponents bad, but also to subvert and distort whatever factual, esthetic, and moral assertions the other side may make.

At the most simplistic level, opposing ideological assertions merely contradict each other, with authorities typically claiming superior or privileged access to the essential facts. A somewhat less obvious tactic is to oppose the opponent's facts with seemingly contradictory but actually incommensurate facts. That is, if radical critics assert extensive and increasing poverty, racist oppression, or police harassment of dissidents, establishment apologists may point to rising average incomes and welfare payments, case histories of educationally or occupationally successful minority persons, or the numbers of police officers assaulted in the course of duty.

Or one may simply disseminate selected "out of context" statements by the opposition (the more "extreme," the better), with careful excision of any qualifying, conditional clauses and sentences. A dissident party calling for "revolutionary changes in our crime-control policies" may be caricatured as a "subversive movement" aiming at "revolution." An official call for "innovative ideas about improving the administration of justice" may be ideologically filtered to become a sinister gambit to trick dissidents into betraying themselves, and/or a signal of approval to those who want more punitive measures. In the stereotyping of information and exhortation, no communication emanating from the enemy is to be credited.

Yet another tactic is to use stirring slogans and other imagery to inspire and direct action, and to minimize any inclination to analyze the rationales of action. Situations and events as well as people and communications can be depicted in stereotyped ways, as with, for example, the bloody clash of May 1886 in Chicago's Haymarket Square. Three months earlier, the struggle for higher wages and an eight-hour shift at the McCormick reaper factory culminated in a strike. Both sides were adamant, tens of thousands of people were eventually on strike against McCormick and other employers, and there were numerous instances of violence against and by the strikers. On May 3 several demonstrators were killed by the police after an officer was reportedly fired upon.

August Spies, editor of an anarchist-socialist newspaper, called for a mass meeting to protest the killings. Because of an imminent rainstorm the crowd was rapidly dwindling and the speakers preparing to end the meeting when a formation of 176 policemen marched up the street to the speakers' wagon. The commander ordered the meeting to disperse; the speakers readily complied, climbing down from the wagon and indicating their peaceable intentions. Someone threw a bomb over the crowd into the ranks of the police, killing at least one of them and wounding others. The police attacked the crowd and killed or wounded an indeterminately large number of people. Many people attacked the police. Seven officers died in the melee; days later, eight known radicals, including Spies, were arrested. Spies and three others were hanged November 11, 1887; one committed suicide, two had their death sentences commuted to life, and the eighth was sentenced to fifteen years instead of death. The bomber's identity was never learned, nor the origin of the bomb. These appear to be the established, agreed-upon facts. What "really" happened?

To radicals and sympathetic labor historians, and probably to most workers, the Haymarket bombing was the act of an irresponsible individual, and the ensuing riot an assault by the police upon innocent working people. The convictions and executions were acts of vengeance in the absence of "a shred of evidence linking these men to the bomb" (Brooks, 1971: 70). Those responsible for the tragedy were the callous and recalcitrant employers, biased journalists, and brutal officials of Chicago specifically and the state and nation generally. The police were the destroyers of law and order.

To conservatives, officials, and trade union opportunists such as Samuel Gompers, and probably to most nonunion people, the Haymarket bombing and riot were the work of anarchists and socialists (the distinction minimal and irrelevant anyway) interested only in chaos. "Their concern was less with the 8-hour movement, the ballot, and peaceful techniques of trade unionism than with the obliteration of ordered government" (Trible, 1978: 18). Responsibility for the tragedy is attributed to the fanatics who promoted upheaval, and who were duly convicted for conspiring to murder the officer immediately killed in the explosion. As symbolized by the commemorative statue, the police fought and died in discharging their duty to preserve law and order.

To summarize, the point of all this stereotyping of people, communications, and events is, for authorities, to reinforce people's confidence, fatalistic acceptance, or unthinking assumption that the government is in control and the familiar routines of social life are continuing. For revolutionaries, the contrary objective is to force or induce people to believe that the government is losing its grip and that the persistence of the social order cannot be depended upon. If people believe the government is weakening, governance becomes more difficult and costly; if they believe that everything is falling apart, then social life becomes more ambiguous and unpredictable. And, conversely, believing the government is strong contributes greatly to making it so, as believing in the continuing reality of "our way of life" is an essential component of that reality. Events and structural realities can overwhelm and change beliefs or support and strengthen them; but people's conceptions and feelings remain the crucial intervening variables in determining when and how the detailed alternations of social stability and social change will occur.

Characteristics of Political Resisters

Given that the stereotyping of political criminals is an aspect of the political struggle itself, the question to which we return is, "What kinds of people become political criminals?" Or, more specifically, who becomes eligible for political criminalization? The search for an answer is complicated by the problematic linkage between the *behavioral* realities of political resistance and the *definitional* realities of criminalization by authorities. It is obvious that people may resist without being criminalized, and may be criminalized without having resisted. But it is equally obvious that *some* people who resist are criminalized, and that *some* people who are criminalized have indeed resisted.

The simplest way to handle the analytical problem is to consider "kinds of people," "resistance," and "political criminalization" as *variables* that may interrelate, or interact, in causally significant ways. Even though conventional usages and the quality of available evidence force us to use mainly the language of "qualitative" rather than strictly quantitative analysis, the quantitative analogy should at least help in suggesting when and how behavioral and definitional realities coincide.

Kinds of people includes all those attributes of social advantage or disadvantage, learning experiences, situational pressures or inducements, and mental capacities or states which have been considered in studies of persons believed to have engaged in political resistance, or to be prone to do so.

Resistance refers to any form and degree of dissent, evasion, disobedience, or violence in challenging authorities. Acts of resistance may be instrumental or expressive, calculated or spontaneous, organized or unorganized.

Political criminalization encompasses all forms and degrees of punitive attention given to resisters by authorities, with reference to whether such attention is direct or indirect, legal or extralegal, mild or severe. For present purposes, political criminalization is viewed simply as the treatment accorded people who in fact resist political authority. As will become clear in the following chapter, political criminalization is actually a far more complex and problematic matter than is suggested by the imagery of "reaction" to resistance.

Research on the characteristics of political resisters has dealt with the extent and nature of differences both between resisters and nonresisters and, much less, among various kinds of resisters. Some attention has been given to connecting kinds of people to kinds of resistance, but very little to relating either kinds of people or kinds of resistance—much less their relationship—to forms or degrees of political criminalization. Virtually nothing has been done to trace or account for changes over time in any of these variables or their relationships. Apart from some cogent observations about the conditions under which various historical revolutionary efforts succeeded or failed, and scattered discussions of the careers of eventual revolutionaries, scarcely any consideration has been given even to the possibility that such changes may occur. What follows is, therefore, no more than an attempt to construct testable generalizations based as far as possible upon the available evidence.

Resisters and nonresisters have been scored and compared on various measures of status, class, and power, as well as numerous indicators of social attitudes and psychological states or inclinations. There has generally been a presumption that the social, attitudinal, and psychological measures are interrelated, or else that their possible or probable relationships constitute a primary research concern. In particular, investigation has typically centered, or been grounded, on the question of status, class, or power differentials, then moved toward consideration of attitudinal and/or psychological characteristics as correlates of such differentials. Thus, *kinds of people* as a variable may be more specifically defined as "social class," to be examined first in terms of particular indicators and correlates, then in relation to types of political resistance and of official response.

One of the most ancient beliefs about political resisters is that they are likely to come from the lower, most disadvantaged classes. The reasoning goes that people who are deprived will generally be dissatisfied with their lot and envious of their social superiors, and prone to unlawful defiance and incitement if their dissatisfactions and envy reach pathological levels. Whether their pathologies are defined in reference to inadequate class-linked socialization, the frustrating realities of lower-class life, vulnerability to manipulation by demagogic agitators, or some other causal source, political offensiveness and "lower classness" are presumed to be strongly associated. This classic and plausible view does not fit the facts as they have been generated in studies of historic and current revolutionaries, urban rioters and rebels, student dissidents and radicals, and sundry civil disobedients and champions against social injustices.

Apparently, "it takes almost as many kinds of men and women to make a revolution as to make a world" (Brinton, 1965: 119). The evidence from various studies and sources, including his own analysis of the membership of the Jacobin clubs before and after the destruction of the French monarchy in 1792, led Brinton (1965: 105) to conclude that although typically more, rather than less, advantaged, "the revolutionists tend to represent a fairly complete cross section of their communities. . . . This is as true of the Bolsheviks as of the Puritans and the Jacobins." Strauss (1973) has recently provided further evidence of the heterogeneity of political offenders in his study of 73 leading Russian revolutionaries of the 1905-1917 period. From his analysis of biographical materials he identified 6 "role types" (rebel, striker, propagandist, party organizer, upper-level politician, intelligentsia), who varied greatly in such characteristics as class origins, education, and age. Nevertheless, consistent with Brinton's earlier observations, these revolutionaries were found to be disproportionately higher class in their origins.

Although successful in demonstrating the social heterogeneity of known revolutionaries and their generally higher-status beginnings, historical studies such as those of Brinton and Strauss have not succeeded either in accounting for the differentiation of revolutionaries from their class peers or in characterizing followers and allies of revolutionary elites. Brinton (1965: 105-119) considers a variety of possible "character types" (such as "sentimental idealists," "opportunists," "crackbrained schemers," and "disputatious, contrary-minded persons") without reaching any systematic conclusions. Strauss does adduce evidence for linkages between types of revolutionary activities and social characteristics. For example, rebels and strikers tended to be less educated, younger, lower class, while the politicians and intelligentsia tended to be more educated, older, higher class. There is little in his data to indicate what distinguished these people from other less and more educated, younger and older, lower- and higher-class Russians, though he did find that the 73 revolutionists were especially likely to be urban, higher class (and specifically the aristocracy), Jewish (excepting strikers), and educated (with students definitely overrepresented).

Stimulated by the "long, hot summers" of the 1960s, there have been numerous attempts to determine just what characteristics distinguished those black Americans who "rioted" in Detroit, Los Angeles, and several other cities from those who did not. Studies carried out for the United States National Advisory Commission on Civil Disorders (1968) thoroughly devastated the popular view that the militants, or "rioters," were drawn almost entirely from the bottom of the social scale. Fogelson and Hill (1968: 223) summarized the findings of several studies in which various methods had been used:

First, that a substantial minority of the Negro population, ranging from roughly 10 to 20 per cent, actively participated in the riots.

Second, that the rioters, far from being primarily the riffraff and outside agitators, were fairly representative of the ghetto communities. And third, that a sizable minority (or, in some cases a majority) of the Negroes who did not riot sympathized with the rioters.

Instead of standing alone as a minority of "riffraff," the militants clearly expressed and acted out grievances held by a great many people living in the communities, regardless of the ostensible stakes in the security of person and property in those communities.

That resistance to the authorities cut across socioeconomic distinctions within the ghettos proves, of course, only that black ghetto residents share a common experience and resentment of being an oppressed racial minority. It is logically possible, accordingly, that an association between lower social class and political resistance will be found where the special aberration of racism does not override the class relationship. However, evidence from research on (mainly and usually white) student radicals and dissidents does not support this line of argument.

Compared with their nonactivist peers, student activists have tended to come not from the more disadvantaged but from the more advantaged classes. (For a cogent assessment of the literature, see Weinberg and Walker, 1969.) Thus, research on the correlates and causes of "campus unrest" and "activism" has directly encountered the problem hinted at in the historical studies of revolutionaries—that of accounting for a class link with political resistance opposite to that expected by the conventional wisdom. Given that students come disproportionately from the higher classes of the larger society, the class thesis is not, of course, adequately tested by investigation of so truncated a segment of the class ladder. Yet, it is significant that the more materially and educationally disadvantaged students, with the poorest noncollege and postcollege prospects, are less likely to engage in protest actions even on behalf of their most immediate interests—presumably in eliminating the elitism and scholasticism that reduce their chances of academic survival and later "success."

The problem of explaining student dissidence and radicalism has, therefore, been largely the classic one of explaining higher-status "defections" from systems guaranteeing the defectors disproportionate powers and privileges. In general, such defectors have been characterized as either "going through a stage" (something like sowing one's political wild oats) in some presumed natural history of maturation, or else alienated as the result of traumatic or otherwise aberrant emotional and intellectual experiences. A less psychological line of explanation has emphasized the lack of institutional opportunities for high-status persons to accede to the favored positions which they learn to assume are their due.

Specifically in reference to student activism, the first kind of explanation is exemplified by the traditional belief that student activism is a product and expression of natural youthful, that is, naive and impatient, idealism (a frequent theme in the Report of the President's Commission on Campus Unrest, 1971). The second, or "alienation" thesis is offered in either a version stressing the more or less pathological bases of intergenerational conflict (Feuer, 1969) or a version pointing up the more or less normal responses of youth to the combination of humanism and affluence found in some higher-class families (Flacks, 1971: 54-56).

Weinberg and Walker (1969: 80) have provided an example of the "institutional opportunities" explanation in their thesis that "the form, persistence, and consequences of [student activism] are significantly affected by the existing structural relations between the university and the state and between student politics and the environing political system." On the basis of analyses of student political activities in the United States, Britain, France, and Latin America, they suggest that the more extreme forms of student collective politics tend to be associated with the lack of congruence and continuity between campus politics and careers in the environing system.

Tygart and Holt (1972) subsequently found that student activists at UCLA in 1966 were more likely than nonactivists to have experience in conventional politics (precinct work in the 1964 presidential election), which they took to be evidence contrary to Weinberg and Walker's suggestion. However, in his response, Walker (1972) emphasized the distinction between (a) *structural* analyses of linkages between campus and off-campus political organizations, and (b) *statistical* analyses of aggregated data on individual political activities. He also noted that the *timing* of data collection may have been crucial, in that the Tygart-Holt data were obtained just at the point "when student activists had become aware that Johnson did not intend to terminate the war, and reflect the beginning of the delegitimation process to which Skolnick (1969: 99-100) refers" (Walker, 1972: 968). Thus, survey data on past activities are not an adequate basis for predicting future patterns of political activism even in individual biographical terms.

Opposition to American military intervention in Vietnam eventually spread far beyond the arena of student politics to involve large numbers of persons from the world outside the universities. Therefore, studies of these resisters can be expected to provide better evidence on the class and other characteristics of those who challenge political authority.

On the campuses, the initial impetus to challenge the American government's conscription program came from higher-class students from large metropolitan areas (Ferber and Lynd, 1971: 180; see also Gaylin, 1970). As the resistance movement grew, more lower-class and nonacademic individuals became involved; but the membership and especially the leadership of organized "peace groups" continued to be mainly middle or upper-middle class. Lower-class people were typically either progovernment or apathetic, and tended to join the resistance late if at all. Only as Washington's military, diplomatic, and economic failures became overwhelmingly obvious did significant numbers of the more disadvantaged begin to join the resistance. Even then, the increasing lower-class involvement is ambiguous because "everybody" was becoming involved, in ways ranging from participation in demonstrations and other activities as active members of formally organized peace groups to admitting negative attitudes to pollsters. (For an analysis of the resistance movement, see Useem, 1973.)

As the class composition of the resistance movement was, as far as peace groups were concerned, clearly biased upward, the common presumed association between lower classness and political offensiveness has again been disconfirmed. Indeed, the problem appears more and more to be that of accounting for the association between *higher* social classness and political offensiveness.

Bolton (1972) compared each of three (overwhelmingly suburban middle-class) peace groups, a random sample of nonmembers, and a small aggregate of radical pacifists from outside the community in regard to several attitude and alienation scales. The peace-group members were more liberal than the nonmembers in their political attitudes and "had a markedly more internationalist-prodisarmament orientation in foreign-policy attitudes" (Bolton, 1972: 541). However, there was considerable overlap, leading him to conclude that differences in political and foreign-policy attitudes alone did not adequately explain peace-group membership, and to focus attention in his analysis upon alienation.

Using measures of Seeman's (1959) familiar five conceptual types of alienation, Bolton compared his various groups on *powerlessness, meaninglessness, normlessness, isolation,* and *self-estrangement.* No significant differences among the groups were found on *self-estrangement,* probably the most "psychological" of the scale types in terms of standard conceptions of psychopathology. Relative to nonmembers with comparable socioeconomic characteristics, the peace-group members were high on *normlessness* ("alienation from the economic-political structure") and *isolation* ("degree of commitment to popular culture, including the general values of American society"), relatively low on *meaninglessness* ("the condition where the individual cannot predict with confidence the consequences of acting on a given belief"), and especially low on *powerlessness* (feeling that people cannot collectively control their fate, but are subject to some natural or supernatural destiny or at least to powerful elites). The radical pacifists differed little from the peace-group members on political and foreign-policy attitudes, and also scored high on *normlessness* and *isolation* and low on *powerlessness*. But they were, in contrast, highly alienated on *meaninglessness*. Finding that the degree of radicalism among the peace-group members was also directly related to the same three kinds of alienation, Bolton (1972: 556) hypothesized that

> a high degree of meaninglessness, normlessness, and isolation, in combination with a high sense of being able to influence a social environment perceived in terms of a sociological mode of causation, predisposes persons toward radical social action.

Predispositions do not, of course, guarantee that individuals will in fact engage in acts of resistance to political authorities. Bolton's, and other, evidence suggests that political resistance is far more likely to be a product of social involvements and recruitment than of private tendencies and self-selection. Yet, there obviously is an interaction of some kind between the pull and push factors, instead of either alone causing resistance behavior. If the key predisposition or "push" is alienation (in the senses of normlessness, meaninglessness, and isolation) conjoined with a feeling of present or potential efficacy, or power, then the conjunction must somehow be related to higher classness, as must the kinds of social network involvements that interact with alienation *cum* efficacy to produce not only *acts* of resistance but also varying degrees of commitment to resistance *roles.*

Mueller (1973) has provided a fairly systematic theory that plausibly links variations in class socialization to variations in political consciousness and orientation. Developing a theme consistent with studies by Keniston (1965, 1968), Flacks (1967, 1971), and others, he argues that middle-class people in advanced industrial societies typically learn modes of communicating ("elaborated language codes") that encourage and facilitate reflective, analytic reasoning, while lower-class people learn "restricted codes" that instead promote nonreflective, descriptive reasoning. Equipped with better tools for critically understanding the abstract complexities of political affairs, middle-class youth are strongly encouraged or allowed to use and sharpen their analytic skills by their characteristically democratic, participatory, permissive family environments. Lower-class youth are, on the other hand, socialized in family environments marked by parental authoritarianism and rigid, restrictive patterns of control. Accordingly, middle-class youth learn to think for themselves and to question authority; lower-class youth learn to defer to authoritative others and lack the motivation and means to challenge the bases of others' authority.

There are also, of course, variable features of the nonfamily environment (such as educational and peer-group experiences) that may influence personal development. Nonetheless, the class differences in socialization are considered to be the fundamental sources of differences in political orientations. The general thesis is that "the lower classes tend to be the principal scaffolding of existing institutions in advanced industrial society and . . . the middle classes appear as those who could potentially articulate alternatives to the political and institutional status quo" (Mueller, 1973: 85).

To articulate political alternatives is, of course, not necessarily to insist upon them. Since not all middle-class youth are equally sensitized to political and related economic and cultural failures and wrongs, there must be something more distinctive—at least in quantitative, if not qualitative, terms—about the experiences of the more sensitive. Why are they more sensitive? How does sensitivity come to be expressed in acts of political resistance?

The most sensitive appear to come from families that emphasize "the primary importance of commitment to the world of ideas and the arts rather than to personal material success or religious devotion" (Flacks, 1971: 54). Youth from more materialistic middle-class families may be less likely to develop as finely tuned an awareness of political issues and possibilities, but they will presumably still share the more general resentment of authoritarianism and arbitrary restraint resulting (if Mueller's theory is correct) from middle-class socialization. They may, then, be more likely to develop a varient of *ressentiment*—a seething discontent with what life offers, associated with an "identity crisis" marked by feelings of aimlessness, negativism, and ultimate futility (see Scheler 1961: 45-48).

Both the politically ultrasensitive and the resentful may be alienated, but the alienation of the politically sensitive seems more likely to be a focused response to social institutions than a diffuse expression of personal malaise. The former appears more likely to result in deliberate and sustained political resistance, the latter more likely to lead to apolitical hell-raising or poorly considered and sporadic political defiance (see Scheler, 1961: 24, 31). Alliances between the two types of alienated middle-class youth can be expected to be stormy, which may help account for the quarrels between the "serious revolutionaries" (SDS) and the more moderate participants in the Vietnam war draft resistance (Ferber and Lynd, 1971: 155, 162, 164, 176-77, 267), as well as the disdain of traditional "structural" Marxists and neo-Marxist "cultural" revolutionaries for each other.

Plausible as all this may be, it is still far too much of a simplification merely to invert the conventional theory of lower-class political rebelliousness. The majority of middle-class youth do not become politically rebellious; and it seems obvious (in the absence of any contrary evidence) that even the most intellectual and liberal middle-class families produce far more political establishmentarians than rebels.

To complicate matters further, it seems that alienation in the sense of powerlessness may be associated with political resistance even when more generalized feelings of alienation (normlessness, meaninglessness, isolation) are not particularly salient. Less than a year before the French rebellion of May 1968, Seeman (1972) found a large majority of French workers—whether manual or nonmanual (that is, lower or higher status)—to be alienated in the sense of feeling "power-less" vis-à-vis the government against which they, collectively speaking, later rebelled. Yet, their most specific concern apparently was their "lack of control in the work sphere" rather than their general political helplessness in Gaullist France. As Seeman observes in trying to sort out the inferential relation-ships between his 1967 attitude data and the 1968 "events of May," it is necessary to distinguish powerlessness from distrust—that is, to distinguish feelings of helplessness from those of no confidence in the intentions or skills of officialdom. The French workers apparently felt powerless in the sense of having little political trust, but not in the sense of having lost their capacity to give political expression to their distrust.

Paige (1971), cited by Seeman, found evidence in Newark, New Jersey, that self-reported black "rioters" similarly com-bined political distrust with "a strong sense of personal political competence." Compared with voters (relatively high on trust) and civil-rights activists (moderately trusting), riot participants were the most distrustful among politically sensitive respon-dents (that is, those high on political information). The *com-bination* of distrust and high information, rather than either separately, distinguished rioters from nonrioters.

Moran (1974) applied a "developmental model" in analyzing the case histories of twenty persons who committed major, often violent acts of political resistance in the United States between 1965 and 1972. His subjects were Jane Alpert, Dwight Armstrong, Karl Armstrong, Bill Ayers, Daniel Berrigan, Philip Berrigan, Stanley Bond, Kathy Boudin, H. Rap Brown, Stokely Carmichael, Bernadine Dohrn, Daniel Ellsberg, Ted Gold, Samuel Melville, Diana Oughton, Katherine Powers, Terry Robbins, Mark Rudd, Susan Sax, and Cathlyn Wilkerson. All were political criminals according to Moran's (1974: 61) criteria (using Schafer's concept of the "convictional" offender): "1) the individual must be motivated primarily by a sense of con-viction, and 2) his unlawful act must be designed to attack the social structure for the purpose of bringing about a reorganiza-tion of the social system." Excepting Oughton (millionaire's daughter) and Melville (laborer's son), these individuals were middle class in origin. Unlike the majority of other politically sensitive resisters, these became fully dedicated to bringing about social change even at the price of physically endangering others and themselves. Moran concluded that these revolutionaries had generally gone through the following process— which he hypothesizes is characteristic of all political criminals as defined (see Moran's summary, 1974: 139-140):

(1) Experienced personal strain because of perceived discrepancy between ideal and actual social conditions, and resolved that the discrepany (and therefore the strain) had to be eliminated.

(2) Developed a political-institutional view of the problem, emphasizing the need to destroy and replace existing institutions.

(3) Concluded that every alternative to violence had been tried and had failed, that violence was morally and pragmatically justified, and that to stop short of violence meant to abandon the just cause.

(4) Felt an overwhelming sense of personal responsibility and commitment that made it seem an unbearably dishonorable cop-out not to commit the necessary acts.

(5) Committed a serious crime in the belief that it would contribute in any of several direct and indirect ways to the destruction of the institutional sources and devices of exploitation and repression.

Despite some diversity in backgrounds and the nature of the offenses, Moran's case descriptions show in every instance a person who was encouraged to develop a strong sense of personal worth and efficacy, to seek and use information, and to view the social world as manipulable and improvable. More to the point, these people appear to have shown an unusual integrity—or rigidity—in examining and accepting the implications of their social understanding. For them, looseness of understanding was unacceptable; personal inconsistency between conclusions (or impressions) and actions was intolerable. When they had reached an intellectual position attuned to their moral sensibilities, they felt no need for further reflection and delay.

It can be said that the twenty cases refused to grow up and learn better. To them, maturity meant exchanging their youthful idealism, moral sensitivity, and hope for a better world for adult responsibility with its accompanying need for conciliation, selective morality, and emphasis on settling down [Moran, 1974: 94].

The known members of West Germany's upper-middle-class "Baader-Meinhof gang" generally followed the same developmental path as their American counterparts, but seem to have gone farther into "the politics of nihilism." Even though Becker's (1977) psychologistic interpretations must be heavily discounted, her descriptive accounts do suggest that some leading figures of the group moved beyond radical chic and the stage of considered, limited acts to a posttheoretical, essentially anti-intellectual war against all authority structures, that is, social life itself. The individual careers of Ulrike Meinhof, Andreas Baader, and their eventual comrades-in-arms began with their participation—with thousands of other young Germans—in specific campaigns against university authoritarianism and the Vietnam war policies of the United States. As some university reforms were instituted and popular opposition to the American military effort mounted, most youthful militance was defused. This isolated in time a minority whose greater alienation and/or political sensitivity made its members unable to be satisfied with reforms. Nothing short of the total collapse of all Western (including Soviet Marxist) social structures—political, economic, cultural, familial—would be tolerated.

Not even Herbert Marcuse, that most eminent philosopher-friend of the radical students, was considered worthy of a hearing by 1968 (Becker, 1977: 59-61). After all, he himself had told them that they were the most enlightened people in the world and just as exploited as everyone else, so what else did they need to know? (For a highly critical assessment of Marcuse's offerings, see Marks, 1970: 132. Marks concludes that "the possibilities of revolutionary change from a repressive society to one of abundant beneficence are as nebulous after the Marcusean analysis as before.") With all now so obvious, the point was (in a common misconstruing of Marx) not to bother further with understanding the world, but to get on with changing it. Henceforth, any attempt to analyze the options for effective social action was not only unworthy of consideration, but even a pernicious distraction from full commitment to the "praxis" of revolution. Marcuse's own concept of "repressive tolerance" was invoked to justify the abandoning of all debates and calculations in favor of an unlimited commitment to violence. Success was to be equated with the magnitude and political-economic impact of destruction.

Despite the rhetoric of the persisting Baader-Meinhof tradition and the commission of occasional crimes of resistance, few West German or other Western revolutionaries have yet reached the level of total alienation and total war consciousness exhibited by the "outlaw ex-intellectuals" of the Japanese *Rengo Sekigun,* or United Red Army. To them, discussion is ended; all facets of the bourgeois world system must be obliterated. Extreme, suicidal violence anywhere in the world is their trademark, as in the Tel Aviv Lod airport massacre of Puerto Rican tourists. Everyone who consciously or unconsciously accepts, uses, or contributes to the bourgeois culture of capitalism or state socialism is considered worthy of death—which effectively means all of us. Even members of their own organization have been horribly tortured to death for such offenses as "displaying bourgeois tendencies by wearing make-up and showing affection for the opposite sex," wearing earrings, and "asking for the 'luxury' of a Kleenex tissue while enjoying the 'bourgeois warmth' of a sleeping bag" (McKnight, 1974: 158-170). It is hard to imagine any greater degree of rejection of every dimension, basis, correlate, or product of authority and social activity.

Out of the zero-sum conflicts of the desperate Third World have emerged many revolutionaries whose names have come to stand for implacable resistance: Carlos Marighella, the supreme tactician of urban terrorism; Fidel Castro and Che Guevara, strategists and exemplars of rural guerrilla war; George Habbash, Yasir Arafat, and others of the Palestinian Arab opposition to the Israeli state and the West; Frantz Fanon, who surpassed Georges Sorel as prophet, analyst, and advocate of revolutionary violence; Ho Chi Minh, symbol of perseverance against the military might of Western imperialism; Vladimir Ilych Ulianov (far more renowned as Lenin), Leon Trotsky, Joseph Stalin, and Mao Tse-tung, who engineered the most awesome revolutions in history. (Though the Russian revolution predates the conception of "Third World," it too was a struggle against capitalist exploitation in an underdeveloped, largely agrarian setting.)

Virtually always such remarkable individuals have originated in the more educated, traveled, generally privileged classes of their respective societies. Awakened by parents, studies, peers, or personal experience to the inequities and miseries of social life around them, they have been unable to follow the usual route of separating their personal interests from their social concerns. Though altruism is too simplistic a term for their motivation, it is clear that the meaning of their lives has been fused in their consciousness with the struggle to eradicate disprivilege. Their own life chances are in a sense forfeited on behalf of the collective life chances of those with whom they identify in struggle. The damned, the "wretched of the earth," cannot possibly deserve their fate, so whatever and whoever is believed responsible for their miserable, hopeless lives must be destroyed. Freed, "the people" will do good and not evil to one another, and thus to themselves.

> When we speak of the people, we do not mean the comfortable ones, the conservative elements of the nation. . . . When we speak of struggle, the *people* means the vast unredeemed masses, to whom all make promises and whom all deceive . . . who long for great and wise changes in all aspects of their life [and who] are ready to give [even their lives to reach those changes] [Castro, 1968: 27-28].

> We are nothing on earth if we are not, first of all, slaves of a cause, the cause of the people, the cause of justice, the cause of liberty [Fanon, quoted in Geismar, 1971: 185].

We are now in a better position to suggest some propositions about the kinds of people who resist political authorities. First, the "riffraff," or lower classness theory of political criminality must be rejected. The safest generalization from the available evidence is that higher-class as well as lower-class people may become political resisters. Perhaps a less safe generalization, but one supported by considerable evidence, is that higher-class people are *more* likely than lower-class people to become resisters. The link between higher classness and resistance may well be attributable to class-linked patterns of socialization that provide individuals with the motivation, confidence, and means to resist authoritarian restraint and manipulation. The more that humane and intellectual, rather than materialistic, values are emphasized in their home environments, the greater the sensitivity of people to political domination seems likely to be. Therefore, the sharpest articulation of political challenges and the first philosophically rationalized actions against domination can be expected to come not from the lower but from the higher classes, and the most "enlightened elements" at that.

Although outstanding exceptions appear (for example, Big Bill Haywood), when lower-class people do become resisters, it seems that they are more likely to be joiners than initiators, and to be similarly characterized by the combination of cultural and political alienation with political sensitivity and a sense of personal efficacy. At each stage of radicalization they seem likely to be more focused than higher class resisters upon immediate problems of economic well-being and security. Analogously, the resisters of the poor Third World appear generally more concrete in their motivations and objectives than do their sometime allies in the affluent Western nations.

What triggers alienation into action? Gurr's (1970) work on a theory of violent political resistance suggests that the main factor may be *relative deprivation,* which he defines as "actors' perception of discrepancy between their value expectations and their value capabilities" (p. 24). When life does not appear to offer what it should, people of any class are disposed to challenge the right of those who dominate to do so, and to transfer their allegiance to "other groups, other causes, other nations" (Grodzins, 1956: 131). (Ruthless suppression, destitution, and failure to effect improvements by even the most heroic efforts may, of course, stifle the disposition to resist—a subject to which we shall return in the following chapters.) However, there are limits to the explanatory power of the relative deprivation theory.

The most obvious limitation is that it does not fit the facts as we understand them: Those who take the lead in political resistance are relatively *privileged,* not deprived. Alienation that leads to consciously political action is more characteristic of the advantaged. At least in the earlier period of an organized resistance, the advantaged take the lead, to be joined eventually by the disadvantaged if they can be mobilized. It may well be that the relative deprivation thesis is more useful as a mobilizing device than as an explanation of the process of mobilization itself. Whatever the degree of differential life chances, those who are disadvantaged will find it hard to reject a patently true description of their position. Nor will they readily disagree with moral assessments of their relative position that (1) define it as undeserved, (2) laud them as more virtuous than the advantaged, (3) blame not them but the advantaged and "their" institutions for the persistence of injustice, (4) inspire them to believe that revolutionary overthrow of the dominant classes and their institutions will bring the good life, and (5) promise inevitable victory if the disadvantaged will join in all-out revolutionary struggle. That the meanings of "deprivation" and "justice" are fully elastic makes some form of the relative deprivation theory supremely useful for mobilizing those whose combination of alienation, political sensitivity, and sense of efficacy is not enough to move them to serious revolution.

Add only an appeal to the ethnocentrism found in some form or degree among all peoples (Levine and Campbell, 1972), and the developmental path of individual resisters may be replicated on a grand scale in an analogous development of masses into movements of resisters. As Laqueur (1977a: 376-377) makes the point, any ideology combining socialist and nationalist elements is sufficient for tapping and channeling popular discontent if it is used in an environment where grievances are felt and governmental controls are weak. When the connection is made, via an ideology of relative deprivation, between (a) the generalized (or transferred) political identities of sensitive higher-class revolutionaries, and (b) the grievances of resentful lower-class rebels, organizing and carrying on revolution becomes (in the absence of successful repression) increasingly everyone's business. Class and other distinctions dissolve as political resistance becomes the normal behavior of the many instead of the deviant behavior of the few. Recalling Brinton's observation, it does indeed take all kinds of people to make a revolution.

Given that political offenders may be of any age, higher or lower class, politically sensitive or merely resentful, and broader or narrower in their focal concerns and objectives, the task remains of trying to link the kinds of people who resist political authorities to (1) the forms and degree of resistance in which they engage, and (2) the varied responses of the authorities who criminalize them.

Political Resisters and Resistance

Although the detailed tactical possibilities are limitless, there appear to be four basic forms of political resistance: *dissent, evasion, disobedience,* and *violence. Dissent* includes any mode of speaking out against the personages, actions, or structures of authority. *Evasion* refers to any attempt to avoid being constrained by the expectations and demands of authorities, as in hiding or fleeing to avoid military conscription. By *disobedience* is meant any explicit nonviolent rejection of such expectations and demands; *violence* is, then, the most extreme form of disobedience. Each form of resistance may vary in regard to whether it is calculated or spontaneous (or "instrumental" versus "expressive") and organized or unorganized (the product of a deliberate collective opposition, or an idiosyncratic act or program that may coincide with similar or complementary actions by others to result in an aggregate opposition).

Research evidence is lacking. Yet, several linkages between (a) these forms and dimensions of resistance and (b) the social class and related characteristics of resisters appear to be plausible enough to warrant consideration. Given considerable evidence, on the other hand, that the reactions of authorities to political deviance vary with the nature of the challenge and with the social characteristics of the challengers, an effort will be made not only to identify such linkages between resistance and resisters but afterwards to relate them to variations in political criminalization.

Our earlier discussion suggests that the most salient attributes of political offenders are whether they are politically sensitive or merely resentful in their alienation and whether they feel a sense of personal efficacy. The combination of being sensitive to political arrangements and their effects and feeling able to do something about those considered to be intolerable is (it was tentatively concluded) associated—but not perfectly—with having the socialization of novitiates in the relatively privileged and powerful classes. To be considered first, then, are the various possible combinations of sensitivity/resentment, presence/absence of a sense of personal efficacy, and higher/lower social class of resisters in relation to the forms and dimensions of political resistance.

(1) Dissent is a characteristically higher-class form of resistance, especially insofar as it is an articulate elaboration of a reasoned political philosophy. Grumbling, diffuse complaints, or emotional rhetoric with little if any empirical grounding or logical coherence are more likely to characterize the "dissent" of those lower-class persons who do speak out against the given order. (Perhaps it should be emphasized that lower-class people may have quite valid comprehensions of political situations and issues regardless of whether they are able to articulate that understanding in complex terms and whether they dissent or resist in some other way.)

In the absence of a developed political consciousness, or sensitivity, dissent is likely to be an expression of a more or less vague resentment of one's political fate rather than an instrumental action intended to achieve any specific changes in the political environment. If more a spontaneous outcry than a calculated move in a program of resistance, it is probably less likely to be the product of an organized resistance than an episode or isolated event in an unorganized history of struggle against the bonds of political subordination.

The expressive political defiance of some may, of course, be accompanied or promoted by the instrumental actions of others. An essential feature of programmatic resistance to authority is the effort to capitalize upon whatever discontent exists, by promoting minor into major grievances and by orchestrating what may for the participants be spontaneous protests. Only empirical inquiry can determine the extent to which any specific challenge reflects the authentic feelings and views of those who speak, and whether the voicing and phrasing of dissent are spontaneous. That such research is both methodologically and politically difficult has already become obvious in our examination of political stereotyping and of studies of political resisters. The problematic relationship between expressive and instrumental dissent reflects the complex and essentially hierarchical relationship between higher-class and lower-class political dissenters.

Immediately authentic cries of protest are more likely to come from the lower class; but the words they use and the stimulus to use them are very likely to be generated by the higher class, for whom their own and the dissent of others may well be significant only in tactical terms. Higher-class resisters tend to exaggerate the relative importance of dissent, especially of reasoned dissent derived from elaborate theories implying long-term strategies. In contrast, lower-class resisters seem prone to favor nonverbal over verbal resistance, and to trust emotional commitments undertaken in faith more than reasoned commitments derived from theoretical conclusions and predictions.

The distinction between dissent and expressions of resentment is variable. Levels of political sensitivity or consciousness
are not easily measured, and depend considerably upon subjective criteria of understanding and commitment. Assuming for
now the equating of consciousness with active commitment to
radical social change, one might score people according to
whether they ask and how they answer the following questions:

LEVELS OF POLITICAL CONSCIOUSNESS

Highest
"*How* can we transform social life?"
"Why not *all* of us together?"
"Why not *us* instead of *them?*"
"Why not *me* instead of *him*?"
Lowest

The ordering of questions implies that self-interest alone
provides no basis for a truly political critique of the given order
and that group parochialism is no more than self-interest
multiplied—especially in a heterogeneous and complex society.
That is, expressions neither of selfishness nor of tribalism would
alone constitute dissent as a mode of political resistance. On the
other hand, accounts giving some kind of reasons and possibilities for cooperation within, among, or across groups would
presumably be scored as dissent, as would analyses of how
resistance might be appropriately and effectively mounted. A
higher-class Californian merely demanding lower property taxes
and a lower-class Canadian postal worker merely demanding
higher wages are alike in that their political awareness stops at
selfishness and tribalism. Contrast them with an Ivy League
university chaplain declaiming against military conscription and
American policy in Vietnam, or a Chicano spokesman calling
upon organized labor and the general public to join migrant
farm workers in their struggle against exploitation by boy-
cotting grapes and lettuce. Elements of self-interest are un-
doubtedly still present, but do not constitute the terms in
which protest is expressed. An even clearer example is Martin

Luther King's appeal to whites to help end legalized racial oppression in order to free themselves as well as blacks from the brutalizing, self-defeating impact of racism.

(2) Evasion has been a characteristically lower-class form of calculated resistance, for those experienced in powerlessness learn to avoid rather than to seek confrontations. Unlike higher-class people, lower-class people do not generally experience freedom and encouragement to review and contest the actions of authorities. Lower-class socialization promotes a fatalistic acceptance of subordination as a fact of life. When relative deprivation sparks resistance, the most deprived are still likely to fear exposing themselves to the anticipated wrath of their rulers, so that the most immediately appealing form of resistance is to conceal oneself, one's activities, or one's resources from them.

Resenting intolerable demands placed upon them for goods or services, lower-class people typically develop ingenious ways of minimizing their conformity. Ostensible stupidity, ignorance, laziness, and utter destitution have been standard devices for resisting authority without the dangerous appearance of doing so. Slaves, peasants, and proletarians have all learned how to play the game of withholding at least something of what their overseers force from them—which is always basically their labor. Pilfering (theft) and hustling, or conning, are bolder methods of keeping (or taking) something back; though they may be more dangerous, they still do not constitute an open challenge to authority as such.

As long as the lower class is unable to organize, evasion will be largely an expressive means of resistance. Even if their experiences lead them from generalized resentment to greater political sensitivity, the lack of organization will keep evasion from becoming systematic rather than idiosyncratic. Without coordination on a sufficiently wide scale, techniques of evasion are unlikely to have much instrumental significance as far as political impact is concerned.

Historically, the instrumental use of evasion by lower-class people has been associated with the clustering of erstwhile slaves and peasants as workers in factories, and with their subsequent unionization. Unionization is interpretable in the present context as a process in which slowdowns, make-work, sabotage, pilfering, and myriad other older and newer devices for withholding labor come to be institutionalized in a legal and/or customary arsenal for routinized, even ritualistic, conflict monitored by the authorities.

Short of suicide, the ultimate form of evasion is to become a fugitive, withdrawing physically from the distressed social position in which one has been kept. That lower-class suicide rates are relatively high may reflect the inability of many lower-class resisters to find a tolerable alternative form of resistance. Those who do succeed in slipping out of the social control nets of the authorities may become politically irrelevant or relevant, depending largely upon whether they find collective support and upon their level of political sensitivity. For those whose political consciousness is at the level of resentment rather than sensitivity, collective evasion will probably lead to "outlawry" or "banditry" (Hobsbawm, 1959). Politically sensitive fugitives are more likely to generate a guerrilla resistance, distinguished from banditry by the primacy given to the goals of political change.

In modern states it becomes increasingly hard to flee beyond the jurisdictional claims of the authorities. Both banditry and classic guerrilla resistance are becoming obsolescent, even tragicomic, as in the New Mexico revolution by Mexican Americans proclaiming in the late 1960s the Republic of Rio Chama (Love, 1969). Consequently, becoming a fugitive means either going underground, possibly to attempt another experiment with urban guerrilla tactics (on the poor prospects, see Oppenheimer, 1969), or seeking asylum in the domain of some other set of authorities. Traditionally, seeking political asylum has been an evasion tactic more likely to be used by higher-class than by lower-class resisters. Similarly, going underground to carry on political resistance has been almost the *rite de passage* for higher-class revolutionaries. It appears, then, that evasion by fleeing is becoming more a higher-class form of resistance, as the lower-class versions are ruled out by the technology of political control. Indeed, it may be that the joint effect of the institutionalization of some kinds of lower-class evasions and the suppression of others is making evasion itself an increasingly higher-class form of political resistance.

(3) Disobedience is characteristically higher class insofar as it involves what are perceived to be high risks of failure and punishment. To disobey authorities openly and nonviolently indicates either a reckless disregard for the possible consequences or considerable faith in the tactical worth of such audacity. Lower-class resistance may erupt in spontaneous disobedience, as when individual workers simply throw down their tools and refuse to work or soldiers refuse to fight under especially inhumane or hazardous conditions. However, deliberately to set oneself up as a target for official displeasure goes against the lessons of lower-class socialization. Such action is likely to seem merely foolish to persons without enough political sensitivity to perceive disobedience as a tactical alternative to other forms of resistance.

Civil disobedience, in particular, is unlikely to be attempted without a compelling faith in its at least potential efficacy. Standing up against the authorities presupposes that political changes are likely to follow whatever painful consequences must first be accepted. Lower-class experiences do not prepare people to accept readily the probability of early pains for the sake of problematic later political gains. Even if some protections are legally or otherwise presumed to be available, lower-class people are less likely than higher-class people to find verbal guarantees of official restraint convincing. Nor are they as likely as higher-class people to risk their "lives, fortunes, and sacred honor" in seeking recognition by the authorities of their moral philosophical rights. The history of "passive resistance" everywhere has pointed up the difficulties met by higher-class strategists (from Gandhi in South Africa and India to King in the

United States) in persuading discontented members of the lower classes to follow them in the path of righteous and instrumental disobedience.

Evidence from the biographies of the notably (or nobly) disobedient suggests, in conjunction with that on passive resistance movements, that the relationship between social class and the organization of calculated disobedience may be curvilinear. Individuals who on their own explicitly refuse obedience to the authorities, especially without taking steps to avoid or fight punishment, are very likely to be persons who have learned to make their own assessments of political truth and to act upon them with confidence. Higher-class socialization is more likely to produce such people. At the same time, higher-class people are more inclined than lower-class people to organize themselves for resistance (as for almost any other activity). It follows that calculated disobedience by lone individuals and by highly organized groups (such as sit-ins) will usually involve higher-class more than lower-class resisters, while less organized and more spontaneous collective disobedience (such as riots) will be likely to involve greater lower-class participation.

(4) Violence has traditionally been considered a lower-class form of political resistance. But the association is more presumed than demonstrated, and stems mainly from the ideological assumptions of authorities and their respectable supporters. As many social analysts have observed, violence *against* the lower class will probably be ignored or defined away, while violence *for* the lower class is likely to be given maximum attention and magnification. Granted the inadequacy of the evidence and the definitional bias, there still do appear to be sufficient grounds to accept the traditional view with qualifications.

Spontaneous, unorganized collective violence expressing resentment of the fact or the consequences of political subjugation is characteristically lower class. The "rabble" or "mob" is a familiar historical phenomenon, as are slave uprisings and peasant revolts. Higher-class people are less likely to participate in such outbursts because of their ingrained reluctance to act without prior calculation of the probable costs and benefits. Though their political sensitivity may lead higher-class resisters to engineer or applaud mob action, they themselves are likely to hesitate to join unless it is defined as tactically necessary (for example, to inspire followers, show solidarity, or gain recruits or sympathizers to the cause).

Lower-class and higher-class persons seem equally likely to commit individual acts of violent political resistance. In either case such idiosyncratic action will probably reflect resentment more than sensitivity with respect to the mechanisms of political dominance. Those who think to make a political difference by a merely personal and isolated violent act may be more likely to be lower class, because their socialization would presumably make the essential futility of such resistance less easily perceived. However, ostensibly the same acts may be committed as more or less reasoned tactical moves dictated by a theory of "the propaganda of the deed" that justifies the occasional destruction of property or lives, whether of key authorities or of randomly unfortunate "noncombatants."

Where episodes of violent resistance are components in some strategy, they are likely to be produced by organized and politically sophisticated resisters who are trying to undermine the bases of political dominance by demonstrating the inability of the authorities to counter resistance and protect supporters. Assassination and terrorism thus acquire tactical justification, signaling the escalation of resistance by the politically sensitive as they opt for war with the authorities. Such calculated, organized, collective violence marks the ultimate commitment of sensitive resisters to significant political changes. Defiance in this form and intensity is irreversible, and usually leads to either a full-blown revolution or annihilation. At some not precisely determinant point in the escalation and spread of resistance and the deterioration of political controls, the meaning of "political criminality" becomes too problematic for the concept to be applicable. "Criminal" resistance becomes "military" (as well as cultural, economic, and even diplomatic) opposition.

In abstract analytical terms, dissent, evasion, disobedience, and violence by political resisters are moves matched by countermoves in a "conflict game" with the authorities of a specified arena (or "matrix" of possible move combinations with their probable outcomes). It is the countermoves of authorities which are now considered.

Political Criminalization as Reaction

Reaction by authorities to resistance may, in very general terms, be direct or indirect, legal or extralegal, and severe or mild. *Direct* reaction is by officials without involving non-official sources of pressure or restraint; *indirect* reaction involves the use of such sources (employers, creditors, news media). *Legal* reaction utilizes legal norms and procedures to deal with resisters; *extralegal* reaction refers to any form or degree of punitive response that is beyond legal review and the legality of which is clearly dubious even by the criteria of political crime laws. *Severe* reaction is any degree of punitive response that involves physical assault, imprisonment beyond a few days, and/or the loss of material resources for either the resister or persons emotionally significant to the resister, such as relatives, friends, and sympathizers; *mild* reaction is anything less. While considering variations in the reaction of authorities to political resistance, it is essential to keep in mind that authorities cannot be assumed to wait for actual political deviance to occur before acting to control it, and that police actions will not necessarily be directed solely against individuals actually engaged in political resistance.

The reaction of authorities to political challenge varies with their perceptions of the contextual significance of particular acts. If an act is believed to be no more than a spontaneous idiosyncratic "deviation" by a few resentful individuals, the kind and degree of criminalization will vary fairly directly with the openness and the violence of the resistance. Calculated acts as part of a program of resistance by an organization will elicit a relatively severe response, with the choices of legal or extralegal and direct or indirect control tactics depending upon the degree of perceived threat. The perceived relative power (more or less correlated with social class) of the opposition will be an additional contingency affecting the form and degree of official response to calculated and organized resistance.

Given that (a) resistance is spontaneous, unorganized, and limited to a few individuals, and (b) such individuals are far more likely to be politically resentful instead of sensitive, the severity of reaction will probably be greatest for violence, less for disobedience, somewhat less for dissent, and least for evasion. The more public and explicit the challenge, the more the authorities will feel constrained to make an example of offenders. For instance, a few eccentric voices crying ineffectually against wickedness in high places will more likely be tolerated than influential critics articulating dissent in specific terms. Similarly, unpublicized draft evasion by a few apolitical rural boys will probably be dealt with more leniently than highly publicized refusals by numerous politically sensitive or resentful college students. Irrespective of the form and degree of resistance, lower-class resisters are likely to receive more severe treatment than are higher-class resisters.

The use of legal methods alone will be more likely in such cases where the form of resistance is dissent or disobedience instead of evasion or violence. There are several necessary qualifications to this generalization. First, public and articulate but nonviolent resistance will usually involve higher-class people, who are able to invoke whatever legal rights of challenge may be officially available. Second, individualized dissent and civil disobedience offer no great threat (except perhaps in some theoretical or long-term respects) and therefore can be used as occasions for illustrating the presumptive willingness of authorities to play by the legal rules. Third, evasion is likely to be more easily ignored or handled by extralegal means except in publicized instances of defection by higher-status politically resentful (rather than sensitive) individuals such as Patricia Hearst (the nature of whose later political development is still unclear).

Fourth, violence by higher-status resisters seems more likely to be met by a strictly legal reaction than is violence by lower-class resisters, who may be repressed with little or no legalistic ceremony. And fifth, in all such small-scale and low-threat cases, regardless of the form and degree of resistance, any legal response is likely to treat them as conventional criminality with little or no political significance. Unless the politicality of resistance is undeniable or needs to be emphasized for propaganda reasons, the standard legal response to spontaneous and unorganized resistance will be to minimize its political significance.

Direct methods are more likely to be used against lower-class individuals to the extent that indirect methods are more cumbersome. It may be, too, that the propensity of higher-class resisters for more open and explicit challenges will make it less of a nuisance for authorities to neutralize them by indirect means that involve more possibilities for negotiating quiet dispositions—for controlling the situation without any possibly embarrassing fuss. In any case, the more open or violent the resistance, the more likely will be a direct response instead of or in addition to an indirect one. Open challenges require not only that authorities respond but also that they be seen to respond; violent resistance challenges the need and presumptive right of authorities to monopolize the ultimate means of control.

Given that resistance is calculated and organized, and therefore likely to be the work of politically sensitive instead of merely resentful people, reaction can be expected to be relatively severe largely irrespective of the form and degree of resistance. Variation in severity will depend more upon the perceived threat and the power ascribed to the opposition. Where social discontent is widespread, deliberate resistance will be viewed as especially threatening and met with marked severity. Under conditions of political stability, whether more or less consensual, some variation by social class is more likely: Lower-class resisters will generally receive a harsher reception than will higher-class resisters.

Legal controls will be supplemented or supplanted by extralegal ones, and are particularly likely to be deemphasized as resistance becomes more widespread and violent. Public collective acts of dissent or disobedience will probably be repressed with scant regard for restraining legal formulas; violent acts will be ferociously punished, with legal formulas invoked only as *post factum* rationales. Higher-class resisters may be somewhat more likely than their lower-class counterparts to be punished by "due process of law"; but insofar as they are seen as class renegades their punishment may be even more severe.

Direct controls will be emphasized, but will be supplemented by indirect ones because authorities will usually mobilize their full range of controls in order to curtail serious political resistance. The greater the threat, the greater the range of mobilization.

The countermoves of authorities in particular instances of resistance cannot be adequately understood, much less predicted, without understanding the contextual nature of political policing. Therefore, the hypothesized relationships between (a) combinations of resister characteristics and moves, and (b) types of countermoves by authorities have to be viewed in light of the more detailed analysis of political policing which is presented in the next chapter. "Outcomes," in the game theoretic sense, are discussed in the concluding chapter.

Summary

The criminality of political criminals has been analyzed as a complex product of (a) more or less deliberate stereotyping (favorable as well as unfavorable), in conjunction with (b) combinations of resister characteristics and modes of resistance, interacting with (c) variations in control measures used by authorities.

The manipulation of perceptual realities is crucial for both successful political resistance and successful control of such resistance, because the authority structure of a polity ultimately depends upon there being a prevalent assumption that the government is in control and the routines of social life are firmly established. Consequently, both resisters and authorities use stereotyping (of themselves and each other, and of communications and events) to lead people to believe what is required. At the extremes, revolutionaries require people to believe the government is weak and social life precarious; authorities need people to believe the government is unchallengeable and the social order is nature itself.

Social class origins are significantly related to political resistance, but not in the simple way traditionally assumed. Higher-class as well as lower-class people become political resisters; in fact, the evidence indicates that higher-class people are even more likely to become resisters. The explanation offered is that higher-class socialization is the more likely to induce the requisite degree of political sensitivity (as distinguished from relatively unfocused resentment) and strong sense of personal efficacy. In particular, higher-class resisters tend to plan and initiate, taking the lead, while lower-class resisters tend to require mobilization—largely and usually through the efforts of the higher-class "vanguard."

Dissent, evasion, disobedience, and violence are the major alternatives for resisters. Cries of protest do not necessarily constitute dissent, which is defined operationally as speaking out against perceived injustices in a relatively articulate way— reflecting a level of political consciousness above selfishness and tribalism. Given the differences between the characteristic socialization of higher- and lower-class people, dissent in this sense tends to be more a higher-class than a lower-class mode of resistance. Evasion has historically been the recourse of lower-class people, because of the real and perceived risks of challenging the dominant classes. However, the control technology of modern states appears to make it increasingly difficult for lower-class people to evade by fleeing their condition; only resisters (such as the famed "Carlos") with ample resources who are highly knowledgeable about such complexities as banking records and procedures, electronic surveillance methods, and international travel arrangements have any real chance of avoiding modern monitoring and detection systems. Consistent with the class socialization thesis, calculated disobedience—the open but peaceable refusal to accept the claims and demands of authorities—is typically a higher-class more than a lower-class resistance alternative. Spontaneous violence is the way the poor disobey when aroused beyond the subterfuges of evasion, while the planning and mobilization of an ongoing revolutionary effort is the work of higher-class resisters irreversibly alienated from society as they find it.

How the authorities react to resisters depends upon the contextual significance of who is doing what. In general terms, direct, extralegal, severe methods are most likely to be used when resistance is violent and/or calculated and when resisters are lower class and/or organized. Indirect, legal, mild control measures are most likely to be used when resistance takes the form of dissent and/or evasion, is spontaneous rather than calculated, and is attributed to higher-class people. The greater the commitment of resisters to revolution, the greater will be the range of countermoves adopted by authorities.

Though some patterned variations have been described or hypothesized, it is obvious that political resisters are extremely diverse in their origins, motivations, character traits, sophistication, activities, and effectiveness. Contrary to the negative stereotypes, political deviants are frequently admirable and politically sensitive, well-informed persons whose experiences and investigations have led them to more or less radical conclusions about the unacceptability of the status quo and the necessity to change or replace it—by legal means if possible and illegal means if necessary, perhaps including assassination and terrorism (see Sorel, 1950; Fanon, 1968). As for positive stereotypes, many political resisters are neither very admirable nor informed, and may act out of vague resentment, hypocrisy, or pathology instead of any firm knowledge or exceptionally sensitive convictions. Certainly only a minority of resisters— quite probably higher class—would fit Moran's (1974: 52-53) definition of a political criminal as "an individual who, motivated by his conviction, commits an unlawful act designed to attack the social structure in order to bring about a reorganization of the system."

To generalize Gary Marx's (1974) comment regarding *agents provocateurs,* the motivation of any one political resister— whether in the broadest sociological or the narrowest legal sense—"is no doubt exquisitely complex, varying both from one situation to another and from stage to stage in his career." In some cases it may even be hard to decide whether the individual is "really" engaged in political crime or in political policing (Donner, 1972; see also Marx, 1974).

Given the diversity of resisters and resistance, and the problematics of official response, we are led to conclude that there simply is nothing empirically distinctive about *all* political "criminals" other than the fact that they happen to have been labeled as current or potential political threats. They may or may not have developed a consciousness of themselves as political resisters and/or acted so as to defy or subvert the authorities: Their only common attribute is that they are the targets of political policing. Therefore, to understand, even to define, political *criminality* we must understand political *policing,* and quite independently of any official descriptions and justifications of this crucial mechanism of political-legal control.

CHAPTER 4

POLITICAL POLICING

Methods of compulsion and suppression have ever
been used in political life. . . . [The] modern
political myths . . . did not begin with demanding
or prohibiting certain actions. They undertook to
change the men, in order to be able to regulate
and control their deeds.
                                        Ernst Cassirer (1955: 360)

All policing is political, in that the ultimate rationale and
purpose of policing is to preserve against radical changes those
cultural and social structures which are congruent with some
historically specific polity. "The creation of police forces is to
be understood in political terms; police forces are the creatures
of politics" (Bayley, 1971; see also Bowden, 1978a). More
precisely, policing is the institutionalized development and use
of "methods of compulsion and suppression" for the control of
those who live within a polity's jurisdiction. The jurisdictional
claims and normative demands of authorities acquire social
reality insofar as an "enforcement staff" is generally perceived
as able to impose or defend those claims and demands against
resistance (see Weber, 1968: 34-35, 313-315). Never really
neutral, police forces are designed for use on behalf of the
politics of social order and continuity.

Even as the police stage or dimension of the process of
political organization is realized, policing becomes an increasingly more complex and subtle control effort. Methods of
physical coercion are supplemented—eventually overlaid—by
strategies aimed less at "demanding or prohibiting certain ac-

tions" than at controlling the motivational springs of action (for a brief historical review of punishment, see Sellin, 1976). The emphasis shifts from detection and punishment after crime to preempting the possibility of crime. Foucault (1977: 216, 218) sees this shift (marked by the eighteenth-century organization of the French police) as the key element in the historical movement toward "the disciplinary society," in which "a tactics of power" minimizes the economic costs and political risks of control, while maximizing its intensity, scope, and completeness. The result is "to increase both the docility and the utility of all the elements of the system" (Foucault, 1977: 218).

To some this image of policing will seem to be one-sided in one or all of at least three ways: (1) in emphasizing the negative side of policing without recognizing the positive; (2) in implying that policing is the same in democratic as in totalitarian societies; (3) in assuming that police officers are always the unquestioning servants of the dominant classes. It is, therefore, essential to address the issue of "good" versus "bad" policing and police before going on to discuss the specific features of political policing.

The Primacy of Control over Service

Policing may be thought of as a continuum of activities ranging from a pole of service, protection, and concern for individualizing justice to a pole of domination, exploitation, and concern for maintaining order. The "service functions" include *emergency assistance, guidance,* and *protection,* and may or may not be mandatory on a universal basis. Where the institution of policing has been most highly developed (as in the major capitalist and state socialist nations), service is mandated. It is the duty of the police to provide initial help to victims of any accidents, attacks, or natural disasters. When people need guidance in vehicular or social traffic, the police are supposed to show them where and how to go, or else to refer them to the appropriate agency or party. And it is the particular obligation of the police to guard and warn against threats to persons or property, to come to the aid of anyone being "unlawfully" threatened or victimized by another, and to stop any inter-personal violence of which they become aware.

The "control functions" are *intelligence gathering, informa-tion control, neutralization of offenders* ("specific deterrence"), and *intimidation of the general population* ("general deter-rence"). Each of these will be explored more fully later. For now, it should first be noted that they are *always* mandatory for policing as an institution, though not necessarily for every officer and agency. Secondly, there is no "strain" or "contradic-tion" between the service and control functions in policing. While instances can easily be found of situational, momentary conflict (for example, an ordinary patrolman arrests an under-cover agent for carrying a concealed weapon; security officers are charged with illegally gathering intelligence from medical and tax records), the performance of service functions contri-butes directly and indirectly to the control effort. Directly, assisting people gives police ready access to many kinds of information about them: physical attributes, mannerisms, opinions, relationships, locations, movements, occupations, financial resources. Indirectly, the more helpful the police are found to be, the less people are likely to "make trouble" or to support "troublemakers," thus making it easier for the police to set control priorities and to deploy their resources accordingly. Whatever increases the openness of a population to surveillance and intervention contributes to its control.

The proportionate allocation of police resources to service and control functions varies both among and within polities, depending upon two main factors: the degree of perceived threat and the established theory and practice of control. When authorities feel relatively secure, considerable resources may be devoted to service; where they believe themselves to be seri-ously threatened within their jurisdiction, all available resources will be directed into maximizing the control effort. However, the perception of threat and the specifics of the control re-sponse will be determined by the knowledge and instruments available to them. Authorities interpret threats according to their understanding of social deviance, and of human behavior in general. In trying to counter threats, they use the control technology generated out of their historical experience, and upon which they have learned to depend.

It follows that the authorities both of relatively democratic and of relatively totalitarian polities can be expected to act in much the same way in highly threatening situations. There is ample empirical evidence to support this conclusion, as will become clear in the remainder of this chapter. It also follows that differences between democratic and totalitarian contexts are to be expected in the timing, directness, magnitude, mode, and other aspects of control. Where a more democratic legal system has been established, the control effort will generally be channeled through at least the formal machinery of due process and public accountability. Where a more explicitly autocratic, or authoritarian, system is the historical product, the control effort will tend to be more devastating, less inhibited by any niceties about subjects' rights and rule of law. Again, there is evidence; but it is far less easily evaluated. As will be seen, democratic safeguards have often been suspended or ignored in the policing of political deviance.

For now, the most tenable generalization is that the image of the police officer as "friend and servant of the people" has empirical substance, especially in more democratic polities, only as long as elite group interests do not appear to be endangered. Ordinarily, most police work may well involve providing services in response to citizen requests and complaints (Manning, 1977: 108-109). However, when "civil disorder" or "terrorism" threaten, service will quickly be displaced by, or subordinated to, control. The police image hardens, and the reality of policing as violence becomes inescapable. Britain, Canada, and the United States, sharing the common law tradition, are among the most democratic polities the world has seen. Yet, each has provided numerous examples of how rapidly and drastically the service emphasis of ordinary policing can be shifted to control minimally restrained by the safeguards for which that tradition has been especially notable.

Unemployment in Britain having reached more than two million by 1920, the National Unemployed Workers' Movement was organized to press for relief. People were helped to obtain benefits due them under existing laws, and there were demonstrations and petitions protesting the inadequacies of current programs and calling for new policies. But even though marching, petitioning, and making speeches were quite legitimate activities, the leadership was infiltrated and spied upon; the "hunger marches" were met with baton charges, arrests, and shootings; and dossiers were compiled on "militants" and sympathetic civil libertarians. The authorities noted communist influence at the national policy level as justification for the repression (Bunyan, 1977: 120-122). Bowden's (1978b: 210-235) historical analysis suggests that such repression has continued to be the pattern of British police response to "crisis politics."

During a period of rising protest against the economic subjugation of French Canadians, separatist radicals of the *Front de Liberation du Quebec* (FLQ) kidnapped two people in late 1970: the British trade commissioner, James Cross, who was freed unharmed after two months; and Pierre Laporte, Quebec labor minister, who was found dead after one week. The circumstances of Laporte's murder remain unclear and controversial (Vallières, 1977: 84-163) even though three members of the FLQ were convicted. Governmental reaction to "the October crisis" was to invoke the War Measures Act, permitting detention of anyone for up to three weeks without warrant, legal assistance, or court appearance. About 20,000 warrantless raids were conducted; and some 465 persons were detained in the first few hours, of whom 16 were eventually charged (unsuccessfully) with seditious conspiracy and other offenses. Since then, there have been strong criticisms from across the political spectrum regarding the use of the Act in peacetime, the lack of evidence that Quebec's secession was at all imminent, and the obvious need for legal alternatives to all-out war measures in dealing with such limited emergencies (see Grosman, 1972; Toronto *Star*, feature on the War Measures Act, October 4, 1975; Vallières, 1977; Mann and Lee, 1979: 256; see also

Sawatsky, 1980: 238-247, 252-266). Nonetheless, the War Measures Act is still Canada's emergency law.

Black resentment of institutionalized barriers to changing or escaping ghetto living conditions erupted once more in Detroit in the "long hot summer" of 1967, as in several other American cities. Over 7,000 people were arrested, and most interned in makeshift jails: Some were kept as long as 30 hours on buses, others spent days in an underground garage without toilet facilities (National Advisory Commission on Civil Disorders, 1968: 106-107). Usual and legal procedural norms regarding arrest, booking, detention, charging, pretrial release, preliminary examination, and court disposition of cases were administratively relaxed and altered so that virtually no one was able to obtain release in less ‘than 3 days—normally, in that length of time over half of all felony defendants are out on bail (Balbus, 1973: 113-147). At least 44 people died in the course of the "riot," including a police officer killed accidentally in a scuffle and 3 young black men evidently executed, by Hersey's (1968: 195) account,

> for being thought to be pimps, for being considered punks, for making out with white girls, for being in some vague way killers of a white cop named Jerry Olshove, for running riot—for being, after all and all, black young men and part of the black rage of the time.

Balbus's (1973: 255) detailed analysis of the Detroit and other cases indicates a continuing pattern of combining severe measures to "clear the streets" with later minimal sanctioning by formally legal procedures, a pattern consistent with the authorities' "long-run interest in maximizing their legitimacy and minimizing the revolutionary potential of the revolts."

That the control function ultimately defines the nature and purpose of policing does not mean that every police officer and agency will be a blind servant of the regime of the day. As the events of Watergate and the Nixon Administration's consequent downfall illustrate, the apparatus of policing is not necessarily monolithic. Different components may work against each other, and some officials or agencies may be subverted or criminalized by others more committed to legal ideals, or at least more politically alert or fortunate. Also, some police officers may identify with the disadvantaged classes to the extent of either tacitly or openly refusing to criminalize particular offenders, quite apart from discretionary nonenforcement because of corruption or low morale. In revolutionary crises, the odds are great that some police will join the resistance.

Despite all these qualifications, however, it still appears that, under conditions of relative political stability, even the most enlightened policing (in the sense of neutrality in conventional politics and a dedication to public service) will have the effect not of facilitating political changes but rather of helping to stabilize "the existing political and economic structure through efficient 'engineering' of social conflict" (Center for Research on Criminal Justice, 1977: 41). Contrary to the particularistic emphasis of the Center collective upon characterizing policing in capitalist societies, their conclusion is equally applicable historically to socialist ones. Whether the threat is defined as "communism" or as "capitalist mentality," as revolution or as counterrevolution, the authorities of all polities invariably act to defend the cultural and social structures within and by which they achieve power and,privilege.

The priority of the control over the service function implies the priority of population control over the control of individual deviants. This priority is most emphatically asserted in political policing in the narrow and usual sense—that is, legal control activities intended to eliminate or neutralize intolerable political opponents. The complex issues of individual guilt-innocence, liabilities-immunities, and powers-privileges—and of human needs-desires—are in political policing most explicitly and thoroughly subordinated to the mandate to ensure that the given order, of structured advantage and disadvantage, will continue. Regular policing necessarily involves some concern with such issues; political policing involves concern with them only insofar as they become pertinent to the business of population control. From the perspective of political policing, the population is made up of actually and potentially intolerable dissidents, whose technical status in terms of confirmed law-breaking is of no more than tactical significance. Thus, political policing is less concerned with merely suppressing actual political offenders than with accomplishing this in ways that maximize the deterrent impact upon potential offenders, that is, everyone else.

To foster the myth of their omniscience and, omnipotence—a key objective, as Bramstedt (1945: 176-180) has pointed out—political police have encouraged the widespread belief that they use secret methods known only to the masters of political policing. In fact, political police adapt and extend techniques of regular policing, albeit to extremes ordinarily disallowed in law and often even in practice. Nonetheless, there are significant differences: political policing involves the systematic, routine, and skilled use of control techniques which in regular policing are unsystematically and even idiosyncratically, haphazardly, and crudely employed. Where "excessive" measures may be officially and sometimes informally frowned upon or punished in regular policing, they are informally and perhaps even officially expected and rewarded in political policing—as long as they work, in terms of superiors' judgments regarding acceptable cost-benefit ratios (on use of the "suicide tap" by FBI agents, see Navasky and Lewin, 1973: 277). Such judgments may, of course, rest in part upon some degree of commitment to "the rule of law"; but the nature of the task makes it unlikely that such scruples will have much operational import.

> Deeply embedded within the clandestine mentality is the belief that human ethics and social laws have no bearing on covert operations or their practitioners. . . . The determining factors in secret operations are purely pragmatic: Does the job need to be done? Can it be done? And can secrecy (or plausible denial) be maintained [Marchetti and Marks, 1975: 240]?

To summarize, the service functions of policing are real, but are always subordinate and complementary to the control functions. Specialized political policing differs from regular policing only in the *degree* to which gathering intelligence, information control, neutralization of resistance to authority, and general deterrence are emphasized over the assistance, guidance, and protection of individuals.

Intelligence

Authorities always seek intelligence—an information base enabling them to detect potential as well as actual resistance. The more threatened they feel, the greater will be the effort to monitor thoughts and feelings as well as behavior and relationships. Failure to find significant resistance usually leads not to relaxing the drive to know, but rather to increasing the scope of surveillance. A kind of "paranoia of office" goes with the administration of a structure of legal control, because lack of adequate information can result in futile, counterproductive, and ultimately disastrous moves in the struggle to maintain class dominance. Strategies of information control (counterintelligence), neutralization of resistance, and general deterrence depend upon authorities' understandings of realities and probabilities. Indeed, authority is distinguished from power in large part by the greater concern in authority relationships with knowledgeable manipulation, versus steamrolling, of subjects and rivals. Without intelligence, authority cannot exist.

Detecting potential crime is, of course, an inherently limitless task: There can never be enough information on the doings of people if one is concerned with preventing their doing something. "The chain of inquiry which starts with searching out 'loyalty' and 'subversive activities' is an endless one" (Emerson, 1973: 226). Consequently, the process of intelligence gathering always tends to flow through and around legal restraints, and to be limited only by political considerations and the available technology.

Legal constraints such as requiring judicial warrant or top-level administrative approval for specific surveillance operations are typically and ultimately ineffectual. This is not because officials are unconcerned, but because of the inordinate difficulty of (a) anticipating precisely what bits of information may prove useful on some future occasion, (b) setting criteria for distinguishing between potentially useful and other information, and (c) ensuring that agents will or can always use the criteria. It appears that in practice authorities everywhere try to limit the volume and maximize the quality of intelligence by "targeting" the most obvious resentful or politically sensitive persons, groups, and sectors of the population, in conjunction with routine checks upon the transactions and movements of the general population.

"Targeting" means, in principle, focusing upon the high-probability cases and situations. Probability estimates, and therefore targeting decisions, result from authorities' perceptions of prior events and their assumptions about the kinds of people most prone or sympathetic to evading to challenging legal authority. Though the specific targets vary with the history, human geography, and politico-military environment of the polity, authorities have been in notable agreement in targeting the following: radical activists; dissidents of the left and extreme right; labor leaders and organizations; racial and ethnic minority persons and organizations; foreign-born persons; persons frequently abroad or having foreign contacts; civil libertarians and other human-rights "idealists"; artists, intellectuals, and students; persons exemplifying "deviant" life-styles; and politically influential individuals, in or out of office. The only generalizations to be ventured here are that the more actively resistant will be given priority attention, and that more democratic, sophisticated, and/or secure authorities tend to target a smaller proportion of those eligible by criteria other than active (especially violent) resistance.

In more democratic polities there is likely to be a greater public commitment to restraint in the name of civil liberty, and the political repercussions of illegal intelligence activities are probably greater. However, it is difficult to find convincing evidence of any real desire on the part of authorities to curtail intelligence because of belief in democratic principles. A far stronger case can be made for the view that such principles, and the laws reflecting them, actually inhibit intelligence work only insofar as violations ("excesses") may cause serious trouble for the organization or high-level careers. The CIA and FBI curtailed illegal domestic surveillance and other operations only after the post-Nixon purge and congressional investigation signaled that the political bounds had been overstepped.

Regardless of variations caused by shifts in the political climate, the scope of intelligence activities in all modern polities is enormous and very unlikely to be reduced significantly. In the United States, files are maintained on millions of people whose political orientations are of concern to the FBI, any of several intelligence agencies, the Civil Service Commission, the Atomic Energy Commission, or myriad other agencies. By the mid-1960s there were 187,762,000 federal security investigation files (Orlansky, 1969: 293). In addition to files produced by routine security checks and active surveillance, federal investigators have access to hundreds of millions of police (including private agencies), medical and psychiatric, banking and credit, communications, and other records (see Wheeler, 1969; Miller, 1971; Rule, 1973). The monitoring powers of the American police have recently been greatly extended by the Currency and Foreign Transactions Reporting Act, which provides both civil and criminal penalties for persons failing to report the importation or exportation of funds exceeding $5,000, and for banking institutions failing to report transactions of more than $10,000. While reported cases have involved narcotics, foreign payoffs by multinational corporations, white-collar crime, and alien smuggling (Chasen and Sinai, 1979), the law can obviously be useful in tracking and inhibiting the transmission of funds for politically questionable purposes.

When routine monitoring, informers, or investigative leads indicate possibly significant (that is, suspicious) persons or situations, active surveillance is undertaken. Techniques of surveillance are essentially the same in political and regular policing, with greater latitude to be expected in political policing. In each case the problem is that of detecting offenses and of apprehending offenders where the nature of the offense is such that victims, complainants, or voluntary witnesses are not likely to appear, or even to exist. Thus, the techniques for policing vice, business-world, and political offenses are largely interchangeable.

Characteristic techniques include the recording of communications, meetings, and movements through the analysis of news media and other secondary sources, mail, tax records, material obtained from live and electronic informants, and official agents' observations. As has already been implied, an important feature of intelligence operations is to develop and maintain cooperative working relationships with other governmental agencies (such as other police and investigatory organizations, the military services, tax, postal, licensing, and other regulatory agencies, legislative investigating staffs), as well as certain private organizations (such as banks, telephone and telegraph companies, credit and other business associations, veterans' organizations, progovernment citizens' groups, private security companies). A file is developed by following "audit trails" and other "paper routes," as well as by physical and (increasingly) electronic observation.

The ultimate product is a dossier containing "good evidence," or information which is legally and/or politically usable. Legally usable evidence is sufficient to bring a formal accusation with a high probability of conviction; politically usable information is perhaps sufficient to bring charges, but its real value is to provide the police with "leverage." In the context of political surveillance, leverage means information which can be used either to make connections (persons to acts, persons to others, events to organizations, funds to sources) or to pressure the subject to furnish such connecting information. Illegal phone taps of conversations involving the person under surveillance might be leverage of the first kind; evidence of unconventional sexual activity might be leverage of the second kind. Because (1) no legal control system can formally process more than a small fraction of the potentially eligible cases, and (2) overly frequent public recognition of political resistance tends to be counterproductive, leverage is more important than legal evidence in political policing. Keeping track of the chang-

ing patterns of alignment and conflict is the main purpose of
political intelligence work, far more than is generating formal
evidence for the occasionally necessary political trial.

Leverage sometimes leads to what some people may regard as
ridiculous extremes—products of official paranoia—but which
others may see as worthy of at least routine attention. An
example is the FBI's coverage of the 1970 Earth Day demonstration in Washington, D.C. (Elliff, 1973: 239-243). To most
people, presumably, the Sierra Club's concern for environmental protection is obviously legitimate, and no justification
for political surveillance exists. Nonetheless, the FBI had information linking two local environmental activists with the Communist Party and the SDS, and there was also an agent observation of some environmentalists picketing a hotel where the
Secretary of Transportation was to address lobbyists for the
highway construction industry. Rennie Davis (who apparently
was under surveillance) appeared on the same platform with
Senator Edmund Muskie (who was not), both of whom were .
therefore mentioned in the report on the event. From the FBI's
perspective, the Earth Day rally was an event where they might
learn something about possible connections between environmental pressure politics and the subversive activities of political
radicals. Probably to cover himself politically as much as for
other reasons, Senator Muskie himself made public the FBI's
Letterhead Memorandum (LHM) on "National Environmental
Actions, April 22, 1970."

Electronic surveillance has become especially worrisome to
civil libertarians in recent years, as official and unofficial disclosures have made it obvious that illegal invasions of privacy
have been common practice. Determined legislative and judicial
efforts are being made to eliminate the use of illegal taps and
bugs by the FBI and other agencies, private as well as public.
The present legal situation, as understood by FBI writers
(Burke, 1976; Laturno, 1976), is that the use of electronic and
mechanical devices to obtain intelligence is generally forbidden
unless authorized by procedures established by federal law,
excepting cases where one of the parties in a communication

(whether a legal control agent or a private individual) consents to the use of such a device. Other parties involved need not to be made aware; and presidential discretion in ordering electronic surveillance in any case thought to involve "a foreign power" is unlimited. The exceptions are not reassuring; discussions by such observers as Navasky and Lewin (1973) and Bunyan (1977: 196-229) suggest that police agents and officials are adept at finding ways to evade legal restraint and public accountability (for example, by temporarily "shutting off" detection devices before testifying about the extent of their use; by getting nonagency persons to install devices; by attributing data from them to unknown informants). Especially when pressed by higher authorities or the general public to obtain results, investigative agents readily avoid legal restraints. In sum, there seems to be little chance that legal procedural requirements can effectively limit surveillance.

Paradoxically, the single most important recent effort to bring political intelligence activities under legal control is a major source of evidence indicating that the effort may be futile. In 1976 the United States Senate committee chaired by Senator Frank Church reported that federal investigative agencies, notably the FBI and CIA, regularly disregarded legal issues and limits, gathered information far beyond any legitimate governmental interest, excessively used intrusive techniques such as warrantless break-ins and electronic surveillance, tried with much success to discredit and disrupt legitimate political activities, obtained and used information to serve the partisan political interests of the agency or the administration of the day, improperly disseminated or illegally kept information, and were never subjected to serious hindrance by anyone legally responsible for "overseeing, supervising, and controlling" their activities (U.S. Senate, 1976: Book II, 137-288).

Even if legal restrictions cannot seriously impede political intelligence gathering, one view is that the intelligence capability of any legal control system is inevitably limited because of the physical and financial impossibility of keeping everyone, or even very many people, under surveillance. "Total surveillance, under anything like the present state of technology and social organization, is impossible" (Rule, 1973: 319). However, great advances in the technology not only of gathering intelligence but also of storing, retrieving, condensing, and analyzing it are virtually inevitable. As Rule (1973: 322-324, 338-339) goes on to note, sampling and stop-check procedures are increasingly effective in identifying probable "deviant cases"; and centralization of computer record systems is strongly encouraged by the general public's desire for rapid access to credit and medical records, the provision of "fine-grained" social services, and efficient crime control. Because intelligence gathering will clearly not be limited by technological any more than by legal restraints, the unavoidable conclusion is that total surveillance technology will most probably be perfected, and used to a degree inconsistent with traditional conceptions of privacy and freedom.

The only effective source of restraint appears to be the political interests of the authorities themselves. Conventional politics depends upon widespread belief in the efficacy of law; demonstrations and disclosures of skullduggery by legal control agents undermine political authority in several ways. Violations suggest that people have no hope of legal recourse against illegal state interference in their lives. Alienation, resentment, and resistance are fostered by the perception that the law is meaningless even to those who are its agents. Recognizing that unconstrained police intelligence activities are especially open to partisan use, conventional political participants may, in mutual fear and suspicion, begin to distrust one another's commitments to the ground rules, leaving less and less room for the essential compromises possible only within such rules. And eventually the elites are forced to show their hand in trying to regain control over an organizational tool whose unrestrained snooping endangers them directly, in addition to subverting the authority structures that cloak and enhance their power.

Information Control

Information control is indoctrination. Free thinking and criticisms are to be suppressed; celebrations and apologias are to be broadcast. From the perspective of authorities, the ideal is for educational, research, religious, and media institutions to accomplish such control without police assistance. In these, the knowledge institutions, are concentrated the specialists in generating and inculcating accepted orientations, doctrines, reality models, and intellectual skills (or lack thereof). However, the knowledge institutions have developed around core conceptions of truth seeking and reporting—which makes them something other than trustworthy agencies of social control. They may stimulate thinking instead of merely channeling thought, and may encourage change instead of only justifying the status quo.

Enlightened authorities accept the risks because of the expected practical and esthetic benefits, and the usually conservative impact of study, worship, and media presentations. But no authorities feel secure unless intolerable views and reports can be suppressed, with or without the help of the intellectuals. Therefore, while most of the work of promoting the dissemination of favored ideas and information is left to the knowledge institutions, as well as the task of discouraging disfavored ones, their work is complemented and "corrected" by the legal control agencies.

Wilsnack (1980) has offered a formal definition of information control as "the processes used to make sure that certain people will or will not have access to certain information at certain times." He suggests there are four main methods, or processes, of controlling the production and dissemination of factual (objectively verifiable) information: *Espionage* is obtaining information against resistance to its disclosure; *secrecy* is denying others access to information; *persuasion* is ensuring that other people obtain and believe certain information; *evaluation* is learning more from information obtained than others wish you to know. Wilsnack's consideration of these processes and their interrelations leads him to hypothesize (paraphrasing loosely) that agencies specializing in (that is, assigned to) one control process will become involved in the others as well; that any agency in conflict or competition with others will resist any effort to limit its information-control activities; and that control agencies will collaborate as much as possible with one another in performing intelligence and information-control functions, even if on opposite sides in a conflict. It will be useful to keep these general propositions in mind as we now consider the specific features of information control in political policing.

Police control of information tends to emphasize suppression of disapproved communications more than the dissemination of favored ones; but the latter is not neglected—particularly when it serves the agency itself. The American FBI and the Canadian RCMP are outstanding examples of control agencies nurtured in large part by their public imagery: the stereotyped clean-cut, dedicated, brave, and resourceful G-men and Mounties who "always get their man" and never make mistakes.

From the Post Toasties cereal "Junior G-men" of the 1930s to television's Efrem Zimbalist, Jr., and *The FBI* of the 1970s, the FBI public relations program has always been carefully orchestrated. And, despite forty years of criticisms and recommendations by criminologists, the Bureau's published *Uniform Crime Reports* have continued to reflect greater concern with media impact and appropriations hearings than with research needs (Sherrill, 1973). Criminologists and other social scientists have, in fact, frequently been the targets of vitriolic and grossly misleading accusations that they sought to blame the statistics instead of their own theories and projects for the ever rising tide of crime (see Ottenberg, 1965). Director J. Edgar Hoover objected to even a scholarly and generally sympathetic conference on the FBI's problems and needs (held at Princeton University in 1971), and refused to cooperate on the grounds that the outcome was prejudged (Watters and Gillers, 1973: 414-425).

The Royal Canadian Mounted Police, the national police of Canada, enjoy a legendary status. As John Hogarth (a noted law professor and former chairman of the British Columbia Police Commission) observes somewhat ruefully, "We are the only country in the world that I know of that has the police officer as a national symbol" (Hogarth, 1979: 10). The glamour of the

Mounties' frontier origins is sustained by colorful entertainments such as the "musical rides"; the invariable pictures (posters, calendars, mugs, key holders, and so on) of Mounties as red-coated handsome young men on horseback; and fictional portrayals of Mounties as lone rangers in the wilderness who overcome all hardship and resistance to bring villains to justice. Criticisms of the Mounties by scholars, reporters, trade unionists, native people, and immigrants have been rejected as communist-inspired or uninformed (Brown and Brown, 1973: 104-105), and extraordinary pressure has been put on individual officers to keep secret any disclosure—even under judicial or parliamentary questioning—that might tarnish the image (Mann and Lee, 1979: 146-149).

Public relations ploys, though not insignificant, constitute a much less crucial dimension of information control than efforts to chill or stifle other than approved discourse, or try to influence directly policy decisions by higher authorities. As is indicated by Wolfe's (1973: 125-173) distinction between "private" and "public" ideological repression, restrictions upon the flow of ideas can be accomplished directly, explicitly, officially (as in the appointment of censors to judge the acceptability of books, films, newspapers, and other media), or else indirectly, surreptitiously, unofficially (and sometimes illegally) by, for example, the circulation of confidential "advisories" or anonymous "tips" resulting in the denial of licenses, permits, space for assemblies, printing contracts, and other facilities needed to produce and distribute intolerable messages and statements.

Among the standard forms of suppression are censorship and confiscation, disruption of resistance or conventional opposition activities, and the punishment of receivers as well as transmitters and originators of prohibited communications. In 1933 and subsequently, the German Nazi police demonstrated how far direct suppression can be taken: No unapproved publications, speeches, discussions, meetings, entertainments, travel, letters, telegrams, radio transmissions and receptions, or any other communicative acts were allowed, on pain of property confiscation, imprisonment, torture, and/or death for offenders and their associates (Delarue, 1964: 17). Since then, most modern states have become somewhat more subtle and less blatantly ferocious—at least within their own official jurisdictions.

Censorship of political statements is universal, regardless of the Helsinki accord on the human right of free expression (among others). Every polity has some version of an "official secrets" law that prevents public disclosure and discussion of matters that authorities prefer to keep to themselves. And there are always additional legal and extralegal measures used to intervene in the flow of public and private communications. Britain's three Official Secrets Acts (1911, 1920, and 1939) have been interpreted as covering "anything in an official file," and have been invoked to justify suppressive actions ranging from the harassment of a Member of Parliament (for discreetly inquiring about the lack of antiaircraft guns in 1938!) to the prosecution and jailing of civil service clerks, postmen, police and military officers, reporters, students, and others for such offenses as "not taking proper care" of trivial documents stolen from them (Bunyan, 1977: 5-27).

Canada has followed suit in making the "freedom of information" law a virtual farce (Leighton, 1978), and in using the Official Secrets Act to prosecute individuals such as the editor of the Toronto *Sun*—for publishing "secret" information on entirely open and legal Canadian-Soviet business and scientific dealings (Mann and Lee, 1979: 159-161). In a bizarre, almost comical recent case, Peter Treu was convicted for possessing without authorization scientific documents which he himself had written, even though it appears that his security clearance had never been formally withdrawn. "The court decided that Treu was a loyal Canadian and no security threat, but sentenced him to two years as a deterrent to other possible offenders" (Mann and Lee, 1979: 159). Though the government has decided not to appeal the reversal by the Quebec appellate court, it has also ruled out any compensation to Treu for his legal defense costs.

The American Senate's Church committee documented the use of a wide variety of information control tactics in the FBI's counterintelligence program (COINTELPRO). These included giving derogatory and often false information to the media anonymously or through "friendly" contacts, and ordering agents to find information disproving "allegations by the 'liberal press, the bleeding hearts, and the forces on the left' " that the Chicago police used excessive force during the 1968 Democratic Convention demonstrations (U.S. Senate, 1976: Book II, 15-16). Similar campaigns were waged against the Black Panther Party and the New Left movement (for details of these and the King case see U.S. Senate, 1976: Book III; also Elliff, 1971: 83-152, 153-226).

Spreading favorable information and misinformation, disrupting and blocking disapproved communications, and generally perverting the public's access to the full range of political beliefs and opinions has been even less restrained abroad than at home, and in dealing with foreign nationals (on the CIA, see Marchetti and Marks, 1975: 165-231; Agee, 1975). Whatever one may conclude about the necessity or inevitability of such activities, it is worth noting at this point that the line between domestic and foreign intelligence, information control, and neutralization activities has been exceedingly blurred in practice no matter how clear it is in law (for example, the CIA's domestic activities and the FBI's "liaison" agents abroad). Especially when the fruits of such operations have been used to shape rather than merely inform high-level policy decisions, they have contributed to disastrous errors. External, foreign policy consequences of misinformation, as in the 1961 attempted invasion of Cuba, are important in an analysis of political policing mainly because of their repercussions for internal control decisions and practices. For example, fictionalizing or exaggerating links between political resistance and foreign relations difficulties encourages witch hunts and precludes accurate assessments of the nature and sources of resistance.

Effective response to legitimate black protest in the United States was made even less likely by over 25 years of treating the

NAACP as possibly "communist-infiltrated" (against consistent evidence of that organization's anticommunism), and by the distortions and confusion produced by the propaganda campaigns against both King's movement and the Black Panthers. That information control took precedence over intelligence is clear. In one instance, when a field office reported that Martin Luther King was unsympathetic to the communist cause, FBI headquarters responded with a classic example of misdirection: "While there may not be any evidence that King is a Communist, neither is there any substantial evidence that he is anti-Communist" (U.S. Senate, 1976: Book II, 7). In another case, when an agent assigned to investigate an Afro-American bookstore in Washington could find nothing wrong, he was told to buy a copy there of Mao Tse-tung's "little red book." Because the bookstore had no copies left, and because having a copy mailed to his superior would have been too cheeky, he simply bought the book (readily obtainable everywhere) from a Brentano's shop. The file on the Drum and Spear Bookstore thereafter noted that radical literature, including the "little red book," could be bought there (Wall, 1973: 343-344). From such investigative sources were derived the impressions and "facts" in which have been grounded the appallingly counter-productive "ghetto policing" and "nigger control" programs of the past and present.

Needless to say, in more totalitarian polities intelligence and information control are even less restrained than in the more democratic ones. Whether China, Cuba, or the Soviet Union on the left, or Argentina, Iran, or South Korea on the right, detailed official and public investigations of political policing such as the Americans and Canadians have been experiencing are unimaginable. Among such polities the Republic of South Africa is unusual in that some degree of public scrutiny is still possible even though severely limited by legal and extralegal intimidation.

The South African government does publish some information on security activities; and other scraps are occasionally elicited in parliamentary questioning. It is known, for instance, that, in 1977, of 2121 "publications or objects" examined by the censors, 1246 were deemed undesirable and decisions on another 62 were pending at the year's end (SAIRR, 1979: 128). Several people were prosecuted for possessing banned items such as *Detention Without Trial,* a publication by the Institute of Race Relations. In other actions various African and student newspapers and magazines were banned; some editors and reporters were prosecuted and jailed; films were banned or edited; and the prime minister threatened the already tightly supervised press for supposedly irresponsible reporting on the covert activities of the Department of Information—which a commission of inquiry found had secretly used and misused enormous sums to generate favorable publicity for South Africa throughout the world (SAIRR, 1979: 128-137). Adding to the government's embarrassment is the case of Eschel Rhoodie, former director of the propaganda effort and author of *The Third Africa,* who has recently been extradited from France to stand trial for stealing millions of rands from the secret fund.

Although political information control involves much more than the control of factual communications, Wilsnack's (1980) hypotheses are supported by what is known about political policing. It is an ever-expanding process, the logical end of which is total surveillance and total information control. There is firm resistance to even the most authoritative efforts to limit or oversee that expansion. And there is collusion as well as some conflict among political control agencies (including those of hostile as well as friendly nations), between political and regular police, and between public and private agencies. Again, the evidence warrants pessimism more than optimism. Intelligence and information control operations tend to decrease, not increase, the availability of accurate information which authorities, legal control agents, political resisters, and everyone else need to make realistic and effective moves. To the extent that political policing corrupts all channels of communication in a society, it contributes greatly to destroying the cultural foundations of the polity which it is intended to secure. Further, the distortions generated and amplified by information control feed back to subvert both intelligence gathering and the control policy decision-making process. (On the social costs of secrecy, see Lowry, 1972.) The logical outcome is the collapse of control, legitimation, and, therefore, the polity. There is a lesson not yet learned in the words inscribed in the lobby of CIA headquarters: "And ye shall know the truth, and the truth shall make you free" (John 8:32).

Neutralization: Specific Deterrence

Perhaps the most characteristic police activity is the physical and psychological coercion of specific individuals, who may themselves be actual or suspected deviants or else surrogates representing actual or putative disreputables or rebels. Political policing is distinguished from regular policing by the greater extent to which surrogates are given punitive attention, both as a means of indirectly pressuring or punishing actual offenders and as a tactic independent of any immediate concern with the apprehension of particular offenders. The aim is to neutralize resistance in ways that ensure that offenders will not repeat (specific deterrence), and that contribute to inhibiting any inclinations others may have to resist the authorities (general deterrence). Thus, *how* political resistance is neutralized is as important to authorities as neutralizing it.

There are two alternative but complementary approaches to maximizing the deterrent impact of the control effort: *terror* and *enclosure*. *Terror* involves making the consequences of political resistance so gruesome that no one who has experienced them is psychologically and/or physically capable of further resistance—if he or she survives—and no one who becomes aware of them would dare to risk them. *Enclosure* is analogous to "persuasion" in information control, in that it involves using every means to convince resisters and everyone else that the resisters never had and will never have any chance of success in either achieving their goals or avoiding punishment. Terror tries to make the costs of resistance too high; enclosure tries to make their payment inevitable. Both approaches are used in every modern polity, though in more democratic or secure polities terror is used less than in more totalitarian or insecure polities.

Intelligence and information-control activities are part of the neutralization effort. Control agents may deliberately let subjects become aware that they are under surveillance, or make them think they are when they are not, to frighten or confuse them. Others significant to a person or organization (employers, creditors, contractors, customers, members, neighbors, associates, relatives) may be made aware, or led to believe, that the subject is being watched. The expected result, of course, is that the target's capabilities will be reduced by others withdrawing their material or emotional support, whether out of fear, outrage, suspicion, or merely the very common desire not to risk having one's life touched, that is, disturbed, by anything out of the ordinary. Individuals and organizations can not only be immobilized by the loss of support, but also paralyzed and destroyed by the structured distrust that is created by the objective and perceptual reality of investigations and information control. As the following accounts show, the relationship between neutralization and the other control functions is very intimate; and the ways in which various operations reinforce one another are limited only by the resources and inventiveness of control agents—and of those whom they seek to control.

The FBI's counterintelligence activities have involved the use of all sorts of "dirty tricks" to disrupt the lives of individuals and organizations. Some leading examples noted in the U.S. Senate study (1976: Book II, 10-12): Anonymous attacks were made on people's political beliefs to get them fired. Sometimes successful efforts were made to break up marriages by sending anonymous letters to spouses. Tax audits were encouraged—in one case to deter a protest leader from going to the national convention of the Democratic Party. Members of violent groups were falsely and anonymously accused of being informants, exposing them to attack. Demonstrations were disrupted by broadcasting fake orders on the same radio frequencies used by demonstration marshals trying to maintain order and prevent violence. Forms requesting housing for demonstrators were duplicated and falsely completed to cause "long and useless journeys to locate these addresses." An anonymous letter was sent to the leader of a "violence-prone" Chicago gang, falsely telling him that the Black Panthers had a contract out on his life, in the hope that he would "take retaliatory action." Communications were anonymously directed to Martin Luther King trying to induce him to commit suicide, and to his wife picturing him as a sexual deviant.

An FBI memorandum called for "more interviews" with persons engaged in New Left politics "to enhance the paranoia endemic in these circles" and "get the point across there is an FBI agent behind every mailbox" (U.S. Senate, 1976: Book II, 17). Other moves against the New Left (whose "paranoia" was certainly warranted) included an anonymous attempt to prevent a supposed "Communist-front" organization from conducting a forum at a Midwestern university (and investigation of the judge who upheld the rights of assembly and free speech); use of a friendly contact in a foundation to pressure a recipient college to fire an activist professor; an anonymous communication urging a university administrator to "persuade" two professors to discontinue financially supporting an activist student newspaper, to "eliminate what voice the New Left has" there; and "targeting" the New Mexico Free University for teaching "confrontation politics" and offering "draft-counseling training" (U.S. Senate, 1976: Book II, 17-18). An ex-agent of the FBI revealed that before antiwar demonstrations agents wrote and gave the media "often fanciful press releases warning that violence was expected on the day of the rally, or that the organizers of the march were in contact with Hanoi, or that some known Communists were active in organizing the march" (Wall, 1973: 341).

Discrediting the sources of intolerable views and information is, of course, a classic device that may involve both substantive counterpropaganda and the public or subpublic (as in "leaks") revelation of presumably damaging information about an individual or group. Obviously the information may be true or false, or even true information manipulated to give false or misleading impressions—for example, the "revelation" of J. Robert Oppenheimer's "left-wing" past associations as an argument for revoking the security clearance previously granted him, with assurances that his past memberships and activities did not preclude his directing the atomic bomb research project (Archer, 1971: 156).

That even relatively mild and indirect neutralization tactics, as in such information control, can have extremely painful consequences is illustrated by the news accounts of the Jean Seberg case (Toronto *Star,* September 15, 1979; New York *Times,* September 16, 1979). Seberg, at the time a rising American actress, exemplified the least formidable kind of political resister: the more or less active sympathizer—in this case with the Black Panther movement. Her political deviance was anything but idiosyncratic; the Panters were, for a while, virtually lionized, one might say, by many in the celebrity entertainer circles in which Seberg moved. Leonard Bernstein even hosted a gala fund-raising party on their behalf. Nonetheless, as a move in its campaign against the Panthers, the FBI in 1970 concocted and disseminated the story that Seberg was pregnant by a Panther leader (whose name is still being censored). Gossip columnists were sent a fake letter, purportedly from someone in whom Seberg had confided. The result was that at least one report was read by Seberg, who (according to Romain Gary, then her husband) was seven months pregnant at the time and immediately went into labor. The child was stillborn. Seberg was awarded $5000 in a libel suit. Her marriage collapsed, as did her career. After numerous attempts (reportedly each year on the anniversary of the infant's death), Jean Seberg nine years later committed suicide in Paris, where the earlier tragedy had occurred. A former Director, Clarence Kelley, has condemned the FBI's smear of Seberg and others as indefensible—and repeated the official assurance that such things are not being done anymore (Toronto *Star,* September 27, 1979).

Another avenue of neutralization is through informers, who may be used not only to obtain intelligence but also "to demoralize a target or handicap political activity" by such means as planting forged papers compromising a leader, promoting quarrels (for example, between blacks and antiwar activists in the 1960s), spreading rumors or charges that some member of an organization is a spy, and promoting or instigating violence (Donner, 1973: 314-315; see also Donner, 1972). When informers are overly zealous, dishonest, stupid, or even mentally ill, they can still be valued for providing usable misinformation, disrupting the circles that they have infiltrated, or committing acts—especially publicly repellent and, ideally, violent, ones—for which they may (as unwitting sacrificial pawns) be punished as ostensible representatives of the target groups. A double agent may be particularly useful as a conduit for disruptive information and misinformation, and a source of intelligence regarding the information-control tactics as well as other activities and plans of political resisters. The importance of informers in neutralization is salient in judicial or legislative hearings, when they surface to give testimony weighted with the presumptive authority of an insider's knowledge. In conspiracy cases, especially, the impact of informer witnesses is maximized by the combination of vague substantive law with the procedural rule that evidence against any one conspirator is admissible against all others—thus permitting informers to be used even against people they have never heard of (Donner, 1973: 317).

So far, the focus of discussion has been on enclosure more than on terror, especially on the relatively indirect and mild methods of neutralization by information control by which persons are portrayed or treated as offenders without being designated as such, and without the authorities revealing themselves. That criminalization is occurring becomes clearer when authorities move more directly, openly, and severely against individuals or groups. However, the scale of criminalization includes a dimension in which persons may be subjected directly to punishment by the state's agents without any official acknowledgment.

Known or suspected offenders (or surrogates) may be neutralized by threat instead of public accusation, secret torture instead of formal interrogation, assassination instead of official execution. Such practices characterize the gray area between surreptitious "dirty tricks" and explicit political policing, and are resorted to when the political or other costs of adhering to legalities are considered excessive, yet neutralization can be accomplished only or most effectively by direct repression. Unofficial repressive acts are especially likely to be ordered or condoned when authorities feel that more open and legal neutralization cannot be achieved with sufficient certainty and dispatch, and/or without further raising an already dangerous level of political consciousness in the general population.

Brazil's notorious unofficial and unacknowledged police "death squads" have demonstrated the extremes to which surreptitious repression can be carried. At least 177 homicides in a single district of Rio de Janeiro, in the first 4 months of 1978, were attributed to the squads (Amnesty International, 1979: 106). Thousands of people have been threatened, beaten, kidnapped, and tortured because of their actual or suspected political orientations. Many others have suffered similar treatment as the license to repress social deviation has been ever more broadly used. Such death squads have been active in several other countries as well: In Guatemala, for instance, they have killed over 20,000 people since 1966 (Amnesty International, 1979: 123).

As the line between illegal or extralegal practices and legal ones is crossed, the only really significant difference is that more or less public legal justifications are now offered "for the record." What is done to people is still the same: Violence is threatened and used against individuals or groups to produce fear and pain—which is the precise meaning of neutralization as terror. To be the object of direct police action is to be threatened with deadly violence, even if the threat is not immediately stated, or is supposed to be contingent upon (especially violent) refusals to defer to the demands of police, judicial, or other authorities. Officially acknowledged or not, the repression of political deviance has always been characterized by human suffering.

During the late thirteenth century and early fourteenth century, in Florentine Italy the Guelph and Ghibelline parties alternated in savagely repressing each other, as first one and then the other prevailed. "Whether an individual was beheaded, banished, or merely fined was frequently dependent upon his importance in a political revolt, the strength of his personal influence, and most often on the arbitrariness of the judge or court that pronounced the sentence" (Wolfgang, 1954: 564). Michelangelo was relatively fortunate in merely being outlawed (deprived of all property and all legal rights and protections), then eventually permitted to return to the city with the further penalties of a fine of 1500 ducats and exclusion from the Great Council for three years. Machiavelli was less fortunate, being tortured on the rack and sentenced to the galleys before finally being declared "not guilty" and released. Many thousands of other people died, often in excruciating ways: burning, racking, exposure, mutilation, impaling, as well as hanging and beheading.

Over six hundred years later, medieval barbarities continue to be matched in kind and surpassed in scale by modern ones. Governments of the left, right, or center have in every continent resorted to terror in attempting to impose and preserve the hierarchical structures of politically organized social life. With tragic monotony, reports are disseminated of official torture and annihilation in the name of necessity: to counter the (presumably) otherwise unstoppable activities of terrorists, subversives, saboteurs, dissidents, or however else the internal enemy is characterized.

In Europe, authorities widely regarded as being among either the most barbaric or the most enlightened have used "extreme measures" to ensure their respective structures of power. Germany in the 1930s and 1940s developed the technology of terror to unexcelled levels, including gruesome medical experimentation on prisoners (Delarue, 1964: 316-327). Stalin and his successors in the USSR have continued traditions of political repression established by the Czars, consigning millions to the "Gulag Archipelago" of interrogation centers, prisons, and labor camps (Solzhenitsyn, 1974), augmented by mental institutions (Medvedev, 1971; U.S. Senate, 1972; Amnesty International, 1979: 242-244). Britain's long struggle with "the Irish problem" includes frequent accounts of torture by the police and of gross mistreatment of prisoners in Northern Ireland's Long Kesh prison (Amnesty International, 1979: 235-237). France, Spain, Portugal, Italy, both Germanies, Czechoslovakia, Hungary, Albania, Greece—the list includes virtually every nation on the continent, each with its own histories and moments of notoriety for ruthless treatment of political opponents.

Greece was a place of special horror from 1967 until late 1973 under the rule of "the Colonels" (Amnesty International, 1977). Torture was practiced with unusual ferocity, marked by sexual mutilation and degradation as well as the infliction of pain and death in other and quite terrible ways. "Social jealousy" was a factor in the particular viciousness shown toward students, former superior officers, and higher-status individuals in general. Contrary to stereotypes of the torturer as a moronic and sadistic brute from the dregs of society, the torturers were mainly young middle- and working-class men who were conscripted, and trained to the job by a combination of rightist indoctrination, gross physical abuse, including torture, and environmental controls. Of those charged in the first and most fully reported trial—that of the military police—15 were acquitted; 11 officers were given sentences ranging from 6 months to 23 years, plus 10 years deprivation of political rights; 5 soldiers received sentences from 5 months suspended for 3 years to imprisonment for 6 years. Because torture is not a crime under Greek law, the defendants could only be charged with misdemeanors involving "insults," "abuse of authority," and "bodily injury."

American national, state, and local authorities have often demonstrated their readiness to use and promote violence "with extreme prejudice" against political resistance wherever encountered. A recent domestic example is the 1975 extermination of six Symbionese Liberation Army rebels trapped in Los Angeles (Center for Research on Criminal Justice, 1977: 95-96).

Externally, from 1962 until the retreat from Vietnam the United States government was "intimately involved" in funding and training the South Vietnamese police—for whom torture was standard operating procedure, whose targets rarely survived interrogation and detention, and whose infamous Con Son "tiger cages" were replaced by cells (two square feet *smaller*) designed and built by an American corporation with a grant from the U.S. Navy Department (Amnesty International, 1973). The United States continues to provide counterinsurgency training for the security forces of many governments— particularly in Asia, Africa, the Middle East, and Latin America.

Governmental terror is commonplace throughout Latin America. In Argentina, an estimated 15,000 individuals (*los desaparecidos,* or "the disappeared ones") have vanished after being picked up by the security police (Amnesty International, 1979: 99; see also Hoeffel and Montalvo, 1979). From Bolivia, Brazil, Chile, Colombia, and so on through the alphabet of nations to Uruguay and Venezuela, every year thousands of doctors, lawyers, engineers, journalists, academics, students, farmers, workers, and others—men, women, and children— experience the police and prison routines of fear, pain, and death.

The Uruguayan case of the courageous Nuble Yic is illustrative of the cruelty which has become standard (Amnesty International, 1978a: 4-5). Yic, a 52-year-old worker in a meat packing factory, was convalescing from a heart attack. He was arrested at dawn on October 21, 1975, and held incommunicado until March 1976. During his family's second visit, Yic shouted to everyone in the visiting area that all should know prisoners were being tortured and killed; that he himself had suffered four months of electric shock, *submarino* under water and excrement, suspension by his feet or hands, and the forcing of sharp objects under his nails; and that he could not survive much longer because his heart condition had returned. The next day, March 14, Yic's torn and battered body was delivered in a coffin to his wife. A witness reported that after his outburst Yic was taken to *El Infierno* ("Hell") and suspended for hours above dogs, who savaged him until the ropes were cut. Then Nuble Yic dropped painfully on his swollen limbs, and died.

Equivalent reports come from the Middle East and North Africa: torturing and massacring of Kurdish adults and children in Iraq; Israeli interrogators beating, sexually assaulting, shocking, and hanging by the wrists Arab detainees in the occupied territories; the abduction by Syrian security forces of hundreds of persons arrested in Lebanon to be imprisoned in Syria; torture, executions, and inhumane prison conditions in every country (Amnesty International, 1979: 249-276).

Conditions are the same in sub-Saharan Africa, whether the stories be of Amin's terror in Uganda, Bokassa's butchery of schoolchildren in the Central African Republic, the rape, torture, and slaughter of thousands of people in Ethiopia's "Red Terror" on behalf of "revolutionary justice," or the frequent deaths of persons in the custody of South Africa's "security branch" (Amnesty International, 1979: 33-94).

The Republic of South Africa may well have the world's most elaborate legal structure for the repression of political resistance of all kinds (see Matthews, 1972; Amnesty International, 1978b). As protest and criticism find new forms and channels of expression, laws and procedures are modified or invented to facilitate the effort to stop them. Under the "sabotage" laws alone, persons may be arrested, detained incommunicado, and convicted for any activity that— "objectively considered"—is intended to promote "any social or economic change." The burden is upon the accused to *disprove* the assumption of such intent (Matthews, 1972: 164-169). Despite the relative ease with which convictions can be obtained, between September 5, 1963, and September 12, 1977, at least 45 persons died while being held by the security police—without any charges ever being laid or evidence brought forth (Woods, 1978: 6-7). The last of these was Stephen Biko, whose death precipitated major demonstrations and riots, as well as renewed international opposition to South Africa's legal control policies and practices.

Steve Biko was a founder and the leading symbol of the Black Consciousness movement in South Africa. Through the now-banned South African Students' Organization and the Black People's Convention, he worked to generate pride and hope among Africans—especially the young—and to encourage nonviolent efforts to transform South Africa into a democracy (Woods, 1978; Arnold, 1979). For his activities Biko was banned: restricted to a small "dorp" in the Eastern Cape (King William's Town) and forbidden to speak to more than 1 person at a time or to be published or quoted. Breaking the banning order by traveling, Biko was arrested when stopped on August 18, 1977, at a police roadblock near Grahamstown, then taken to district security headquarters in Port Elizabeth. Chained and in leg irons, Biko was for 22 hours continually tortured by 2 interrogation teams, which caused severe brain damage and other injuries. Kept naked in his cell for weeks, he was finally in such poor condition that the authorities decided to move him to the prison hospital in Pretoria. Placed on the floor of a police van, he was driven the 700 miles to Pretoria; he died a few hours after arrival—at the age of 30. A 2-week inquest ended with the magistrate's deciding that "on the available evidence the death cannot be attributed to any act or omission amounting to a criminal offense on the part of any person" (Woods, 1978: 261).

Court and administrative decisions exonerating legal control agents are to be expected in any polity. For official repression even to be subjected to legal review is an accomplishment; and for a regime to punish its own agents for using harsh tactics against its political enemies is unthinkable in most countries. By such minimal standards of accountability, South Africa still is one of the minority of polities today where some official concern for "rule of law" ideals persists. In 1977, 95 white and 155 black South African police officers were convicted for assaults—8 whites and 14 blacks for culpable homicide, and 4 blacks for murder; 32 persons were paid a total of about R22,500 for unlawful arrest; and nearly R90,000 was paid to people who had been assaulted by policemen (SAIRR, 1979: 74). Steve Biko's family was in 1979 awarded compensation equivalent to about $120,000—which his widow declared would as "blood money" be donated to a memorial community project (Toronto *Star,* July 30, 1979).

A less charitable interpretation of such compensatory actions by repressive governments is that they suggest analogues to certain manipulative techniques often used by interrogation teams. The essential coerciveness of policing techniques aimed at neutralizing resistance may be obscured by acts of seeming (or even genuine, at the moment) kindness and decency. Control objectives are sought through a program of deceptive interruptions and suspensions of the pressuring, including sometimes extreme alternations of the harshest torture with the most comforting and reassuring treatment. In political policing, there may be added a dimension of intellectual debate in which the subject's theoretical and factual assumptions and beliefs are explicated, argued, and refuted. (The validity of the refutation is irrelevant in most instances.) When the subject's intellectual powers have been weakened by physical and mental anguish, he or she may say or sign whatever is demanded, and may even be "brainwashed" into an inauthentic conversion to the interrogator's viewpoint. Such conversions usually lead to a ritual confession, and possibly—though rarely—to subsequent renegadism, that is, "working for the enemy" (on the techniques and limitations of brainwashing, see Brown, 1963: 267-293; London, 1969: 84-92).

Supplementary techniques involve credibly threatening personally significant others with anything from harassment to torture, or employing some other form of emotional blackmail that plays upon the individual's own sense of what may be personally discrediting. The particular approach is keyed to the subject's self-esteem, material concerns, or deeply held political, religious, or other social attitudes and convictions. The head of the Greek Colonels' security police prided himself on his skill in pressuring strong and honorable individuals into signing statements denouncing emotionally significant others and firmly held beliefs (Amnesty International, 1977: 82).

Whatever combinations of enclosure and terror may be used, most people and all governments evidently take it for granted that neutralization will be accomplished if enough resources can be devoted to it. The success of neutralization programs is commonly assessed in two ways: by the "body count" of those dealt with by control agents, and by the diminution of resistance activities. The first measure assumes that ending or limiting the social existence and participation of some number of people leaves fewer opponents. The second assumes that a decline in the number or rate of resistance acts, as designated by legal or other criteria, indicates a decreasing resistance propensity or capability in the population. Both assumptions are questionable because they imply ignoring alternative possibilities and contrary historical evidence.

While neutralization efforts in political policing clearly do incapacitate and deter many people, such efforts also radicalize and enrage many. Enclosure and terror can indeed generate a sense of hopelessness and dread. However, human beings so blocked or terrorized may, instead of giving up, become implacable foes who no longer expect or show any mercy—for example, the fanatical Japanese Red Army (McKnight, 1974: 158-170). The Czar's Okhrana did not stop the Russian revolutionaries, nor have the Cheka and its successors down to the KGB succeeded in eliminating opposition to the state tyranny of Soviet Marxism. And in a spectacular recent example, Mohammed Riza Pahlevi of Iran was forced to flee ignominiously after pouring enormous resources into the savage efforts of his political police and army to stamp out resistance to his rule—which lasted only 26 years after the CIA helped him to overthrow Mossadegh's elected government and proclaim himself Shah (Marchetti and Marks, 1975: 46, 49, 51).

Declining counts of resistance acts, whether calculated as actual frequencies, rates, or rates of change, may or may not be statistically valid. Counting bodies and cases is a matter of perceptions, purposes, judgments, and technical skills. Even if the counts are valid, they have (as every criminologist knows) no necessary significance beyond the summarizing of control activities as recorded. What may be happening is that resisters are becoming more skilled in avoiding detection and neutralization, that alternative tactics of resistance are being used, or that resistance is temporarily in abeyance while a more effective strategy of resistance is being planned. The point is that casualty and encounter figures are not necessarily useful indicators of how the war is going (as the United States military demonstrated in Vietnam).

Estimates of the effectiveness of neutralization are, therefore, meaningless unless they take into account the possibilities that resisters may be incensed rather than deterred, that the data may be faulty, and that declines in the incidence of resistance acts may be illusory or temporary. The most crucial test of control effectiveness, however, is not whether resisters are deterred from further resistance, but whether the potential for resistance by others is reduced. Are old resisters being replaced by new ones? Is the probability of new resistance increasing? Is further resistance likely to involve an increasing and more representative proportion of the population? In short, is *general* deterrence being accomplished?

Intimidation: General Deterrence

People may refrain from dissent, evasion, disobedience, or violence because they have no grievances or concerns not satisfied within the structure of conventional politics. Or they may acquiesce out of fear and ignorance—which is the meaning of general deterrence. General deterrence is the ultimate goal of political policing; it is the anticipated product of intimidation. Because they are intended to influence potential as well as present resisters, programs of intelligence gathering, information control, and neutralization go beyond what might be expected if the detection and neutralization of dangerous political enemies were the only objectives. Instead of limiting surveillance and intervention to activities constituting "clear and present dangers," authorities are very likely (though perhaps regretfully) to accept the premise that effective political policing requires open-ended monitoring, censorship, and maximal credibility of threat. The implication is that fear and ignorance are necessary elements in political socialization.

Research on political and legal socialization suggests that fear and mystification are more likely outcomes than is a developed political consciousness. Children generally learn early to emphasize the fear of violence and chaos as the main reasons for government and rules, and to view police officers as harshly punitive authority figures (Tapp and Levine, 1970; Tapp and Kohlberg, 1971). Their knowledge of governmental structures and rules tends to be meager, and their level of political concern tends to be correspondingly low. Caldeira (1977) recently found that a sample of 10-14-year-old American children knew and cared very little about the federal Supreme Court, consistent with the level of ignorance commonly found in studies of adults—and contrary to the Easton and Dennis (1969) thesis that the Court's high prestige derives from the knowledge and appreciation of the Court acquired early in life by most Americans.

Adults in several nations have been found to have relatively low average levels of political knowledge, often along with what might be seen as unrealistically high levels of perceived subjective capacity to challenge and influence their respective governments (see Elcock, 1976: 58-73). From their comparative study of five democracies (Britain, Germany, Italy, Mexico, and the United States), Almond and Verba (1963: 346-374) concluded that persons who report having participated significantly in family, school, and job decisions tend to report being more politically active and confident of their effectiveness. However, as the authors recognize, *actual* effectiveness in the hierarchical structures of political authority does not necessarily follow from experiences in decision making in more egalitarian subpolity structures. The trend toward more democracy in such structures as the family and school

> will increase the individual's "availability" for political participation. But whether or not this will lead to an increase in effective political participation is problematic [Almond and Verba, 1963: 374].

Studies of legal beliefs and attitudes indicate that people in widely differing political contexts generally have little specific knowledge about laws or legal procedures, and often hold views about right and wrong that differ notably from those asserted explicitly or implicitly in the workings of legal institutions.

That most people know little about the legal systems impinging upon their lives is empirically indisputable. However, the extent and significance of discrepancies between legal norms and popular sentiments has long been at issue. In a major recent study, Newman (1976) interpreted his findings as evidence of high value consensus within national cultures, and possibly suggestive of a universal values scale. Yet, his survey data (some urban and rural residents of India, Indonesia, Iran, Italy, Yugoslavia, and the New York area) also revealed noteworthy dissensus and variability in regard to the perceptions of certain acts as deviant, knowledge of the relevant laws, beliefs about levels of law-enforcement activity, and opinions on appropriate penalties (see Newman, 1976: 123-153, 165-166, 210-211, 225-248). In any case, the problem at hand is not how much consensus is found, but how it is produced. Specifically, to what extent does public consensus reflect deterrence—that is, fear and ignorance—rather than informed judgments?

A review of the literature on the impact of legal control efforts has led to the conclusion that legal coerciveness in Western democratic nations has generally been effective in keeping interpersonal and collective violence at manageable levels, though ineffective or counterproductive for most other offense categories (Turk, 1972b: especially 27-70). With respect to political crime, legal control programs were assessed as having been largely effective in repressing the more overt and violent forms of political resistance, but counterproductive and probably ineffective in suppressing dissent (pp. 59-66). However, the generally poor quality of the available evidence makes it impossible for such conclusions to be much more than plausible hypotheses.

Analyses of data on political conflict in various polities have demonstrated within-nation and across-nation variations in the frequencies and levels of "strife," "turmoil," "disorder," and so on, but provide no clear evidence regarding the effects of general deterrence programs. Graham and Gurr (1969: Vol. 2, 483), for instance, found that "the size of military and police establishments has no consistent effects on strife." For the

Western group of nations there was, in fact, a direct association:
The larger the military and police force, the higher the levels of
strife. However, some evidence suggests that consistency in
using coercion, rather than the size of the force using it, may be
significant in reducing strife. Substantively and methodologically diverse efforts by other analysts of crime, collective
violence, and political assassination were no more successful in
establishing the causal significance of control forces and policies
(see Graham and Gurr, 1969; Kirkham et al., 1969).

Most recently, in a detailed comparative historical study of
four cities (London, Stockholm, Sydney, and Calcutta) Gurr
found that the effects of "policies of public order" varied
greatly both among and within the cities, depending on complex factors "only dimly understood" (Gurr, 1976: 183; the
case studies are in Gurr et al., 1977). The unresolved methodological problem was (and is) that associations between changes
in levels of public disorder and in control policies could have
resulted from other cultural, political, and/or economic
changes. He concludes that

> there is little empirical basis for confidence about the contemporary
> effects of policies informed by humanitarian faith in equalization of
> opportunity and rehabilitation, or by conservative reliance on strict
> authority and firm punishment [Gurr, 1976: 183].

Similar problems have been encountered, and similar conclusions reached, in research on the deterrent effects of specific
legal sanctions upon specific crime rates (Zimring and Hawkins,
1973; Gibbs, 1975; Blumstein et al., 1978). The basic proposition tested in deterrence studies has been, in Gibbs's (1975:
222) formulation, "the greater the celerity, certainty, and severity of punishment, the less the crime rate." Despite its plau-
sibility, and the investment of considerable resources in verifica-
tion studies, the research evidence bearing upon the proposition
has recently been evaluated as

> still not sufficient for providing a rigorous confirmation of the
> existence of a deterrent effect. Perhaps more important, the evi-

dence is woefully inadequate for providing a good estimate of the
magnitude of whatever effect may exist [Nagin, 1978: 135].

Perhaps the most intensive efforts have gone into confirming
or disproving the deterrent effect of capital punishment. After
being widely cited as finally demonstrating a deterrent effect,
Ehrlich's (1975) econometric analysis was subsequently found
to be flawed by data quality, sampling, and computational
problems that vitiate his findings (Nagin, 1978: 109-110; Klein
et al., 1978; see also Vandaele, 1978). "The deterrent effect of
capital punishment is definitely not a settled matter, and this is
the strongest social scientific conclusion that can be reached at
the present time" (Klein et al., 1978: 359).

Whether or not intimidation can be shown to produce general
deterrence, authorities always assume that it does, and place
their ultimate reliance upon coercion rather than education.
Gibbs (1978: 113) notes that governmental agencies, particularly in Anglo-American jurisdictions, *as a matter of penal
policy* . . . do very little to further public knowledge of criminal
law," and suggests that *why* is "a central question for the
sociology of law." An answer is implicit in the proposition that
for governments "a belief in the efficacy of deterrent measures
is attractive because it offers crime control measures where
alternatives appear to be unavailable and does so without great
apparent cost" (Zimring and Hawkins, 1973: 21-22). Alternatives to intimidation may simply be unacceptable because
they are perceived to involve intolerable changes in the allocation of resources among competing groups, even to the point of
dismantling the existing structures of power and status.

Accordingly, the creation and presence of a "force" is
assumed by authorities (along with most other people) to
constitute in itself a deterrent: The threat of violence is made
real by organizing and displaying persons authorized to use
violence. Intimidation begins, then, in the general understanding
that police officers are distinctively privileged and commanded
to use deadly violence in making their contribution to social
control. Political policing differs from regular policing in the
degree to which intimidation is the explicit and not merely the

implicit goal. This is evidenced in the virtually exclusive investment of specific organizational resources in control instead of
service functions, and especially in the systematic use of actual
and threatened violence against the general population, apart
from its use in the neutralization of offenders.

In addition to the dissemination and encouragement of information and rumors likely to make people afraid or at least
cautious about doing, saying, asking, or thinking "dangerously,"
political policing may generate more convincing evidence of the
general population's vulnerability. The most obvious method is
random terrorism, as reflected in the proverb—historically
attributed to Shaka, ruthless founder of the Zulu Empire—"You
can only rule the Zulus by killing them" (Walter, 1969: 176,
218). A scarcely less barbarous tactic is the public display of
mutilated bodies, or of persons maimed by their ordeals in the
hands of police, such as Duvalier's infamous "ton-ton
macoutes" of Haiti. A less extreme technique is to warn the
public by the humiliation, or worse, of individuals linked by
their own acts or by imputation to publicly denounced views
(for example, the treatment by the USSR of the renowned
physicist and humanist Andrei Sakharov, who has been stripped
of his honors and banished to the "prison city" of Gorky; New
York *Times,* February 17, 1980).

And because it has never been possible to stop entirely the
emergence and diffusion of moral and political dissidence,
authorities have sooner or later hit upon the technique of
punishing those who may possess, quote, discuss, or merely be
exposed to banned communications or ideologically contam-
inated persons. Thus, even if dissenting voices can be neither
smothered nor discredited, the attempt is to make them objects
of fear and aversion with the approximate status of a contagious
disease (exemplified in the "blacklisting" of academics, enter-
tainers, journalists, and others during the McCarthy era in the
United States).

Intimidation may also be achieved by instigating and then
repressing offensive acts, frequently by using *agents provocateurs* (Marx, 1974). And of course legitimate assemblies and

demonstrations may be used as occasions for exhibiting the realities of power, in ways ranging from the mobilization of disproportionately large forces for "crowd control" duty, through ostensibly unwanted "police riots," to deliberate "Cossack charges" in which the aim is to "teach the rabble a lesson" (see Stark, 1972; Kritzer, 1977).

Somewhat analogous to random terrorism is the not-so-random destruction of whole categories of a population. Hitler's "final solution to the Jewish question" is an obvious example, even though its relative secretiveness (abetted by the anti-Semitism and preference for "not knowing" then common throughout Europe) makes it a less than perfect one. A clearer example is the kind of mass purge carried out by the Stalinists in the 1930s, in which political domination was secured by "the manufacture of deviance" (Connor, 1972). In contrast to other methods of political policing, mass purges are characterized by the very high visibility and scale of operations.

A feature of purges and often of other control measures is the punishment of individuals, associates, or entire communities for failure to report suspicious persons or happenings—or even for failing to detect offenses or apprehend offenders in their vicinity. "Guilt by proxy" is an ancient device for promoting cooperativeness in a subject population, as the Anglo-Saxons learned through the "frankpledge" system developed by their Norman overlords (Critchley, 1978: 2-4). Reprisals after acts of political resistance are, of course, common where authorities are unable or unwilling to entrust the task of repression to the established instruments of legal control. More than 3000 people were arrested and some 1350 were sentenced to death when the German "deputy" to the Czech puppet government, Richard Heydrich, was assassinated in 1942 in Prague (Delarue, 1964: 295).

If the idea of *legitimate* government is to be useful to those who govern, at least the explicit, official use of police techniques must usually be justified by authoritative declarations to the effect that whatever was done was "legal." Even though political crime laws characteristically leave the police with great discretionary power, their relationship to political policing is always an uneasy one, because the effectiveness of political policing is still the only real criterion of success regardless of whether particular actions can be adequately justified by the invocation of any law. That political repression must be justified is usually understood better by higher levels of enforcers, especially the judiciary, than by the police, whose tendency is to perceive the "lawyers' talk" as irrelevant nitpicking and obfuscation. Although political police are likely to be better informed than regular police about the complexities of handling social-political conflicts, they still generally share the preference of regular police for relatively direct, unambiguous, and punitive methods for coercing obedience, as against the relatively subtle, complicated, and cooptive methods preferred by the legalists for engineering compliance. Aside from the typical differences in class origins and memberships which may influence their values and perceptions, the differing occupational socialization, role expectations and demands, and working situations of the police and the legalists combine to promote a characteristic "police mentality" and a characteristic "jurisprudishness."

Strained relations between the police and the judiciary in political policing are often apparent in the course of political trials, in which a formal effort is made to justify police actions in terms of the provisions of political crime laws. Relatively few cases, of course, ever come to trial, because (a) "the area of opinions and actions kept under watch by the police of any modern state includes far more than what constitutional governments could and would want to take up with the courts" (Kirchheimer, 1961: 202), and (b) the effectiveness of many techniques used in political policing (as to a lesser degree in regular policing) depends upon their not being publicly revealed or examined—not least because they frequently preclude successful prosecution even under the generous provisions of political crime laws. Of the cases brought to trial, some greater (in more totalitarian polities) or lesser (in less totalitarian ones) proportion will be carefully staged productions, or "showcase trials"—in which the guilt of the defendant, usually involving a ritual confession, is a foregone conclusion, and in which the aim is mainly propagandistic rather than legalistic (for the classic analysis, see Kirchheimer, 1961).

For all their efforts, authorities cannot always manage the complex mechanisms of control so as to avoid occasional embarrassing, though rarely disastrous, errors and failures. Somewhat paradoxically, it is those regimes most concerned with demonstrating their adherence to the rule of law that are most likely to provide "horrible examples" of political trials in which stories and evidence of illegal police practices, stirring orations against the polity's rulers, demonstrations of gross incompetence on the part of officials, acquittals and other expressions of judicial independence, and even official condemnations of and investigations of the police are the fruits of political policing. Nevertheless, barring a general collapse of the polity's control system, the outcome of such setbacks is far more likely to be adjustments of the legal system to accommodate the needs of political policing than the inhibition of political policing to satisfy the restrictive formulas of the system. Recent South African legal history provides examples of just how far the authorities may bend to effect such adjustments (Matthews, 1972). Sachs (1973: 255-256) reports that on one occasion the security police avoided receiving a writ of *habeas corpus* by moving the detainee from one jail to another, until a new law authorizing the detention had been promulgated:

> The judge hearing the matter criticised the action of the police as possibly being in contempt of court, but beyond awarding costs against the police, took the matter no further, and the detainee was not brought before him or released.

Given that the process of political policing is unlikely to be seriously inhibited in the long run by legalisms, it is still true that the interests of rulers imply the need for some limits upon the agents of that process, notably the political police. To create a political police force is to create an instrument capable of suppressing not only intolerable dissidents but also anyone else, including political rivals. Moreover, apart from its potential utility as a weapon in political in-fighting, a political police agency generates its own organizational roles, loyalties, perspectives, and goals (especially organizational survival and welfare)—which may eventually conflict with the expectations and needs of those whose creatures the political police are supposed to be. From being merely an instrument, the political police may acquire such a high degree of autonomous power that they threaten to "swallow up" their political genitor, as in the case of the Soviet NKVD in the 1936-1938 purges (Friedrich and Brzezinski, 1965: 176).

In addition to the need to protect themselves personally and politically against the threat implied in the existence of a political police, rulers also need to maintain control over political policing in order to keep "excesses" from (a) blocking efforts to gain the cooperative acquiescence—if not the respect and regard—of the subject population, (b) upsetting vital military, economic, or other operations; and (c) preventing the adequate resolution of foreign relations problems (such as South Africa's difficulties as "the polecat of the world"). But even "excesses" may sometimes serve a useful function for rulers insofar as the political police may be blamed for social evils and ills, serving as a kind of lightning rod that draws hatred and blame away from the rulers themselves. "If only the king knew" of the evil and stupid doings of his subordinates, then all would (supposedly) be put right.

Of course the "king" (president, prime minister, chairman, chief) usually does know and, perhaps regretfully, approve of the general features and consequences of political policing, and often of the specifics in cases of particular significance. In addition to knowing and condoning, rulers often themselves initiate anticipatory or retaliatory actions against individuals, groups, or movements, including demonstrations of power for the educational benefit of the general populace. If rulers are occasionally troubled by some of the cruder aspects of suppression or by the ethical or legal issues involved, there are always consoling rationales to the effect that the weighty responsibilities of governance sometimes require the performance of unpleasant duties and the facing of harsh realities. The fundamental premise is "that group relations can never be as ethical as those which characterize individual relations" (Niebuhr, 1960: 83). Such rationales are also available to sensitive revolutionaries: "You can't make an omelet without breaking eggs" (on the ethics of communism, see Marcuse, 1971: 161-218). In any case, the transcendence of personal moralities and scruples is integral to the assumption of strategic decision-making roles. Whether or not born to rule, those who reach the pinnacles learn to distinguish (validly or not) between matters of personal morality and those of *statecraft,* the ultimate form of policing.

Statecraft

Statecraft is the art and science of social control as developed and used in the political organization of social life. Narrowly construed as the operations of political police, political policing may be understood as just the sharpest cutting edge of a more encompassing multidimensional effort to accomplish political dominance. More broadly construed as the total process by which intolerable political opposition is prevented as well as punished, political policing finally becomes synonymous with government. It has by now been amply demonstrated that any legal norm and any agency of government are resources which may be used as weapons against the actually or potentially unruly. Gamson (1968: 116-135) has identified three general ways in which authorities try to inhibit political resistance "at the source": insulation, sanctioning, and persuasion.

Insulation strategies seek to block "access to authorities and to positions which involve the control of resources that can be brought to bear on authorities" (Gamson, 1968: 117). Access may be inhibited by manipulating entry or exit in reference to polity or subpolity boundaries. Immigration and visa restrictions are designed to keep out the kinds of people who are considered potentially troublesome, as threats or as burdens. Security checks minimize the chance that "unreliable" individuals will share the knowledge and power available to insiders (especially those who govern), and perhaps deliberately or inadvertently "betray" the politics of stability and continuity. Less obviously, tax and property laws help to ensure that economic resources continue to be disproportionately allocated between the "haves" and the "have nots" (Galanter, 1974). Electoral and other laws regulating political participation have similar consequences (such as property, age, sex, racial, or other requirements for voting or holding office).

If screening procedures fail, troublesome persons may be diverted from "sensitive" positions either vertically or laterally. Demotions and being "kicked upstairs" exemplify vertical diversion; transfers and dismissals, lateral diversion. Extreme forms of dismissal at the polity level are exile and deportation—for example, the shipping of 249 people (mostly radicals detained without charge in the legally questionable "Palmer raids") from the United States to the Soviet Union on December 21, 1919 (Murray, 1955: 207). The transportation of convicts from Europe to penal colonies in the eighteenth and nineteenth centuries is a less clear example, amounting to a kind of forced emigration (Rusche and Kirchheimer, 1968: 114-126).

Sanctioning as a tool of statecraft includes the full range of rewards and punishments available to authorities. In cases where the necessary or desired degree of control cannot be achieved by insulation, an orchestration of sanctions will be tried. Threats and demonstrations of vulnerability are, in some proportion, blended with offers and rewards for compliance. To those who are found "deserving," gratifications and opportunities are granted; the situation of those not so favorably recognized has already been discussed at length. The differential granting, withholding, and withdrawing of status and other resources will, for individuals, be a matter of careers. For the general population, sanctioning will involve policy decisions that increase or decrease the life chances of particular economic, regional, ethnic, or other social categories. The formula is logically simple, though often politically complex: The more

troublesome receive over time fewer rewards and more punishments, if they cannot be insulated, sufficiently rewarded, or
"persuaded to virtue" (Tapp and Levine, 1970; Feeley, 1970).

   Persuasion strategies attempt "to control the desire rather
than the ability" to resist authority (Gamson, 1968: 125). The
intelligence-gathering and information-control techniques of
policing are supplemented by whatever educational, religious,
journalistic, entertainment, and other ideological resources are
available to guide people into cognitive and emotional states
that render them either active supporters or acquiescent subjects. Whether by raising consciousness or eliminating it, programs of ideological control are two-edged swords. Ignorance
and apathy may make people more amenable to direction; but
they may also be less productive and harder to mobilize. As for
consciousness raising, political awareness has, as discussed in
Chapter 3, been associated with relatively high information. Of
course, if societal persuasion fails, the authenticity of resisters'
knowledge and beliefs will usually be denied by authorities and
deferential subjects. At the same time, the "quality" of institutions from or in which such imputed anomalies emerged will
tend to be questioned, and punitive and/or reformative measures adopted—for example, the reported experiences of many
American (especially state) universities in the wake of the
student militancy of the 1960s, as numerous officials and other
establishmentarians demanded (and sometimes got) budget cuts,
program changes, and even faculty and student purges.

   Probably the most effective but also dangerous control tactic
is *cooptation,* the ultimate combination of reward and persuasion. It is most likely to be employed when actual or
potential resistance is highly threatening to authorities, in situations in which other controls are insufficient (Gamson, 1968:
135-142). Drawn into the inner circle, individuals are subjected
to the inducements and responsibilities of decision makers,
while losing the outsider position that gave structural support
and credibility to opposition. However, if they are strongly
committed to resistance, cooptation may be tantamount to
infiltration; and their access to significant resources and the

process of decision making may work against rather than for the figures and structure of authority. A celebrated instance of failed cooptation is the accession by Guy Burgess, Donald Maclean, Kim Philby, and Anthony Blunt to the highest echelons of Britain's security establishment (Boyle, 1979).

Similar dynamics are observable in the rise of formerly subordinate social groupings to join the older, dominant ones. Even as the newcomers acquire the outlooks and interests of the dominant class, they threaten it with the loss of cultural, political, and economic preeminance, even to the point of extinction. Consequently, the relationship between old and new authorities is typically stormy, as they struggle to reach an accommodation which is also an alliance against the rest of society. In social mobility there is always an implicit threat to social stratification.

Whether and how such strategies, or weaponry, will be used depends mainly upon the level of perceived threat and the ability of particular authority figures to mobilize governmental power. A democratic polity is largely defined by the low probability—and a totalitarian one by the high probability—that governmental power can be mobilized without agreement across a wide spectrum of the social groupings found in the population, with and without official standing. Whether statecraft will be successful in either democratic or totalitarian polities is contingent upon such factors as how much power rulers actually can exert, the degree and scope of resistance, and the technical and political feasibility of tolerable solutions to the problems of differential life chances that precipitate and sustain political opposition beyond the bounds of conventional politics. The specific issues in the elemental conflict between authorities and subjects may shift without resolution, and issues thought settled or dead may reappear (for example, Native American resistance to cultural destruction). New dimensions and intensities of conflict may be generated by the actions of either resisters or authorities. Suppression or conciliation may only fuel resistance to authority, while the overthrow of authorities may lead to the institutionalization of even greater mystifications of the processes by which authority structures are accomplished. Clearly, the strategies and tactics of both political policing and resistance may be confounded by processes and events beyond effective manipulation.

Summary

Ensuring the politics of stability and gradualism is the function of all policing, more obviously in control operations and less so in providing emergency assistance, guidance, and protection. The priority of control over service functions becomes evident whenever authorities perceive dominant group interests to be endangered. Proportionate allocation of policing resources to control and service functions depends upon not only the perceived threat, but also the historically established theory and practice of social control. Excepting periods of heightened perceived threat, more democratic polities are characterized by a relatively greater investment in service than is to be found in more totalitarian polities. The more democratic the polity, the more probable it is that control efforts will involve legal rather than illegal and extralegal tactics. Nonetheless, the policing of political deviance can be expected to exceed legal limits wherever it is instituted.

Authorities everywhere pursue the goal of *intelligence,* sufficient information about people's activities and attitudes to detect actual and potential resistance. Because effective countermeasures presuppose adequate knowledge, and because it is impossible to know in advance just what information may be useful, the scope of intelligence gathering is inherently limitless. Attempts to define limits by targeting only the most dangerous persons and situations founder on the impossibility of predefining dangerousness. In practice, intelligence operations generate ever-increasing numbers of dossiers containing both legally and politically useful information. The latter, "leverage," is especially useful because it facilitates the monitoring and processing of far more cases than could be handled by formal legal criteria and means, and without the handicap of publicity. As neither legal nor technological restrictions upon intelligence activities work, the only restraint discernible is recognition by the authorities that unlimited snooping is in itself subversive.

Supplementing and "correcting" the work of the knowledge institutions devoted to study, worship, and media presentations, *information control* in policing is the effort to promote politically acceptable views and to suppress or discredit unacceptable ones. The evidence indicates that censorship moves toward total surveillance and destroys the integrity of communications throughout society—including those of and on behalf of the authorities themselves. The logical endpoint is the collapse of the polity, as its cultural supports dissolve into a cynical "war of all against all."

Methods of *neutralization* are intended to curtail resistance in ways that both eliminate recidivism and promote general deterrence. *Terror,* designed to make resistance unbearably costly, is complemented by *enclosure* tactics to make the costs clearly unavoidable. Enclosure typically involves relatively indirect manipulation through surveillance and information control; terror is characterized by more direct restraint, often involving the most savage assaults upon human bodies and minds. Both enclosure and terror may be overt or covert, depending upon whether the authorities feel open and legal neutralization can be achieved without incurring unacceptable political costs. Despite prevalent beliefs to the contrary, body counts and declining offense rates are meaningless as indicators of effective neutralization insofar as alternative possibilities cannot be ruled out: that repression may drive resisters to greater efforts, that the data may be wrong, and that resisters may change their tactics. Regardless, the incapacitation and specific deterrence of existing resisters is less important to authorities in the long run than preventing the appearance of new resisters.

Intimidation measures—which incorporate and supplement intelligence, information control, and neutralization activities—are used to produce general deterrence: acceptance of authorities' demands because of fear and ignorance, irrespective of whatever consensus may exist between authorities and subjects. Studies of (a) political and legal socialization, beliefs, and attitudes, (b) the impact of legal control programs, (c) factors associated with political conflict, and (d) the deterrent effects of specific legal sanctions have failed to confirm the presence, much less estimate the magnitude, of general deterrence as a consequence of intimidation. Nevertheless, authorities and most other people persist in believing in the efficacy of coercion—possibly because the alternatives imply intolerable social changes. Characteristic techniques of intimidation include creating and displaying military and police forces, random terrorism, punishment for exposure to objectionable persons or ideas, the use of *provocateurs,* purges, and reprisals.

The inconsistency of the intrinsic lawlessness of political policing, in which pragmatics override legalities, generates tension between police and legalists that sometimes erupts in open clashes—with the probable outcome being the accommodation of the law to the requirements of the police. To the extent that authorities understand the danger to themselves and their programs of uncontrolled political policing, they are likely to act periodically to clip the wings of the responsible agencies—such as by making them the scapegoats for the higher-ups' own policy failures. Whatever is done is done according to the ethics of power as distinguished from the ethics of people.

Statecraft is applying the ethics of power to accomplish the political organization of social life. The major strategic options are *insulation, sanctioning,* and *persuasion.* Insulation programs screen persons and groups seeking access to positions and resources, and include vertical and lateral diversionary methods for depriving troublemakers of such access. At both individual and group levels, combinations of positive and negative sanctions are used to induce compliance. Persuasion strategies are designed to win "hearts and minds" by engendering either apathy or enlightenment, both of which may work against as well as in the interests of authorities. *Cooptation,* a hybrid of reward and persuasion, is probably the most effective and most dangerous of all control strategies: Authorities who try it may find themselves either optimally secure or displaced. There is always a chance that nothing will work to sustain, or change, a particular structure of authority and power—at least in the forms or directions envisioned by those who struggle in such deadly earnestness.

CHAPTER 5

TRENDS AND PROSPECTS

All human society amounts to manipulation of human
beings by each other. Everything depends upon who
is doing the manipulating and for what purposes.
                    Barrington Moore, Jr. (1973: 61)

Liberalism is that principle of political rights,
according to which the public authority, in spite
of being all-powerful, limits itself and attempts,
even at its own expense, to leave room . . . for
those to live who neither think nor feel . . . as
do the stronger, the majority.
                    José Ortega y Gasset (1932: 76)

It has been proposed that the political organization of social
life inevitably generates unequal life chances among the various
groupings of people caught up in the process, and further
proposed that any claim that the more advantaged are such by
right, not might, is met sooner or later by the counterclaim. The
struggle over authority is a constant. Thus, instead of aberrations—departures from some hypothesized state of political normalcy—political policing and political resistance are seen
to be the fundamental dimensions of social existence in a
polity. Although the sources, forms, and consequences of both
dimensions of political life have been explored in some detail,
the analysis has not been carried past the point of observing and
explaining the ubiquity and variability of conflict. To consider
whether and how it can be is our remaining task.

Apart from accepting or contesting empirical or analytical
details, one may react in one of four ways to the idea that

conflict is both ubiquitous and variable. First, it is logically possible to deny that conflict exists; but only in some universe of mystic discourse could this alternative be seriously entertained. Second, one may agree that conflict is ubiquitous but deny that it is variable—as does the misanthropic fatalist to whom all striving is meaningless ("vanity, vanity, all is vanity"). Third, one may argue (as do utopians of left and right) that conflict is variable but not ubiquitous—that is, not found in some past, present, or possible society. Or fourth, one may agree that conflict over authority is ubiquitous while also noting that its variability suggests the possibility of manipulating its costs, instead of merely imposing or bearing them. From this fourth perspective, the crucial questions are: Who is to manipulate, who is to pay how much, who is to gain how much—and how are the success and failure of manipulation to be measured?

Both revolutionaries and control strategists tend to define success as the failure of the enemy. Collapse of the control effort is revolutionary success; cessation of political resistance is successful control. In these simplistic terms, the struggle over authority can only be seen as something to be ended as soon as possible, certainly not as an intrinsically valuable kind of social interaction (a notion to which we shall return). If the measure of success were so easily defined, then revolutionists should be eternally optimistic and authorities forever prepared to abdicate, for the ultimate collapse of any particular authority structure may well be inevitable. No one, however, should be prematurely outraged, disturbed, or exhilirated. As will become evident in considering the decay of authority, the meaning of success in political struggle, and patterns of change in political resistance and policing, it is not easy to predict authority's disintegration, or its impact upon the distribution and security of life chances.

The Decay of Political Authority

The preceding analyses of society, law, criminality, and policing have indicated or implied that though political authority structures may last for generations, several factors strongly suggest that no technology of control can forever prevent their deterioration—independently of the prowess or luck of political resisters. First, internal contradictions in the process of political policing not only preclude eliminating all resistance but even help to create it. Second, the functional consequences of political policing are in crucial ways incompatible with the conditions needed for resolving social conflicts. Third, physical and social environmental contingencies cannot be fully anticipated and controlled. Fourth, the sources of conflict over authority lie not only in objective differences in material life chances but also in varying subjective perceptions of both material life chances and cultural dissimilarities. And finally, there may well be a biological basis of human competitiveness that, in conjunction with group loyalties, makes conflict over actual or potential allocations of resources inevitable. After each of these propositions has been examined, we will return to the problem of measuring the relative success of the imposers and the resisters of political authority.

CONTRADICTIONS IN POLITICAL POLICING

Because the modes of political policing are inherently contradictory, trying to make them complementary is an extremely difficult and unending administrative problem. The basic dilemma is that although explicit force mitigates against subtle persuasion, occasional demonstrations of potency are needed to maintain general awareness of the hierarchy of power—in order to reduce the likelihood of escalating challenges which must be met with greater and more costly exercises of force. Another contradiction is that covert surveillance and manipulation become increasingly less so insofar as they bear fruit. Control actions taken as a result of what is learned tend to point back to their informational bases, and targeted people are forced to become more alert and sophisticated. This in turn makes secret policing more difficult, which reinforces the inclination of political police to assume the worst and to move toward more open repression.

Even if the police are cautious and restrained in moving from monitoring to more actively repressive control efforts, the insatiable nature of intelligence gathering—along with the programmed need for ever-increasing efforts to inhibit the spread of dissident views—eventually generates a volume of covert activities too great to remain hidden. The more people under surveillance, the more data collected, the more communications are watched and manipulated, the more activities of all kinds, the more probable it is that leaks will occur and that awareness of what goes on will spread—from the more to the less resistant, from the politically sensitive to the merely resentful, and so on to the politically conventional and the politically unaware. Thus, covert intelligence and other operations almost inevitably blow their own cover as a function of apparent success.

Furthermore, political policing tends to produce not only awareness but also resentment. In the course of monitoring and intimidating the populace, manipulating the quality and flow of information, and neutralizing resisters, control specialists are led by the totalistic logic of their enterprise to actions tending to disturb people's lives. Persons who directly or vicariously experience loss, or even inconvenience, because of police activities are prone to raise the question, "Why me?" no matter how politically conventional they may be. Depending upon how tolerant the authorities are toward grumbling, individuals initially just annoyed may be prodded into increased resentment and sensitivity by further disturbing experiences (such as questioning, employment troubles, or neighbors' remarks). Even conciliatory approaches by authoritative figures frighten many people, who thus come to see that they are under scrutiny, and therefore at risk whether or not the proffered advice or inducements are accepted. It appears that personal insecurity stimulates a process beginning in fear, soon expressed in resentment, then heightened sensitivity, and culminating in a more critical concern about the possible grounds for resentment and possible avenues for seeking relief. Whatever they do, the authorities cannot help provoking resentment in the course of trying to detect, deter, and neutralize resistance.

An especially ironic contradiction of political policing is that it leads to distrust and cleavages among those most advantaged by the structure it is designed to maintain. Although they may argue or hope otherwise, elites well understand that the inexorable logic of the process is to encompass the whole of society. Consequently, the more successful the specialists are in extending and strengthening the control net, the more apprehensive will be enlightened members of the dominant class who do not have proximate control of the policing apparatus. They know that factional struggles are usually won or lost because of the relative ability of contending parties to obtain and control information, to reward friends and punish opponents, and to manipulate the impressions of outsiders such as the electorate or the authorities of other polities. And the stakes may be high: the rise or decline of one's own sector of the dominant class, or even continued class dominance itself. Because whoever controls political policing obviously has the edge, elites struggle among themselves over its control, while at the same time seeking to devise their own protective and alternative security agencies (as will be discussed below). Political policing is indeed a two-edged sword; those who live by it always risk dying by it.

POLICING VERSUS RESOLVING SOCIAL CONFLICTS

A recent analysis of "conflict management" indicates four basic options: prevention by facilitating "legitimate" struggle; prevention by removing the causes of "nonlegitimate" struggle; resolving or terminating "nonlegitimate" struggle—that is, inducing the contenders to stop fighting (give up violence) and begin negotiating trade-offs; or suppressing irresolvable "nonlegitimate" conflict (Himes, 1980: 190-282). However useful the idea of conflict management may sometimes be, at the level of a polity it has definite limitations. A crucial one is that the concept of management implies someone external to a conflict who might be able to compel or persuade the conflicting parties to end their struggle. Though foreign intervention may be possible, no one in a polity (including the judiciary, as was shown in Chapter 2) stands external to the conflict over authority. A second limitation is that efforts to manage such conflicts are compromised by the problematic, malleable nature of the legitimate-nonlegitimate distinction—which is impossible to apply in any truly objective sense to the actions of either resisters or enforcers. (For a discussion of problems in defining "deviant" political policing, see Turk, 1981b.) Without either an external manager or established criteria for differentiating legitimate from nonlegitimate modes of struggle, resolutions of conflicts over authority are notoriously difficult and more or less unstable.

The resolution of conflicts presupposes at a minimum a mutual desire for resolution, a willingness to forgo annihilation of or withdrawal from the opponent, and the ability of opposing parties to reward one another for concessions. But in a polity the basic structure of power and privilege is not negotiable, as far as the authorities are concerned. Political policing begins with the premise that disagreement with the terms of a polity's foundation is intolerable, there being simply no acceptable grounds for questioning the structure of social life itself. As has been pointed out in an analysis of the Canadian French separatist movement:

> The very nature of such dissent makes it difficult for the political authorities to cope with it.... It is relatively easy to pressure a government to modify one of its decisions; it is more difficult to bring about changes in the social composition of those who hold positions of authority; but it is still more difficult to bring a political community and its authorities to accept its own dismemberment [Breton, 1972].

There is, then, little desire or ability on the part of authorities to bargain with radicals—other than the terms of their surrender or departure. As for violence, authorities insist upon retaining the option, in principle and fact, while demanding that their opponents give it up, in principle and fact. Serious resisters are, of course, hardly likely to see this as in any sense a "resolution" of the conflict.

What is "serious" resistance? To the agents of control, all resistance is at least potentially serious, and therefore to be discouraged. The idea of facilitating political conflict is antithetical to that of inhibiting dissidence, and likely to be met with skepticism by control specialists—who are occupationally inclined to view as ridiculously naive such notions as "participatory democracy," or even "democracy" itself. It is also significant that political policing is designed not to remove the causes of resistance to authority, but to deter and neutralize resistance irrespective of its causes. And to the extent that the sources of resistance lie in the political economy as such, prevention of conflict by removing its causes is, from the standpoint of the authorities, obviously out of the question. Their purpose is to inhibit, not facilitate, any effort to remove the causes of "nonlegitimate" conflict.

By elimination, therefore, the only form of "conflict management" compatible with the realities of political policing is suppression—but of the opposition, not of the conflict as such. As long as a potential exists for resistance, policing continues; and the potential continues in large part because, given the premises and functions of political policing, challenges to the material and ideological postulates of authority must be answered by repression instead of negotiation. Insofar as authorities and resisters consider their respective life chances to be at stake (as they are) and cannot ultimately trust each other (as they cannot), polarization is inevitable and the issue of who shall prevail is irresolvable except by tests of strength.

ENVIRONMENTAL CONTINGENCIES

It is one thing to establish a polity and quite another to control variability in its environment and the effects of such variability. Internal control—attained by statecraft in general and political policing in particular—does not itself constitute a solution to the problems created by nature or external social influences. At best, it can help in mobilizing efforts to deal with such problems; at worst, it impedes the quest for solutions. To the extent that political considerations override technical considerations, the process of ordering social life into hierarchical and inegalitarian structures is very likely to impede more than help those trying to solve a polity's "ecological" and "foreign relations" problems. (The following is partly adapted, though considerably revised, from an earlier discussion in Turk, 1972a: 176-180.)

(1) One does not have to accept apocalyptic visions of "the limits to growth," of the inexorable exhaustion of nature's resources, to perceive a growing "energy problem" and to agree that the survival of a polity depends upon extracting a living and overcoming threats from nature within a finite time period. Nature does not compromise or grant delays; people either develop and apply the necessary technology to survive, or they do not—whether for technological, ideological, or politicoeconomic reasons. Whatever may be potentially possible, empirically the only resources that count are those available when and as needed. Given that no "mastery" of nature is ever finally achieved, there is always some room for doubt that organismic needs are being met, or will continue to be met, on a scale sufficient for collective survival. Insofar as events and experiences promote doubt that everyone's material needs can or will be met, there will be political as well as other human costs— with respect to both "losers" and "winners."

From the perspective of control strategists, there are two main costs: the declining value of threat and the lessening of "trust" in the mechanisms by which polity-level decisions are made. The first appears to be especially crucial for authorities confronting losers, the second in regard to controlling winners in the struggle to "make a living."

Threats are decreasingly effective with people who are coming to feel they have nothing to lose. As long as the subjugated have the capacity to be deprived of things valued, they are collectively vulnerable to threats of punishment and offers of reward. Their last refuge is the hope of survival and perhaps a better life for themselves or their progeny. If that hope is lost, they can only be forced or killed in the immediate encounter; they cannot be conditioned to participate in the political organization of social life.

The loss of trust is the greater political cost of ecological failure, because it is more common and pervasive, and far more difficult to counter. Ecological failures often take a long time to become evident, and tend to be felt as partial or temporary "problems" instead of "crises," so that only the most clearly and immediately endangered are unable to sustain hope. Moreover, barring overwhelming catastrophe, the effects of ecological failures can be and are generally diverted from the dominant to the subject classes. However, as failures become evident, and especially as diversion becomes more difficult, winners as well as losers are prone to lose faith in the polity as the guarantor of their interests. Adopting an increasingly exploitative and defensive stance, disillusioned and fearful winners tend to abdicate "responsibility" for the polity and to withdraw into private bastions. More and more resources are allocated for private instead of collective purposes, and hoarded for private instead of public defense. But in turning to self-help, they do not increase their security but instead decrease it, for privatization leads to "fiscal crisis" in the polity (see O'Connor, 1973).

The fewer resources available for political policing and other social controls (such as economic improvement, education, or recreation), the more likely are authorities to emphasize violent methods in meeting resistance—which further erodes any remaining trust. As trust crumbles, so does the sense of inevitability and continuity in social life upon which authority rests. In this process the polity dissolves into ever more "primitive" levels of organization. Finally, unable to anticipate a secure future, the more powerful can learn only to capture and exploit the weaker, not to rule them; the weaker can learn only to avoid capture, not to obey or defer to their "superiors."

(2) The other basic environmental problem is that of asserting and maintaining the polity's boundaries: the "foreign relations" problem. Short of the world empire of which many rulers have dreamed, authorities must deal with outsiders (other authorities, and often also bandits, guerrillas, or other "out-

laws") so as to survive and prosper in their company. Warfare, subversion, diplomacy, international law, and all the other devices of "geopolitics" are invented and developed out of the efforts by authorities to ensure the survival and well-being of their respective polities, most especially of the dominant classes within their polities.

Conceptions of strategy grow in subtlety and complexity as authorities gain experience in the arena of foreign relations; but despite calculations and concessions of expediency, at least one principle is maintained as far as possible, and often with ferocity (as many diplomats, journalists, and humanitarians have recently learned painfully in the Middle East, Latin America, and elsewhere): that the authorities of a polity are masters in their own house. Specifically, the authorities of any polity reserve to themselves the prerogative of defining and dealing with "crime." The reason is clear. To allow parties external to the polity to determine the meaning of criminality, in policy or in control practices, is to abdicate or become vassals, and ultimately to allow the polity to be formally or tacitly incorporated into some other polity. Foreign domination implies the possible replacement of incumbents, and perhaps radical changes in the structure of power and privilege. Consequently, astute authorities resist not only military and subversive intervention, but also external criticism and offers of aid in dealing with resistance.

Accepting external assistance is always dangerous because it invariably means some dilution or forfeiture of discretion in making control decisions, and signals the weakness of the local authorities—who can usually expect further trouble, or testing, when their powerful friends leave or reduce support. The greater their dependency upon foreign support, the more likely are authorities to be stamped as weak by friends as well as foes, and therefore the more vulnerable the polity becomes to interference and challenge.

If environmental problems could be finally solved, and assuming a "beyond 1984" control technology, a perfectly stable authority structure would be at least conceivable (ignoring for the moment the other, especially internal, sources of deterioration). Fortunately or unfortunately, there is strong evidence that no final solutions will be found. Even in such relatively stable environments as that of the Pax Britannica, the present or potential insufficiency of resources and the greater or lesser intrusion of alien elements have always been present to work against the effort to generate political authority. From ancient empires to contemporary "superpowers," every set of powerful authorities has tried and eventually failed to solve its ecological and foreign relations problems by imperialist, colonialist, neocolonialist, and other strategies for dominating and exploiting peoples and polities beyond their jurisdictions. Among modern polities, economic and military interdependency—accompanied by political and cultural interpenetration—has been increasing at least since the beginning of the industrial revolution (see Wallerstein, 1976). Particularly since World War II, it has become increasingly clear that most polities cannot survive on their own, and that the more favored and powerful ones cannot retreat into self-sufficiency (largely a mythological notion, anyway). Any serious attempt to do so would involve nearly unimaginable economic, technological, and cultural regression—with horrendous implications for political control and stability. It seems, then, inevitable that polities must become increasingly open to environmental influences, and therefore vulnerable to disruption resulting from environmental changes.

SUBJECTIVITY AND SOCIAL JUSTICE

Conflicts over authority are not over things, but over beliefs and values. Suppose that technological, ideological, and political obstacles were overcome, resulting in the elimination not only of *absolute* deprivation, reasonably defined, but also of *relative* deprivation in regard to material life chances. There would still remain the linked problems of (a) allocating what have been termed "positional goods" (Hirsch, 1976: 27-31), and (b) making life "meaningful"—that is, understandable and acceptable within some framework òf right and wrong actions and goals, leading to just and (at least by implication) unjust outcomes.

Eckstein and Gurr (1975: 414) have defined *stratification* as "the ways in which people in a society are horizontally divided into higher and lower strata in terms of prestige, respect, worthiness, and dignity." Their conception points to the crucial importance of relative social standing as the marker by which people judge how well they are living. The satisfaction of organismic needs at any level of consumption soon comes to be taken for granted. Beyond the most minimal subsistence level, living is synonymous with social interaction—the giving and receiving of signals reinforcing or diminishing the sense of personal worth. Success in living is, then, largely measured by how significant one is in the eyes and lives of others.

Social status involves much more than, and other than, a popularity contest. Within a particular culture, one's standing may depend upon how much one is feared rather than how much loved, needed rather than liked, appreciated rather than admired. Respect (as all *mafiosi* know) may be a function of one's power or strength of purpose, not of whether anyone really cares about one "as a human being." Regardless of the criteria by which status is determined, the problem for those who wish to create and defend authority is that the "goods" are defined in relative, not absolute, terms: One person or group cannot have *more* unless some other party has *less.* Symbolically as well as functionally, not all can be captains; some must be deckhands.

The problem lies only partly in the impossibility of everyone's "doing well" in the polity; people may be relatively content for long periods to do well within their niches (caste, class, clan, or village). More consequential is the fact that the conscious and unconscious competition for status is inseparable from the search for meaning in human existence. Singly and collectively, people seek and find clues to their "nature and destiny" in comparisons between their experiences and situations and those of others. Relatively high or rising status tends to be felt as deserved success, low or declining status as undeserved failure. Although cultures vary greatly in the specific interpretive devices, all offer ultimate—that is, religious— theories addressing the problem of finding meaning in comparative success and failure. Out of this search for meaning arise conceptions of justice and injustice, models of how social relationships ought and ought not to be—with explanatory accounts of how apparent discrepancies are to be understood and handled.

Aside from ethnic and other cultural sources of difference, those who are advantaged and dominant in a polity tend to develop, or find more congenial, religious theories differing significantly from those toward which disadvantaged and subordinate people are inclined. Higher classes have an affinity for more intellectual, authoritative doctrines justifying worldly success and the use of power, and affirming the value of social organization, order, and continuity. Lower classes resonate more to emotional, antinomian orientations denigrating worldly success, condemning the abuse of power, and minimizing the importance of this world's secular forms. Correspondingly, social mobility tends to be associated with religious mobility: The rising gravitate toward intellectualism, the declining toward emotionalism. (A cogent recent sociohistorical analysis of relations among religious outlook, social standing, and political authority is Baltzell's comparative study of "Puritan Boston and Quaker Philadelphia," 1979.) Although such generalizations need considerable refinement in particular cases, the major point is that socioeconomic stratification is associated with religious stratification, as well as other cultural differences.

Differences regarding the most important issues human beings must face—their standing in society and the universe— are, then, simultaneously inevitable and divisive. Authorities cannot both maintain social stratification and impose ideological uniformity. The justice of hierarchy will be perceived differently by "the high and mighty" and "the meek and lowly." Such differences in belief and perception are a volatile source of potential challenge and disruption, and readily fuel struggles to change political and economic structures (for example, the recent Irish, Palestinian, and Iranian histories). Whenever people feel that their religious concerns, their ways of making life meaningful, are not receiving adequate emphasis, regard, or protection by the authorities, resistance is inevitable. Because authorities cannot fully satisfy or selectively eliminate the divergent religious communities generated by hierarchy in social life, religious dis-ease in some form or other is a constant drain on authority—and can easily become a flood, particularly in conjunction with other sources of decay in political authority.

BIOSOCIOLOGY AND ETHNOCENTRISM

The significance of human biological attributes has generally been discounted in social research. For most social scientists and reformers, the causal relevance of biological factors is highly questionable in explaining social phenomena. In addition, biosociological inquiries provoke fears that they may lend credence to racist, eugenicist, and social Darwinist ideologies. Certainly against any version of biosocial determinism, the paramount role of social contexts and forces is empirically well established. Nonetheless, it is also clear that social factors do not eliminate or displace, but interact with, biological factors to produce and shape human behavior and relations (Stark, 1976, 1978; see also van den Berghe, 1975: 25-51). An interaction of particular importance here is that between what may be called "the will to live" and "the social bond."

For several years the evidence has been mounting that human beings are genetically inclined to compete for the means of life, and that this "selfish" disposition is usually reinforced and channeled by socialization to identify one's own interests and desires with those of "significant others" (McNeil, 1965; Levine and Campbell, 1972; Collins, 1975: 90-114; van den Berghe, 1975: 34-37, 44-51; Stark, 1978: 1-31). The evidence does not support any "aggressive ape" theory, for no such theory can make sense of the complexity of ways in which competition is expressed in social processes and structures. Nor can genetically acquired competitiveness be easily distinguished from socially acquired and promoted competitiveness. Irrespective of how the biosocial interaction is accomplished, there does appear to be an irreducible core of self-and-group-centeredness that pushes or nudges human beings to try, singly and collectively, to improve and consolidate their life chances against the threat represented by the proximity—even the *existence*—of other human individuals and groupings.

It follows that some degree of ethnocentrism—the egoism and defensiveness of humans in concert—will keep any polity from ever being fully secured. The more complex and large-scale the polity, the more differentiated into "we" and "they," the more unlikely that authorities and subjects will be able to overcome their biosocially grounded tendency to distrust each other—as well as all others to whom they are not strongly bonded through socialization and mutually gratifying interaction. If the technology of control cannot eliminate distrust across and within social groupings, then subjects will never fully entrust their destinies to authorities, authorities will always fear overthrow by subjects, and factionalism will be a constant threat to both. Thus, the transformation of power into authority will never be completed—or irreversible.

A Measure of Success

Returning to the problem of defining *success* in authority-subject conflict, we face an apparent conundrum. On the one hand, we find that the deterioration of political authority is implicit in the process and problematics of its creation: internal contradictions of political policing; limitations and inconsistencies of political policing as a means of conflict management; vulnerability of polities to physical and social environmental contingencies; the relative and subjective nature of nonmaterial social goods; and biosocially engendered human competitiveness. On the other hand, we earlier established that the process of political organization is an intrinsic feature of human social life (Chapter 1). How are we to deal with the idea that both the creation and the deterioration of authority are inevitable?

For logical purists there are three major alternatives. One might (1) simply view the ebb and flow of authority "philosophically" as an eternal irony of the human condition, "man's fate"; or (2) "optimistically" expect the "contradiction" to be resolved or transcended in some ultimate achievement of social (and perhaps genetic) engineering; or (3) "pessimistically" conclude that civilization must eventually decline and fall into barbarism (and perhaps extinction) as the impossibility and absurdity of a truly just, healthy society become obvious to all. Fortunately, one does not have to choose among such final metaphysical options. In scientific inquiry, as in everyday life, experience has priority over logic; and conundrums are resolved in practice, whether or not in theory.

Within the pragmatic bounds of social science, it is enough to recognize that in the real world things *vary* and *covary,* and are therefore subject to anticipation and manipulation to an initially and ultimately unknown *degree.* Life is forever open to new possibilities of learning and doing, an inexhaustible mystery. Consequently, there is always the possibility that whatever is learned about the dynamics of authority will help human beings to distinguish more from less viable authority structures, and to find more effective and perhaps less costly ways to move toward the more viable ones. This suggests an approach to defining success in political struggle.

In general terms, success is any movement toward a more viable organization of social life (or, minimally defined, the absence of movement toward a less viable form). Degree of success/failure depends directly upon (a) the product of the actions and interactions of the defenders and challengers of authority, and indirectly upon (b) factors beyond the effective control of either party. The tactical efforts of either or both may be impeded or aided by "negative" factors (such as prolonged droughts, plagues and epidemics, invasions or other foreign interventions, or international boycotts, runaway inflation, or other consequences of the geopolitics of investment and trade), or by "positive" factors such as bumper crops, oil discoveries, or major breakthroughs in weapons or other technologies. In either case, the significance of such "exogenous" factors depends upon how they affect the product of authority-subject interaction. Whether the one side or the other is advantaged or disadvantaged is important only insofar as it affects the kind of outcome generated by their struggle. Not the victory of one or the other, but rather the *effect* of victory (or defeat, or stalemate) is the measure. The crucial question, of course, is, "Measure of what?" What, in observable terms, does "viability" mean?

Clearly the viability of a polity has some connection with the life chances of the people whose lives are framed by it. Against the usual assumption that greater life chances simply means more opportunities, Dahrendorf (1979: 30) has recently proposed that life chances "are a function of two elements, *options* and *ligatures.*" *Options* are the number of behavior alternatives, the "possibilities of choice," available to people within the probable limits set by their social situation. *Ligatures* are the bonds or linkages—or "allegiances"—among people which exist, or are likely possibilities, within their situation. Although options and ligatures can vary independently, and in some instances may even work against each other, there is no reason to discount the possibility of an optimal balance between them. Either alone is demonstrably insufficient: "Ligatures without options are oppressive, whereas options without bonds are meaningless" (Dahrendorf, 1979: 31). One can imagine not only an optimal balance, but also an escalation (or shrinkage) of "the entire system of co-ordinates" in reference to which the association between options and ligatures is mapped (pp. 33-34).

Dahrendorf (1979: 35) goes on to observe that the undeniable increase in life chances accompanying the rise of modern polities has been achieved largely by extending options and demolishing ligatures—a one-sided process that may well have exhausted its potential by the early 1970s. The process of "modernization" (that is, the drive to mobilize human productive capacities in maximally efficient operations, regardless of "traditional" and other "noneconomic" values) has begun to be counterproductive, decreasing life chances faster than they are created. As older social bonds have been destroyed, newer ones have become increasingly difficult to establish against the economically, politically, legally, and culturally supported drive to expand individualized opportunities (options) at the expense of enduring, secure social relationships (ligatures). Without the anchoring of stable relationships, people cannot find meaning, standards for choice and action, so that their options dissipate in aimless mobility, frenetic consumption, and "that nausea of disorientation which leads to pointless acts of identity-craving" —perhaps including terrorism as well as suicide, stress, break-down, and other forms of malaise (Dahrendorf, 1979: 36-37).

The utility of Dahrendorf's conception of life chances depends not upon whether his diagnosis of modern troubles is correct, but rather upon whether empirical indicators of options, ligatures, and their relationships can be devised. Dahrendorf (1979: 74-84) himself offers some illustrative exploration of what might be tried, but soon ends "the games" admittedly yet a long way from "operational precision." His brief discussion suggests or implies several possible indicators of options and ligatures, but offers only minimal direction for addressing the problems of determining an "optimal balance," the dimensions of a "system of co-ordinates," and whether a system is expanding or shrinking.

Options are measured by the ability of persons individually or collectively to obtain and mobilize resources—that is, their power. The possible maximum ("horizon") is defined by what is technologically, culturally, and environmentally accessible to the most powerful social position a person can occupy in a particular time and place. Examples of option indicators for individuals include not only such familiar status markers as income, occupation, and education, but also less obvious indicators, such as access to medical care, unemployment safe-guards, leisure time, and civil liberties (such as freedoms of belief, expression, communication, association, residence, and travel). For collectivities, aggregate measures of options are supplemented by qualitative and quantitative indicators of, for example, accessible energy resources, demographics (such as age-sex composition, morbidity and mortality rates), military strength and diplomatic capabilities, productive facilities and productivity, service facilities (such as educational, medical, housing, recreational), support for and level of scientific research and technological innovation, and legal system characteristics (for example, legal traditions and institutions affecting the other indicators). In short, more developed, powerful, and innovative polities have more options, as do the more advantaged people in them.

Ligatures are harder to define operationally, because the quality ("intensity") is more important than the number of social bonds. The key ideas are that people need commitments as distinguished from mere contacts, and open-ended, unconditional commitments more than limited ones. For example, in reference to interpersonal networks, one indicator is the number of others to whom and from whom commitments are made, scored according to the kind and range of obligations involved. A related set of indicators reflects people's senses of their social location in historical and transhistorical context—for example, knowledge and concern regarding genealogy and kinship, intergenerational links of ethnicity and place, friendships, and shared religious beliefs ceremonially expressed. Another set of measures delineates the sense and level of political identity in reference to the polity (such as trust in authorities from the lowest to the highest levels, loyalty to subpolity and nonpolity collectivities such as religious institutions, social movements, or other polities, and forms and extent of political activity). Insofar as ligatures constitute "the foundations of action" (Dahrendorf, 1979: 31), the association between political identity and social location is an especially important indicator for anyone concerned with strengthening or weakening political authority.

Having now a more concrete understanding of options and ligatures, we have still to consider how they combine into life chances, and to specify the relationship between life chances and the viability of polities. One interpretation of the concept of an optimal balance between options and ligatures is that the power of individuals and collectivities declines when open-ended commitments are either too few or too many. And conversely, that bonding is precluded when power is too great or too little. Another interpretation is that the direction and rate of change in the one should not drive the other below some necessary minimum. For instance, economic development should not proceed so ruthlessly and rapidly that people have insufficient resources, opportunities, and time to adapt existing bonds or form new commitments. Similarly, commitments should not increase to the point of inordinately limiting productive effort—for example, by causing consumption to exceed productivity.

To determine an optimal balance requires some measurement technique for mapping the field, the "system of coordinates" within which options and ligatures increase or decrease. However, as Dahrendorf (1979: 80-83) implies, the problem is not only to construct a multidimensional scale or a system of simultaneous equations, but also to develop a theory of transformation from one system to another ("large shifts")—such as from a medieval to a modern political economy, from a capitalist to a socialist one, or from a "high civilization" to barbarism. One might start by trying to estimate the *relative* life chances of politically significant (minimally powerful) social groupings within a polity, or the *relative* life chances of comparable groupings in different polities, and the direction and rate of change in relative position within or among polities. Such estimates would enable testing of propositions about the relationship between life chances and the viability of polities—such as those offered below.

The connection between life chances and viability is not as obvious as it may at first seem. To the extent that an optimal balance between options and ligatures is not achieved, a grouping or polity with greater options will not necessarily be more viable than one with fewer options but stronger ligatures. The difference is analogous to that between having power and being able to use it, controlling resources and being able to mobilize them ("fixed" versus "liquid" assets). Or a strongly bonded collectivity (one highly "cohesive" or "integrated") may lack the resources to deal with more than a very limited range of contingencies, while a powerful collectivity may be able to handle a wide range of contingencies despite considerable "anomie" and/or internal strife. To illustrate the issue: Is Canada less or more viable than the Irish Republic? South Africa or the United States? The American coal miners union or the United Automobile Workers? Granted the methodological difficulties, questions of viability cannot be avoided in the real world; consequently, it is practically and theoretically important to make the effort to generate plausible and testable propositions about movement toward and away from more viable authority structures.

In authority-subject conflict, any action (strategy, tactic) likely to promote increased viability may be termed *progressive*; actions unlikely to do so are *destructive*. Since outcomes are the products of interaction, it follows that an action by one party that encourages progressive action by the other is progressive, and that an action encouraging destructive counteraction is destructive. From what has been learned and hypothesized about the creation and decay of authority structures, it is possible to derive a great many criteria for differentiating progressive from destructive actions. Some of the more readily perceived ones can be stated propositionally as follows.

To begin with the controllers, the more authorities emphasize increasing rather than limiting the life chances of subjects, the more likely are the great majority of resisters to be nonviolent, and the less support they are likely to receive from the general population. In more specific terms, the greater the use of terror in proportion to enclosure and cooptation, the more destructive of political trust and other social bonds encouraging social stability both in the subject population and among the elites themselves. It is also probable that although the options of resisters will be reduced by governmental terror, their ligatures (cohesion, public sympathy) will be strengthened, so that the life chances of the resistance movement may well be improved. Further resistance is not only probable, but also likely to spread. Even if organized violent resistance is stamped out, nonviolent forms (dissent, evasion, disobedience) can be expected to become more common—but less easily detected, thus pushing the authorities to more and more extreme measures. Violent repression of even the mildest resistance is possible; but the historical record of totalitarianism (for example, in Nazi Germany, Stalinist Russia, Haiti, Uganda, or numerous Latin American regimes) suggests that it is destructive. Compared to more democratic polities, the more totalitarian ones have a generally poorer record (as measured by such things as economic productivity, levels of living, scientific advances, human rights protections)—perhaps excepting military strength, which has typically been achieved at terrible cost in human lives and life chances.

In contrast to authorities of more totalitarian polities, those of more democratic ones are more likely (and historically have been more able) to use option increases to counter resistance. At the same time, they have been less ruthless in neutralizing and deterring violent resistance—and possibly less effective in dealing with small-scale terrorist organizations (Laqueur, 1977b: 119). This narrow "carrot and little stick" approach appears to be destructive. The emphasis upon options without corresponding regard for ligatures has promoted movement toward what is described from various angles as a "legitimation crisis" (Habermas, 1975; see also Friedrichs, 1980), "disintegration of the rule of law" (Unger, 1976: 192), "the twilight of capitalism" (Harrington, 1976; compare Wright, 1979: 111-180), or "the return of anarchy" (Black, 1976: 132-137). Whatever the details of evidence and differing interpretation, few would disagree that the authority structures of the more democratic polities are far from being unquestionably viable. Proposition: Control strategies giving priority to ad hoc material concessions over the development of communities, encouraging people to overvalue options and undervalue ligatures, and failing to differentiate between situations where political policing is and is not appropriate (Turk, 1981a) are likely to be destructive.

Resistance strategies may be assessed in similar terms. Any resistance action is destructive that stresses weakening the polity over making it more viable. For example, the more randomly violence is used (especially in more democratic polities)—that is, the more "terrorism"—the more violent and indiscriminate is likely to be the control response. The result is that everyone's political, cultural, and economic options are likely to be reduced, as resources are diverted into control efforts and the views of "hard liners" among authorities gain greater credibility. The matching of "terror from below" and "terror from above" is particularly destructive of social bonds, so that the capacity for mobilizing progressive collective efforts is diminished for both authorities and resisters.

Apart from random violence, other forms of resistance may be either destructive or progressive, depending largely upon whether directed against more democratic or more totalitarian authority structures. Any action is progressive that reveals new possibilities for *both* increasing *everyone's* options *and* establishing congruent ligatures—that is, social bonds that facilitate the creation and use of options, and are in turn strengthened rather than weakened by increasing options. Thus, actions encouraging or forcing authorities to invest more in cooptive strategies and less in repressive strategies, or more in enclosures and less in terror, are progressive. Premising the extermination of abstracted classes of people is destructive. More positively, actions are progressive that promote, for example, economic growth rather than mere consolidation, the reduction of gross economic disparities, more research and technological innovation, conservation and investment more than simply increased consumption or calls for "austerity," and adapting or replacing social bonds, while both minimizing the destruction and discouraging the unthinking perpetuation of existing bonds. To work out the many potential contradictions in such a shopping list is not resolvable in theory, but only in practice.

Workable solutions to the problems of increasing life chances—of optimizing the balance between options and ligatures, and of expanding the bounds of the possible—cannot be reached through a priori logical constructions or mystical revelations of "the" correct program. They can only be reached through the exploration of possibilities, reflection upon the resulting experiences, and the mobilization of enough resources to choose among alternatives. Because human beings can never fully entrust their life chances to others, conflict is not just inevitable at every stage from exploration to choice, but *necessary* to move from exploration to choice. To be unable to choose is to be unable to act. How the struggle is waged largely determines whether less or more viable alternatives are pursued. The process of politically organizing social life may, then, be progressive or destructive, moving toward a more or a less viable structure of power and privilege, and therefore of authority.

If increasing viability of the polity is the criterion of success in political struggle, then both authorities and their opponents may succeed, or neither. Success or failure is a joint product, irrespective of who overcomes whom. Though success is never guaranteed, human experience so far indicates that the chances are better if political enemies *seek* progressive rather than destructive outcomes—and *during* their struggle, instead of deferring the search until the forever hypothetical future when opposition finally ceases. Further, neither authorities nor resisters can expect success—a more viable polity—if their conflict reduces what is possible *now,* regardless of any notions about increasing life chances later. For the people of a polity, tomorrow's life chances do not exist; the only real pie is that on the table or perceptibly on the way, not "in the sky, by and by."

An idea of how the success of authority-subject conflict might be measured has been offered, along with several propositions reflecting the current state of knowledge and informed speculation as far as possible, but clearly demonstrating the great need for research testing ideas about conflicts over authority, and developing better ones. What has been accomplished should at least help us to look with more seeing eyes at current and anticipated developments with respect to changes in (1) the sources and consequences of political resistance, and (2) the methods and effects of political policing. After what appear to be the major patterns of change have been noted, some implications for the viability of modern polities will be suggested—not as firm conclusions, but rather as general hypotheses warranting further detailed study.

Patterns of Change

Any listing of what is occurring, or is likely to occur, in regard to either political resistance or political policing, is debatable because exceptions can always be found for any generalization, and because the quality of evidence is typically poor. Nonetheless, if inquiry is not to dissolve into "uniquism," the hazards of generalization must be risked. The empirical reason is that polities are not isolated from one another. The theoretical reason is that although detailed case studies provide an essential data base for theoretical interpretation, such studies cannot without more general interpretation increase our understanding of the extent and consequences of interdependence, and interpenetration, among polities in the world today. And the most pressing reason is that unless we prefer to drift into disasters, we must do what we can to anticipate them—for the possibilities of extinction or barbarism are now very real.

POLITICAL RESISTANCE

Available evidence indicates that at least five major and interrelated changes are under way or in the offing: (1) a shift from material to cultural sources of relative deprivation, (2) a movement from underinterventionist to overinterventionist governance as a source of political resentment, (3) a widening generation gap in both the sources of political sensitivity and forms of resistance, (4) an increasingly strong and rapid current from political resentment to resistance, and (5) the internationalization of resistance.

(1) Material needs and inequalities are still primary for most people. However, even in very poor countries there is a growing concern with cultural inequalities, and heightening sensitivity to the perils of cultural exploitation, stagnation, and extinction. Old ethnic, religious, regional, and nationalist sentiments are resurgent; at the same time, new experiences have been stimu-

lating new expectations from life—and from those who would govern it ("the revolution of rising expectations"). Ideological hegemony is increasingly problematic, as, in particular, the power and impact of the communications media become more questionable.

On the assumption that social conflicts are largely the products of erroneous or disturbing perceptions, rather than structural differences in life chances, many influential analysts have concluded that "through the organization of the communications process . . . order is established in the sphere of power considerations" (Pye, 1963: 6). Contrary to such views (and to both the claims of enthusiasts and the fears of critics), it now appears that prolonged exposure to the cultural stylings approved by authorities leads to greater—not lesser—awareness of the preeminence of the values and interests of the more powerful, among as well as within polities. After being diverted for a while by such novelties as television, disadvantaged people soon perceive the threat—to their languages, beliefs, and values— implicit if not explicit in the financially and politically selective programming of public communications. Moreover, "the transnational flow of information" promotes greater attention to conflict and the reasons for it, offers information that may inspire and justify violent as well as nonviolent resistance, and provides technical knowledge useful for resistance purposes (see Redlick, 1979: 74-77). It becomes increasingly difficult to divert people from the realization that the communications market is everywhere manipulated for profit—economic, ideological, and political. The resulting skepticism is reflected in demands for "equal time," controlled by and for "our people," and programs running counter to the celebrations of "popular" and "universal" culture through which the realities of conflict and dominance have been obscured. In sum, resistance to every variant of the "melting pot" ideology is emerging in reaction to, and in part resulting from, the process that was once commonly expected to accomplish hegemonic control.

(2) Politically sensitive individuals have always been concerned with the inefficiencies of governments, and the aims of

resistance have generally included the institution of new and better organizational and procedural mechanisms. Whether seeking the improvement or the replacement of the polity, most politically sensitive people have accepted the postulate that life chances are to be improved by means of more effective interventionist political organization. Though some romantics and anarchists have seriously questioned the postulate, their ideas have never been decisive in either conventional or resistance politics. But as the nets of political control have been ever more widely extended, and their connections with the structuring of social advantage and disadvantage have become ever more apparent, the value of governmental intervention has been subjected to critical examination by politically sensitive people emerging from experiential backgrounds other than the rural gentry, uprooted peasantry, and poetic intelligentsia which have traditionally generated romantic and anarchist attitudes toward nation building.

The submergence of localities and local interests to larger and wider political entities and interests has come to be seen by many politically sensitive persons as the inevitable result of the process of political organization. Rather than trying to take control of the process in order to create better political forms, a growing number of resisters are seeking ways to stop the process altogether and in some respects to reverse it. Not more efficient governance but the end of interventionism is now being articulated as the ideal political solution by people whose perspectives come not from rural parochialism but urban cosmopolitanism. Political sophistication, not ignorance, is leading many to a renewed consideration of anarchistic alternatives to political organization and reorganization as these have ordinarily been conceived (see Wolff, 1971a, 1971b; Nozick, 1974; Tifft and Sullivan, 1980; see also Pepinsky, 1980).

The movement from underintervention to overintervention of government as the main focus of concern for resisters reflects a more fundamental shift of emphasis from *efficacy* to *trust* as the criterion by which political decisions are to be evaluated. No matter what the particular form or ideological color of a polity may be, its demonstrated or presumed efficacy is no longer necessarily the paramount concern. The new radicalism, picking up on some of the elements of classic romanticism and anarchism, asserts that *no* polity can be trusted to secure the life chances of those who do not have proximate control of the organizational devices by which political power is achieved and exercised. Where older radicals distrusted governments because they failed to meet the basic material needs of many people subject to them, the new radicals distrust governments because they are (at least in prospect) capable of meeting material needs at the cost of further reductions in local and individual degrees of freedom.

(3) Particularly in the more economically developed polities, there appears to be a widening gap between older and younger resisters in regard to their politically sensitizing experiences and subsequent political behavior. The greater preoccupation of older adults with material life chances stems, of course, from their characteristic experiences with poverty and material insecurity in periods of economic depression and war. Youth, in contrast, have been living—at least until very recently—in relatively affluent times. Their experiences with material scarcity have involved proportionately more *relative* than *absolute* deprivation. They have also been subjected to a much greater mass of communications to stimulate their awareness both of the range of possible goods in life and of class differences in access to those goods.

Cultural goods, in particular, tend to acquire a greater significance for contemporary youth than for older people, whose personal experiences and political education have combined to place greater emphasis upon bread-and-butter issues than upon those of personal and artistic expression. The symbols of political resistance have traditionally stressed economics and politics; the newer resistance is symbolized as much or more in styles of dress and music and in other dimensions of cultural revolution. Instead of truly ascetic rejection of material goods, or the devotion of all available resources to the cause of resistance and revolution, youthful resisters are increasingly likely to express opposition to authority by adopting different and often provocative consumption patterns, and by emphasizing "parasitic" instead of "productive" methods for acquiring economic resources.

In contrast to the older resistance morality that condemned and rejected most forms of conventional crime and social deviance, political resistance by younger people now is likely to include and even emphasize aberrant behavior. Violations of legal and extralegal norms regarding everything from conventional etiquette and sexual expression to theft, vandalism, and interpersonal violence are being reinterpreted as politically significant and therefore often laudable. At the same time, those whose deviant behavior originates in apolitical rather than explicitly political *milieux* are developing greater awareness of the political dimensions of their divergence from conventional norms.

From initial steps to organize for protective reasons, some kinds of people traditionally defined as deviant have been moving toward integration of their narrow concerns with drugs, sex, or whatever, into a common opposition to intolerance and harassment. Moreover, they have at the same time been developing greater political sensitivity and often accepting—if not so much seeking—alliance with explicitly political resistance movements. Since Horowitz and Liebowitz (1968) noted its emergence during the 1960s, the politicization of deviance has in some instances reached the stage of organized lobbying (for example, the gay liberation movement). For other groups, notably the black gang youth of America's cities, greater economic and cultural barriers to organized resistance have tended to promote ordinary crime more than political resistance, and the politics of corruption more than the politics of either reform or radical change (Short, 1974, 1976a, 1976b). Yet, even after the demise of the "new left," the blending of social deviance and political resistance continues. In historical perspective, the possibility is growing of a more thorough radicalism than was possible as long as (1) the deviant lacked the communication channels and sufficient freedom to organize, and (2) the resistant were economically and ideologically unable to extend their resistance to cultural as well as material inequalities. Unlike romantic revolutionaries of the past, the resisters of the future can be expected to have few or no scruples about attacking the moral, intellectual, and esthetic as well as the political and economic foundations of authority.

(4) The exponential growth of communications and of governmental interventionism are exposing people to an almost overwhelming variety of experiences, and—as noted above—stimulating the conjunction of cultural and political concerns, and the blending of social and political deviance. An increasingly strong and rapid current of political socialization is generated, virtually forcing political awareness upon people, and tending to push the disadvantaged and dissatisfied from vague resentment toward greater sensitivity and on to resistance. Indeed, it becomes more and more unlikely that the disadvantaged can exist *without* experiencing relative deprivation, or that their resistance can be easily curbed. Once political consciousness begins, it seems increasingly likely to grow, expressed in both greater sensitivity to inequalities and a greater propensity to resist efforts to preserve them.

Concurrent with the pressures to move from resentment to resistance are pressures to move from dissent and evasion to disobedience and violence. *Praxis* comes to be defined in more immediate and dramatic terms, while more indirect and subtle forms of resistance become suspect as possibly indicating a lack of political understanding and commitment. For many resisters, especially younger ones, resistance programs extending over years, much less decades or generations, are likely to be seen as procrastination or worse. Therefore, the tension between theoreticians of resistance and activists can be expected to become increasingly acute. Within the ranks of activists, there is likely to be growing tension between those who favor violent over nonviolent tactics, and between those who favor confrontation over "the principle of established bases, or liberated areas" (Buckman, 1970: 269).

The pivotal issue is violence. As the formidable obstacles to effective political resistance and radical change are more clearly perceived, willingness to commit violent acts may well become more of a touchstone of commitment than ever before. Insofar as modern authority structures persist against every effort to destroy or radically change them, the dedicated but frustrated resister faces increasing pressure to decide between either exchanging radical visions for reformist hopes or attacking the recalcitrant systems no matter the risks and costs. Despite the lack of a tenable theory (see Boggs, 1977; Aya, 1979) and the minuscule chance of significantly weakening the great polities (see Schreiber, 1978: 199), serious resisters unable to accept reformism will be driven to the alternative: opportunistic violence. Consequently, more terrorism at greater cost in lives and property is to be expected, as both sensitivity and frustration increase, and as scruples are overcome and weapons become increasingly available—including those of mass destruction (Carlton, 1979; Laqueur, 1977b: 215-234; Schreiber, 1978: 199-207).

(5) Quite apart from efforts by various parties to foster and manipulate cooperation among resisters in different polities, the development of a sense of common interests is being encouraged and facilitated by the global communications and transportation networks that make resisters aware of and able to contact one another. Though older ethnic and class lines of struggle within polities are far from being superseded, within-polity conflicts over authority are being recast conceptually as particular cases of a worldwide Manichean struggle—usually but not always depicted in the rhetoric of communism versus capitalism. Irrespective of the ideological rubric and of its accuracy, the fact of growing international cooperation is well established. The more debatable issue is whether the joining of resistance is more a "natural" occurrence in a shrinking world or a "contrivance" of great power rivalries.

Sponsorship appears to be indispensable for anything beyond ad hoc, ephemeral, cooperative efforts. Most public and scholarly attention has focused upon cooperative terrorist and guerrilla violence in recent years. Particular emphasis has been

given to the supporting roles of wealthy radicals such as the late
Giangiacomo Feltrinelli (McKnight, 1974: 174-179), transna-
tional corporations such as the International Telephone and
Telegraph Corporation (Sampson, 1974) and Investors' Overseas
Services (Hougan, 1978: 145ff.), and governments—especially
the Arab states (particularly Libya and Syria), Cuba, the Soviet
Union, and the United States with its allies (Sterling, 1981;
Horowitz, 1969; Center for Research on Criminal Justice, 1977:
160-174).

Whatever the validity or utility of such studies, the preoccupation with violence is misleading. The extension of networks
enabling coordinated diplomatic, financial, and ideological
operations against targeted authorities has much greater demonstrated and potential significance—under present world
conditions—for affecting the viability of polities. For instance,
the "legalization" by the United Nations of the Palestinian
Liberation Organization threatens Israeli interests more than
does PLO violence (Green, 1979). Similarly, the highly organized "anti-apartheid" campaign has directly and indirectly generated far more difficult problems for South Africa's authorities
than have sporadic guerrilla incursions and occasional terrorism
(see Adam and Giliomee, 1979: 1-7, 269, 300-302). It follows
that major political changes in both Israel and South Africa are
likely to result more from nonviolent international pressures
than from internal violence, whether or not externally sponsored.

The details of international linkages and their impact have
still to be solidly established. What is clear is that the line
separating conflicts among and within polities is increasingly
blurred, not only in violent struggles (Carlton, 1979: 222) but
also in every other dimension of conflict between the defenders
and assailants of particular authority structures. Traditional
legalistic conceptions of sovereignty and subversion are increasingly obsolete.

Trends in political resistance imply increasingly difficult
control problems for authorities throughout the world. The

combination of (a) increasing emphasis upon securing cultural values as well as material resources with (b) increasing resistance to ideological control and to government interventionism means that resentful and resistant subjects will be less easily bought off, deceived, or diverted in future. Further, the blending of social and political deviance indicates that resistance will be less clearly and specifically "political," but will be expressed in open and covert assaults (including more violence) upon every facet of institutionalized authority. Internationalization and sponsorship of resistance will render increasingly unworkable present legal and political understandings regarding the autonomy and jurisdiction of polities. Given those implications, to what extent are they reflected in discernible trends in political policing?

POLITICAL POLICING

In part mirroring trends in resistance and in part helping to generate them, the following interrelated changes are occurring or seem imminent, especially or at least in the Western democracies: (1) increasing use of field controls, (2) expanding surveillance coupled with more selective targeting for neutralization, (3) more "subcontracting" of operations, and (4) the internationalization of control policies and programs.

(1) Manipulating the field of opportunities and resources available to people is generally preferable to authorities because such manipulation is more concealable and deniable, often less costly (especially in political terms), and probably more effective than direct "command" controls in deterring political resistance. As the risks and limits of more directly coercive measures become increasingly evident, authorities can be expected to explore more fully the possibilities of "remote" control. For example, tax law changes that benefit the deferent may be linked to welfare law changes that penalize the defiant. Import controls may be used to defuse the labor militance fueled by unemployment; and educational funding or certification requirements may be tightened to undermine student

militance. However, there are limits to what can be accomplished through field controls.

One limit is the state of available knowledge about the field; another is the amount of resources available for the control effort; and a third is the political feasibility of the effort. To the extent that the authorities do not have adequate knowledge of the social structures to be manipulated, the effects of control efforts cannot be anticipated and may be counterproductive. With respect to the examples used above, benefiting the politically deferrent through tax reforms may whet their appetite for further rewards; penalizing the troublesome by tightening welfare laws may further radicalize them; relieving one industry's unemployment problems may increase dissatisfaction in other industries; and reducing educational opportunities may heighten political resentment among youth and their parents. Even with adequate knowledge, authorities may not have the material resources and technicians needed to apply it. And they may be politically unable to adopt certain policies even if the knowledge and resources were available: "Capitalism" cannot be an option for the Soviet authorities, as "communism" is ruled out for their American counterparts. To generalize Carlton's (1979: 215) conclusion regarding terrorists:

> It is impossible for states, particularly in the postcolonial era, to pursue policies that will, except in rare instances, remove many of the conditions and the grievances, real or imagined, that motivate [political resisters].

From the standpoint of authorities, the basic difficulty with field controls is that the ultimate field control is to change the nature of the polity itself.

Since the use of field controls is necessarily limited, authorities will continue to supplement statecraft with political policing in its more specific forms.

(2) The more sophisticated authorities become, the more they recognize the costs in resources and legitimacy of pursuing excessively coercive and indiscriminate programs of control. To

minimize those costs, a shift of emphasis to more effective surveillance and more selective neutralization is increasingly accepted doctrine among control strategists. There is a growing demand for better intelligence and improved procedures for acting on what is learned.

As we have seen, the need for intelligence cannot be satisfied by anything short of total monitoring of the general population. Increasingly subtle yet near-total monitoring is made possible by the computerized recording of social transactions and the development of electronic surveillance technology. Regardless of civil-libertarian objections, authorities sooner or later invade privacy as far as technically feasible. An irony of political sociology is that, in the more democratic polities, and the more concerned authorities are about the costs of repression, the less actual privacy subjects are likely to have. Expanding surveillance is the trade-off for lessening indiscriminate repression. Selectivity depends upon having good enough information on which to base control decisions and make distinctions.

Because no polity can be maintained without political policing, the increasingly crucial distinction between more totalitarian polities is not whether, or even how much, policing of social life is found, but rather what forms it takes. In more democratic and secure polities, more thorough monitoring will enable and therefore encourage more selective targeting of persons and organizations for neutralization and intimidation, and probably a more sparing use of terror. Thus, as surveillance increases, the casualties of political policing are expected to decrease. In contrast, being under less pressure to limit overt political policing, the authorities of more totalitarian polities will find that more thorough surveillance reveals more actual resistance to be neutralized and potential resisters to be deterred. Terror will increase in efforts to counteract the increasingly evident failure of information control and enclosure tactics to deter significant numbers of covert if not overt resisters. As the distinction between democratic and totalitarian polities becomes increasingly consequential, so will decisions on how to draw the distinction.

Methodological note: Any assessment of what is happening or to be expected in a polity involves not only "scoring" it on a democratic-totalitarian scale, but also estimating the direction of change. In particular, scoring a polity and estimating whether it is moving toward more democracy or more totalitarianism requires both structural, or "systems" analysis and longitudinal, or "historical" analysis. To illustrate, first, an analysis of systemic features of the Soviet polity indicates that increasing dissent will probably result not in democratization but in the replacement of "partocracy" by technocracy, with a consequent shift from the "irrationality" of totalitarianism (Shtromas, 1979: especially 241-243). Second, as the widespread and determined resistance of American college students to military conscription became clear (Smith, 1972), and imprisonment of draft resisters failed to end the growth of the resistance movement, the authorities shifted from a more indiscriminately "coercive" (totalitarian) strategy to a more discriminating and "cooptive" (democratic) one (Hagan and Bernstein, 1979). If neither the systemic features of political organization nor the historical contexts of policing are specified, inquiry is very likely to founder in such sociologically uninformed notions as that political policing is a "ritualistic search for imaginary enemies" (Bergesen, 1977: 230), instead of a set of alternative strategies for obtaining and securing power (Connor, 1972; Pelikán, 1971). The basic point is that one cannot assume but must establish the applicability to particular cases of any general conclusions about trends and prospects in political policing.

(3) Consistent with a greater emphasis on field controls, monitoring, and selective neutralization is increased "subcontracting" of political policing. Instead of direct intervention by identifiable governmental control agencies, to be expected are increasingly sophisticated efforts to manipulate nongovernmental institutions and individuals into performing intelligence and information-control tasks, as well as more of the dirty coercive jobs with which authorities often do not wish to be

identified. Subcontracting rarely involves formal arrangements, and people may be unaware that their associates or they themselves are being used to do some of the work of political policing. Whether conscious or not, subcontracting is strongly encouraged not only by its political benefits but also by its financial benefits—especially in the more capitalist and democratic polities, where public control and other service agencies are increasingly underfunded. The shift from direct toward delegated policing of political activity is part of a general transfer of policing functions from public agencies to private parties ranging from corporations to block watch committees.

In the most advanced capitalist and more democratic polities, since the 1960s the growth of private security forces has far exceeded that of public police agencies; and there are now many more privately than publicly employed control agents. By 1977 the number of private security employees in the United States surpassed the million-plus employed by all levels of government in every kind of "criminal justice activity"—police, courts, legal services, public defenders, corrections, and all others such as criminal justice planners and researchers hired under LEAA programs (National Advisory Committee on Criminal Justice Standards and Goals, 1976a: 63, 399-400; U.S. Department of Justice, 1978: 3-9, 15-16). In Canada's province of Ontario, between 1969 and 1978 the number of sworn and civilian police employees increased from 2.04 to 2.99 per 1000 population, but the ratio for private security employment rose from 1.75 to 3.3 (Solicitor General of Canada, 1979: 24).

The rise of private policing is the consequence of economic rather than political control efforts. Under growing pressures from competitors, shareholders, and other interested parties, modern corporations seeking greater control over their environments find that private policing is more efficient and flexible than public policing, much less restricted by laws and public politics, and thus a better investment (Spitzer and Scull, 1977; Stenning and Shearing, 1979; Shearing et al., 1980). Even though not initiated for political control reasons per se, the relative advantages of privatized policing in such control efforts are equally clear. Having shown little reluctance to work through and with private security forces in the past, authorities under growing political and budget pressures are even less likely in future to forgo the advantages of cooperative or exploitative arrangements with private forces. Despite some occasionally embarrassing rivalries and disclosures, the privatization of policing is almost certain to continue with the tacit if not always the public blessing of control strategists.

Most discussions of private policing have focused upon the transfer of regular policing tasks to contracted or in-house security agencies, and the corresponding extension of "private space"–such as shopping centers, apartment complexes, and vacation resorts. However, investigating committees, ex-agents, reporters, and others have documented the at least sometime use of private control agencies and agents–along with other private institutions and individuals–for political control purposes: security checks, surveillance, espionage, neutralization by violent and nonviolent means, and research. Hougan (1978), for instance, has explored the complex and symbiotic relationships between current and former governmental control agents–often involving various governments, corporations, labor unions, and career criminals. Marks (1980) has documented the CIA's enormous and largely secret direct and subcontracted (knowing and unknowing) involvement in the behavioral sciences over the past thirty years. It is to be expected that authorities–especially in the more open, democratic polities–are becoming more adept at destroying or hiding the kinds of trails uncovered by "freedom of information" laws for private investigators such as Hougan and Marks, and by legislative authority for public investigators such as the Church Committee (U.S. Senate, 1976) and the McDonald Commission (1979). If so, then the use of private resources will become an increasingly routine and significant feature of political policing.

(4) Authorities of different polities have always had to cooperate to some extent to deal with internal control and

foreign relations problems arising from the movement and cooperation of political resisters across jurisdictional boundaries. Treatment of fugitives and refugees, differentiating them from spies and saboteurs, police operations in foreign areas, and related matters have historically been the subject of numerous bilateral and multilateral (and frequently secret) agreements, as well as periodic conferences under the auspices of such organizations as the International Prison Commission and the International Penal and Penitentiary Commission. Formation of the United Nations gave impetus to internationalization by formally establishing the view that crime and its control are not exclusively national concerns and prerogatives; and after several congresses "the notion of crime as a problem of an increasingly socio-political character is taking shape" (López-Rey y Arrojo, 1978: 5).

In recent years the internationalization of political resistance has been reflected in privately and governmentally sponsored international efforts to define and deal with such problems as "air piracy," "political kidnapping," and especially "international terrorism" (Bassiouni, 1975; Cooper, 1976; Crelinsten et al., 1978; United Nations Secretariat, 1978). Not surprisingly, authorities (notably of the Western capitalist nations) who feel most threatened by such resistance activities are most eager to obtain revisions of international law that will facilitate their repression. Authorities (notably of the Soviet bloc, and some Arab and other Third World states) who feel less threatened— and who may expect to benefit from such activities—are not as concerned. Related in part to the political divisions are the differences of view that have so far prevented the United Nations Ad Hoc Committee on International Terrorism, created in 1973, from producing any recommendations (United Nations Secretariat, 1978). Some members argue for the priority of specific definitions, causal research, and combatting state terrorism, colonialism, racism, and other political and economic causes. Others prefer to emphasize a general mandate, action on an ad hoc basis, and combatting antistate terrorism. Whether or not formal international control policies beyond particular conventions on such matters as air piracy are established, the most concerned authorities are going ahead with their own programs for cooperative as well as national efforts against sponsored and unsponsored political resistance.

In the United States, frequently depicted by all sides as the ultimate target of "international terrorism," the effort to promote international policing is increasingly supplemented by programs to deal with the widely anticipated eventual rise in serious terrorist activity. Because greater coordination of control efforts is viewed as increasingly essential, proposals for such innovations as a presidentially led "crisis management team" (Kupperman, 1977: 16-19) are being implemented. And American police agencies at every level are being strongly encouraged to "create, maintain, and develop links with their counterparts overseas," with emphasis upon the exchange of intelligence, control technologies and techniques, operational experiences, and personnel (National Advisory Committee on Criminal Justice Standards and Goals, 1976b: 224-227). However necessary they may appear to be, such innovations and programs do not fit traditional legal assumptions regarding either the internal allocation of governmental powers or the distinction between internal control and foreign relations problems.

Although the internationalization of political policing has been given impetus by that of political resistance, it is also encouraged by more general social processes promoting the blurring and expansion of polity boundaries. Though often reluctantly and despite international agreements, authorities of every ideological color have frequently been led by economic, military, and other considerations to trespass upon one another's prerogatives. Specifically, the needs to secure capital investments, open up new investment and trade opportunities, protect or improve military positions, and respond to the pressures of internal or external politics have led not only to international cooperation and conflict but also to "interference" by some authorities in the "internal affairs" of others. As such pressures increase, so will interference. Whether accomplished crudely or politely, coercively or cooperatively—and regardless of United Nations deliberations—political policing will be organized more and more on a multinational if not international basis.

Observed and expected patterns of change in political resistance and its policing indicate possibilities for both progressive and destructive actions. Insofar as authorities give priority to field controls instead of direct coercion, and focus upon violent resistance without attempting to deter or neutralize every form of resistance, resisters will have more room to develop and offer alternative and perhaps better ideas for the more viable organization of social life. Insofar as resisters seek to persuade by evidence and example rather than to impose their ideas, and can forgo direct—especially violent—assaults upon political authority as such, authorities will have more opportunities and time to try cooptive and less costly control strategies. Not least in importance, each side will be better able to learn from the other, even in opposition.

Against the progressive possibilities are the pressures upon resisters to use violence and to mount offensives against even the most sacred institutions of social life—which will not only encourage governmental and public fears of change, but also destroy cultural resources needed to allay those fears. From their side, authorities risk provoking the spread of resistance as people become aware of expanding surveillance and the subcontracting of operations. For single polities as we now know them, the internationalization of both resistance and policing implies their decreasing viability—as it becomes less and less possible for the resisters and authorities of one polity to keep their struggle separate from conflicts over authority elsewhere. It will be increasingly difficult to resolve or even manage conflicts in one place unless they are resolved or can be managed in other places.

Summary and Conclusion

Conflict over authority is intrinsic to politically organized social life. Authority structures are constantly undermined by the internal contradictions of political policing, its incompatibility with conflict resolution and management, environmental variability, the subjectivity of social justice, and the biosocial bases of human competitiveness and ethnocentrism. Yet, equally universal is the process of political organization—of constructing and reconstructing authority structures. Instead of viewing the simultaneity of decay and construction as merely an irony of life, a contradiction to be resolved, or the dynamic of civilization's collapse, one may pragmatically accept the duality as simply another way in which things vary and covary in the real world, and are consequently predictable and manipulable to a never fully known degree. This makes it possible to consider the viability of an authority structure, a polity, as an empirical issue instead of a philosophical or ideological one.

Success in political conflict is any movement toward a more viable polity, or the absence of movement toward a less viable one. The degree of success is determined by the *product* of authority and resister actions and by factors beyond their control. A polity's viability—its capacity to survive—is associated with the life chances of the people whose lives are oriented and bounded by it. Life chances depend, in turn, upon the availability of both behavior alternatives (*options*) and social bonds (*ligatures*), at maximum levels in some optimum balance. Actions by either authorities or resisters, or both, may be *progressive* or *destructive*—that is, likely to promote greater or lesser viability. Actions aimed at increasing rather than limiting or reducing life chances, avoiding instead of precipitating violence, or increasing the life chances of everyone instead of only some people are likely to be progressive. Random violence, exploitation, and the weakening of social bonds are likely to be destructive. However actions are characterized, working solutions to the problem of creating a more viable polity are attainable only through the struggles that move human beings from thought and exploration to action and choice.

Both progressive and destructive possibilities inhere in current patterns of change. With respect to political resistance, the

changes include: (1) a growing emphasis upon cultural in relation to material deprivation; (2) a resurgence of anarchist
sentiment for less rather than more effective government; (3) an
increasing youth-based orientation more to cultural values,
consumption, and the blending of social with political deviance
than to material needs, production, and the sharp differentiation of social deviance from political resistance; (4) increasing
pressures to move from resentment to resistance, and from
nonviolent to violent forms; and (5) the internationalization of
resistance. Changes in political policing include: (1) greater use
of field controls as alternatives and supplements to command
controls; (2) increasingly extensive monitoring of political activities, in conjunction with more selective and less directly
coercive neutralization and deterrence operations; (3) increasing
use of "subcontractors" to accomplish control objectives; and
(4) the internationalization of policing. Efforts by authorities to
use field controls and limit direct coercion to violent resisters
will probably be progressive, as will resisters' efforts to avoid
violence and dogmatism. Violent actions by authorities or
resisters, and attempts to conceal coercive or subversive actions,
are likely to prove destructive. For any specific polity, the
internationalization of political resistance and policing will
make it increasingly hard for both authorities and resisters to
choose progressive and eschew destructive actions.

CONCLUSION

Wherever people must live together as "strangers" will be
found a conflict over whose life chances will be greater and
whose lesser. That conflict will be acted out in the dialectical
process of political organization—which creates resolutions
while at the same time undermining them. Or, from the
opposite perspective, it generates "revolutionary situations" but
also authority structures that impede the transition to "revolutionary outcomes," and the conversion of revolutionary power
exchanges into postrevolution major structural changes (Tilly,
1978: 189-222). Perhaps there is, as Moore (1978: 7) suggests,
an innate human propensity to avoid or resist certain kinds of

deprivation universally felt as "injustice." However, as he also notes, human beings exhibit "fundamental ambivalence toward social rules and regulations," so that

> there is likely to be an undercurrent of grumbling and opposition to just about every moral code, a discontent that is at least a potential source of variation and change [Moore, 1978: 47].

Variation and change are what conflicts over authority are finally about: whether the benefits and risks of diversity and change outweigh those of homogeneity and stability. Underlying and cross-cutting particular authority-resister conflicts, the fundamental struggle is between (a) those who see human freedom as a better risk than regimentation, and (b) those whose fear of freedom motivates attempts to limit and regulate it. Both sides can adduce impressive evidence supporting their respective views; neither can validly discredit the other's evidence. This suggests that the most viable polity may be one in which neither party is able to overpower and destroy the other. Politically, this is the meaning of genuine liberalism; economically, it is the meaning of genuine socialism. Together they constitute genuine democracy. Proposition: The greater the life chances of the least powerful subjects in a polity, the more viable is that polity.

REFERENCES

Adam, Heribert (1971) Modernizing Racial Domination: The Dynamics of South African Politics. Berkeley: University of California Press.
——— and Herman Giliomee (1979) Ethnic Power Mobilized: Can South Africa Change? New Haven, CT: Yale University Press.
Adamek, Raymond J. and Jerry M. Lewis (1973) "Social control violence and radicalization: the Kent State case." Social Forces 51 (March): 342-347.
Agee, Philip (1975) Inside the Company: CIA Diary. London: Penguin.
Akehurst, Michael (1970) A Modern Introduction to International Law. New York: Atherton.
Alexander, Yonah [ed.] (1976) International Terrorism: National, Regional, and Global Perspectives. New York: Praeger.
Allen, Francis A. (1974) The Crimes of Politics: Political Dimensions of Criminal Justice. Cambridge, MA: Harvard University Press.
Almond, Gabriel and Sidney Verba (1963) The Civic Culture: Political Attitudes and Democracy in Five Nations. Princeton, NJ: Princeton University Press.
Amnesty International (1979) Amnesty International Report, 1978. London: AI Publications.
——— (1978a) Uruguay Deaths Under Torture, 1975-77. London: AI Publications.
——— (1978b) Political Imprisonment in South Africa. London: AI Publications.
——— (1977) Torture in Greece: The First Torturers' Trial, 1975. London: AI Publications.
——— (1975) Report on Torture. New York: Farrar, Straus and Giroux.
——— (1973) Political Prisoners in South Vietnam. London: AI Publications.
Andreski, Stanislav (1968) Military Organization and Society. Berkeley: University of California Press.
Archer, Jules (1971) Treason in America: Disloyalty Versus Dissent. New York: Hawthorne.
Arnold, Millard [ed.] (1979) Steve Biko: Black Consciousness in South Africa. New York: Vintage.
Arnold, Thurman (1962) The Symbols of Government. New York: Harcourt Brace Jovanovich. (First published in 1935.)
Aya, Rod (1979) "Theories of revolution reconsidered: contrasting models of collective violence." Theory and Society 8 (July): 39-99.

Balbus, Isaac D. (1973) The Dialectics of Legal Repression: Black Rebels before the American Criminal Courts. New York: Russell Sage.

Baldus, Bernd (1975) "The study of power: suggestions for an alternative." Canadian Journal of Sociology 1 (2): 179-201.

Baltzell, E. Digby (1979) Puritan Boston and Quaker Philadelphia: Two Protestant Ethics and the Spirit of Class Authority and Leadership. New York: Macmillan.

Bandura, Albert and Richard H. Walters (1964) Social Learning and Personality Development. New York: Holt, Rinehart & Winston.

Barnet, Richard (1971) "The twilight of the nation-state: a crisis of legitimacy," pp. 221-242 in Robert P. Wolff (ed.) The Rule of Law. New York: Simon and Schuster.

Barton, Allen H. (1970) Communities in Disaster. New York: Anchor.

Bassiouni, M. Cherif [ed.] (1975) International Terrorism and Political Crimes. Springfield, IL: Charles C Thomas.

Bayley, David H. (1971) "The police and political change in comparative perspective." Law and Society Review 6 (August): 91-112.

Becker, Howard P. and Harry Elmer Barnes (1952) Social Thought from Lore to Science (Volume 1). Washington, DC: Harren.

Becker, Jillian (1977) Hitler's Children: The Story of the Baader-Meinhof Terrorist Gang. New York: J. B. Lippincott.

Bendix, Reinhard (1964) Nation-Building and Citizenship: Studies of Our Changing Social Order. New York: John Wiley.

Bergesen, Albert James (1977) "Political witch hunts: the sacred and the subversive in cross-national perspective." American Sociological Review 42 (April): 220-233.

Bittner, Egon (1970) The Functions of the Police in Modern Society. Washington, DC: Government Printing Office.

Black, Donald (1976) The Behavior of Law. New York: Academic.

Blumstein, Alfred, Jacqueline Cohen, and Daniel Nagin [eds.] (1978) Deterrence and Incapacitation: Estimating the Effects of Criminal Sanctions on Crime Rates. Washington, DC: National Academy of Sciences.

Boggs, Carl, Jr. (1977) "Revolutionary process, political strategy, and the dilemma of power." Theory and Society 4 (Fall): 359-393.

Bolton, Charles D. (1972) "Alienation and action: a study of peace-group members." American Journal of Sociology 78 (November): 537-561.

Bordua, David J. and Albert J. Reiss, Jr. (1966) "Command, control, and charisma: reflections on police bureaucracy." American Journal of Sociology 72 (July): 68-76.

Bowden, Tom (1978a) "Guarding the state: the police response to crisis politics in Europe." British Journal of Law and Society 5 (Summer): 69-88.

——— (1978b) Beyond the Limits of the Law. London: Penguin.

Boyle, Andrew (1979) "Britain's establishment spies." New York Times Magazine (December 9).

Bramstedt, E. K. (1945) Dictatorship and Political Police: The Technique of Control by Fear. London: Routledge & Kegan Paul.

Breton, Raymond (1972) "The socio-political dynamics of the October events." Canadian Review of Sociology and Anthropology 9 (1): 35-56.

Brinton, Crane (1965) The Anatomy of Revolution. Englewood Cliffs, NJ: Prentice-Hall.

Brooks, Thomas R. (1971) Toil and Trouble: A History of American Labor. New York: Delacorte.

Brown, J.A.C. (1963) Techniques of Persuasion: From Propaganda to Brainwashing. London: Penguin.

Brown, Lorne and Caroline Brown (1973) An Unauthorized History of the RCMP. Toronto: James Lewis and Samuel.

Buckman, Peter (1970) The Limits of Protest. London: Victor Gollancz Panther Edition.

Bunyan, Tony (1977) The History and Practice of the Political Police in Britain. London: Quartet.

Burgess, Robert L. and Ronald L. Akers (1966) "A differential association-reinforcement theory of criminal behavior." Social Problems 14 (Fall): 128-147.

Burke, John J. (1976) "Electronic surveillance: participant monitoring." FBI Law Enforcement Bulletin 45 (October): 11-15.

Caldeira, Greg A. (1977) "Children's images of the Supreme Court: a preliminary mapping." Law and Society Review 11 (Summer): 851-871.

Camus, Albert (1956) The Rebel: An Essay on Man in Revolt. New York: Vintage.

Carlin, Jerome E., Jan Howard, and Sheldon L. Messinger (1966) "Civil justice and the poor: issues for sociological research." Law and Society Review 1 (November): 9-89.

Carlton, David (1979) "The future of political substate violence," pp. 201-230 in Yonah Alexander et al. (eds.) Terrorism: Theory and Practice. Boulder, CO: Westview.

Carter, Gwendolen M., Thomas Karis, and Newell M. Stultz (1967) South Africa's Transkei: The Politics of Domestic Colonialism. London: Heinemann.

Cassirer, Ernst (1955) The Myth of the State. New York: Doubleday. (First published in 1946)

Castro, Fidel (1968) On Trial. London: Lorrimer.

Center for Research on Criminal Justice (1977) The Iron Fist and the Velvet Glove: An Analysis of the U.S. Police. Berkeley, CA: Author.

Chasen, Robert E. and Arthur Sinai (1979) "Currency and Foreign Transactions Reporting Act: a new law enforcement tool." FBI Law Enforcement Bulletin 48 (August): 1-5.

Chkhikvadze, V. M. [ed.] (1969) The Soviet State and Law. Moscow: Progress Publishers.

Clinard, Marshall B. and Richard Quinney (1973) Criminal Behavior Systems: A Typology. New York: Holt, Rinehart & Winston.

Collier, Peter and David Horowitz (1976) The Rockefellers: An American Dynasty. New York: New American Library.

Collins, Randall (1975) Conflict Sociology: Toward an Explanatory Science. New York: Academic.

Connor, Walter D. (1972) "The manufacture of deviance: the case of the Soviet Purge, 1936-1938." American Sociological Review 37 (August): 403-413.

Cooper, H.H.A. (1976) "The international experience with terrorism: an overview," pp. 419-442 in National Advisory Committee on Criminal Justice Standards and Goals, Disorders and Terrorism: Report of the Task Force on Disorders and Terrorism. Washington, DC: Government Printing Office.

Crelinsten, Ronald D., Danielle Laberge-Altmejd, and Denis Szabo [eds.] (1978) Terrorism and Criminal Justice: An International Perspective. Toronto: D. C. Heath.

Critchley, T. A. (1978) A History of Police in England and Wales. London: Constable.

Dahrendorf, Ralf (1979) Life Chances: Approaches to Social and Political Theory. Chicago: University of Chicago Press.

——— (1959) Class and Class Conflict in Industrial Society. Stanford, CA: Stanford University Press.

Delarue, Jacques (1964) The Gestapo: A History of Horror. New York: Dell.

Donner, Frank (1973) "Political informers," pp. 309-335 in Pat Watters and Stephen Gillers (eds.) Investigating the FBI. New York: Ballantine.

——— (1972) "The confession of an FBI informer." Harper's Magazine (December).

Durr, Clifford J. (1965) "Sociology and the law: a field trip to Montgomery, Alabama," pp. 43-56 in Leon Friedman (ed.) Southern Justice. New York: World.

Easton, David and Jack Dennis (1969) Children in the Political System: Origins of Political Legitimacy. New York: McGraw-Hill.

Eckstein, Harry and Ted Robert Gurr (1975) Patterns of Authority: A Structural Basis for Political Inquiry. New York: John Wiley.

Ehrlich, Isaac (1975) "The deterrent effect of capital punishment: a question of life and death." American Economic Review 65 (June): 397-417.

Eisenstadt, S. N. (1969) The Political Systems of Empires. New York: Macmillan. (Original 1963 edition with new preface.)

Elcock, Howard (1976) Political Behaviour. London: Methuen.

Elliff, John T. (1973) "The scope and basis of FBI data collection," pp. 239-273 in Pat Watters and Stephen Gillers (eds.) Investigating the FBI. New York: Ballantine.

——— (1971) Crime, Dissent, and the Attorney General: The Justice Department in the 1960s. Beverly Hills, CA: Sage.

Elwin, Göran (1977) "Swedish anti-terrorist legislation." Contemporary Crises 1 (July): 289-301.

Emerson, Thomas I. (1973) "The FBI as a political police," pp. 225-238 in Pat Watters and Stephen Gillers (eds.) Investigating the FBI. New York: Ballantine.

Epstein, Jason (1971) The Great Conspiracy Trial. New York: Vintage.

Fanon, Frantz (1968) The Wretched of the Earth. New York: Grove.

Feeley, Malcolm (1976) "The concept of laws in social science: a critique and notes on an expanded view." Law and Society Review 10 (Summer): 497-523.

——— (1970) "Coercion and compliance: a new look at an old problem." Law and Society Review 4 (May): 505-519.

Ferber, Michael and Staughton Lynd (1971) The Resistance. Boston: Beacon.

Feuer, Lewis (1969) The Conflict of Generations. New York: Macmillan.

Fine, Sidney (1969) Sit-Down: The General Motors Strike of 1936-1937. Ann Arbor: University of Michigan Press.

Finkle, Jason L. and Richard W. Gable [eds.] (1966) Political Development and Social Change. New York: John Wiley.

Flacks, Richard (1971) Youth and Social Change. Skokie, IL: Rand McNally.

——— (1967) "The liberated generation: an exploration of the roots of student protest." Journal of Social Issues 23 (July): 52-75.

Fogelson, Robert M. and Robert B. Hill (1968) "Who riots? A study of participation in the 1967 riots," pp. 217-248 in Supplemental Studies for the National Advisory Commission on Civil Disorders. Washington, DC: Government Printing Office.

Foucault, Michel (1977) Discipline and Punish: The Birth of the Prison. New York: Pantheon.

Friedman, Lawrence M. (1975) The Legal System: A Social Science Perspective. New York: Russell Sage.

Friedrich, Carl J. and Zbigniew K. Brzezinski (1965) Totalitarian Dictatorship and Autocracy. Cambridge, MA: Harvard University Press.

Friedrichs, David O. (1980) "The legitimacy crisis in the United States: a conceptual analysis." Social Problems 27 (June): 540-555.

Galanter, Marc (1974) "Why the 'haves' come out ahead: speculations on the limits of legal change." Law and Society Review 9 (Fall): 95-160.

Gamson, William A. (1968) Power and Discontent. Homewood, IL: Dorsey.

Gaylin, Willard (1970) In the Service of Their Country: War Resisters in Prison. New York: Grosset and Dunlap.

Geismar, Peter (1971) Fanon. New York: Grove.

Gibbs, Jack P. (1978) "Deterrence, penal policy, and the sociology of law," pp. 101-114 in Rita J. Simon (ed.) Research in Law and Sociology: An Annual Compilation of Research. Greenwich, CT: JAI.

——— (1975) Crime, Punishment, and Deterrence. New York: Elsevier.

Graham, Hugh Davis and Ted Robert Gurr [eds.] (1969) Violence in America: Historical and Comparative Perspectives (Volumes 1 and 2). Washington, DC: National Commission on the Causes and Prevention of Violence.

Green, L. C. (1979) "The legalization of terrorism," pp. 175-197 in Yonah Alexander et al. (eds.) Terrorism: Theory and Practice. Boulder, CO: Westview.

——— (1976) "Terrorism—the Canadian perspective," pp. 3-29 in Yonah Alexander (ed.) International Terrorism: National, Regional, and Global Perspectives. New York: Praeger.

Grodzins, Morton (1956) The Loyal and the Disloyal: Social Boundaries of Patriotism and Treason. New York: World.

Grosman, Brian A. (1972) "Political crime and emergency measures in Canada," pp. 141-160 in Freda Adler and G.O.W. Mueller (eds.) Politics, Crime and the International Scene: An Inter-American Focus. San Juan, Puerto Rico: North-South Center Press.

Guevara, Che (1969) Guerrilla Warfare. London: Pelican.

Gunder Frank, André (1967) "Sociology of development and underdevelopment of sociology." Catalyst (Summer): 1-54 (in Warner Modular Publications reprint).

Gurr, Ted Robert (1976) Rogues, Rebels, and Reformers: A Political History of Urban Crime and Conflict. Beverly Hills, CA: Sage.

——— (1970) Why Men Rebel. Princeton, NJ: Princeton University Press.

——— Peter N. Grabosky, and Richard C. Hula (1977) The Politics of Crime and Conflict: A Comparative History of Four Cities. Beverly Hills, CA: Sage.

Habermas, Jürgen (1975) Legitimation Crisis. Boston: Beacon. (First published in 1973.)

Hacker, Frederick J. (1978) Crusaders, Criminals, Crazies: Terror and Terrorism in Our Time. New York: Bantam.

Hagan, John and Ilene N. Bernstein (1979) "Conflict in context: the sanctioning of draft resisters, 1963-76." Social Problems 27 (October): 109-122.

Harper, Alan D. (1969) The Politics of Loyalty: The White House and the Communist Issue, 1946-1952. Westport, CT: Greenwood.

Harrington, Michael (1976) The Twilight of Capitalism. New York: Simon and Schuster.

Hay, Douglas, Peter Linebaugh, John G. Rule, E. P. Thompson, and Cal Winslow (1975) Albion's Fatal Tree: Crime and Society in Eighteenth-Century England. New York: Pantheon.

Haywood, William D. (1929) Bill Haywood's Book: The Autobiography of William D. Haywood. London: Martin Lawrence.

Hersey, John (1968) The Algiers Motel Incident. New York: Bantam.

Himes, Joseph S. (1980) Conflict and Conflict Management. Athens: University of Georgia Press.

Hirsch, Fred (1976) Social Limits to Growth. Cambridge, MA: Harvard University Press.

Hobsbawm, Eric J. (1959) Social Bandits and Primitive Rebels. New York: Macmillan.

Hoeffel, Paul Heath and Joan Montalvo (1979) "Missing or dead in Argentina." New York Times Magazine (October 21): 44ff.

Hogarth, John (1979) "The individual and state security." Social Sciences in Canada 7 (March): 10-11.

Hoover, J. Edgar (1969) "A study in Marxist revolutionary violence: Students for a Democratic Society, 1962-1969." Fordham Law Review 38 (December): 1-18.

Horowitz, David (1969) Empire and Revolution: A Radical Interpretation of Contemporary History. New York: Vintage.

Horowitz, Irving Louis and Martin Liebowitz (1968) "Social deviance and political marginality: toward a redefinition of the relation between sociology and politics." Social Problems 15 (Winter): 280-296.

Hougan, Jim (1978) Spooks: The Haunting of America—The Private Use of Secret Agents. New York: Bantam.

Hurst, James Willard (1971) The Law of Treason in the United States: Collected Essays. Westport, CT: Greenwood.

Ingraham, B. L. and Kazuhiko Tokoro (1969) "Political crime in the United States and Japan: a comparative study." Issues in Criminology 4 (Fall): 145-170.

Keniston, Kenneth (1968) Young Radicals. New York: Harcourt Brace Jovanovich.

――― (1965) The Uncommitted. New York: Houghton Mifflin.

Kirchheimer, Otto (1961) Political Justice: The Use of Legal Procedure for Political Ends. Princeton, NJ: Princeton University Press.

Kirkham, James F., Sheldon G. Levy, and William J. Crotty (1969) Assassination and Political Violence (Volume 8). Washington, DC: National Commission on the Causes and Prevention of Violence.

Klein, Lawrence R., Brian Forst, and Victor Filatov (1978) "The deterrent effect of capital punishment: an assessment of the estimates," pp. 336-360 in Alfred Blumstein et al. (eds.) Deterrence and Incapacitation. Washington, DC: National Academy of Sciences.

Kritzer, Herbert M. (1977) "Political protest and political violence: a nonrecursive causal model." Social Forces 55 (March): 630-640.

Kupperman, Robert H. (1977) Facing Tomorrow's Terrorist Incident Today. Washington, DC: U.S. Department of Justice, Law Enforcement Assistance Administration.

Laqueur, Walter (1977a) Guerrilla: A Historical and Critical Study. London: Weidenfeld and Nicolson.

——— (1977b) Terrorism. Boston: Little, Brown.

Laturno, Gary M. (1976) "Presidential authority to authorize investigative techniques in foreign intelligence investigations." FBI Law Enforcement Bulletin 45 (June): 27-31.

Leighton, Barry (1978) "Freedom of information legislation in Canada." Presented at the annual meetings of the Canadian Sociology and Anthropology Association, London, Ontario, May 30-June 1.

Lenski, Gerhard E. (1966) Power and Privilege: A Theory of Social Stratification. New York: McGraw-Hill.

Lerner, Daniel (1958) The Passing of Traditional Society. New York: Macmillan.

Levine, Robert A. and Donald T. Campbell (1972) Ethnocentrism: Theories of Conflict, Ethnic Attitudes and Group Behavior. New York: John Wiley.

London, Perry (1969) Behavior Control. New York: Harper & Row.

López-Rey y Arrojo, Manuel (1978) "The Quinquennial United Nations Congresses on the Prevention of Crime and the Treatment of Offenders," pp. 3-10 in International Review of Criminal Policy, No. 34. New York: United Nations, Department of Economic and Social Affairs.

Love, Joseph L. (1969) "La Raza: Mexican Americans in rebellion." Trans-Action 6 (February): 35-41.

Lowry, Ritchie P. (1972) "Toward a sociology of secrecy and security systems." Social Problems 19 (Spring): 437-450.

McDonald Commission (1979) Security and Information: First Report. Ottawa, Canada: The Commission of Inquiry Concerning Certain Activities of the Royal Canadian Mounted Police.

McKnight, Gerald (1974) The Mind of the Terrorist. London: Michael Joseph.

McNeil, Elton B. (1965) "The nature of aggression," pp. 14-41 in Elton B. McNeil (ed.) The Nature of Human Conflict. Englewood Cliffs, NJ: Prentice-Hall.

Mallin, Jay [ed.] (1971) Terror and Urban Guerrillas: A Study of Tactics and Documents. Coral Gables, FL: University of Miami Press.

Mankoff, Milton and Monica Jacobs (1977) "The return of the suppressed: McCarthyism in West Germany." Contemporary Crises 1 (October): 341-357.

Mann, Edward and John Alan Lee (1979) RCMP vs. the People: Inside Canada's Security Service. Don Mills, Ontario: General Publishing.

Manning, Peter K. (1977) Police Work: The Social Organization of Policing. Cambridge: MIT Press.

Marchetti, Victor and John D. Marks (1975) The CIA and the Cult of Intelligence. New York: Dell.

Marcuse, Herbert (1971) Soviet Marxism: A Critical Analysis. London: Penguin.

Marks, John (1980) The Search for the "Manchurian Candidate": The CIA and Mind Control. New York: McGraw-Hill.

Marks, Robert W. (1970) The Meaning of Marcuse. New York: Ballantine.

Marx, Gary T. (1974) "Thoughts on a neglected category of social movement participant: the agent provocateur and the informant." American Journal of Sociology 80 (September): 402-442.

Marx, Karl and Frederick Engels (1962) Selected Works (Volume 1). Moscow: Foreign Language Publishing House.

Massell, Gregory J. (1968) "Law as an instrument of revolutionary change in a traditional milieu: the case of Soviet Central Asia." Law and Society Review 2 (February): 179-228.

Matthews, Anthony S. (1972) Law, Order and Liberty in South Africa. Berkeley: University of California Press.

Mead, Margaret [ed.] (1955) Cultural Patterns and Technical Change. New York: New American Library.

Medvedev, Zhores A. and Roy A. Medvedev (1971) A Question of Madness. London: Macmillan.

Merryman, John (1969) The Civil Law Tradition. Stanford, CA: Stanford University Press.

Michalowski, Ray (1977) "A gentle pedagogy: teaching critical criminology in the South." Crime and Social Justice 7 (Spring-Summer): 69-73.

Miliband, Ralph (1969) The State in Capitalist Society. London: Quartet.

Miller, Arthur R. (1971) The Assault on Privacy. Ann Arbor: University of Michigan Press.

Moore, Barrington, Jr. (1978) Injustice: The Social Bases of Obedience and Revolt. White Plains, NY: M. E. Sharpe.

——— (1973) Reflections on the Causes of Human Misery and upon Certain Proposals to Eliminate Them. Boston: Beacon.

——— (1967) Social Origins of Dictatorship and Democracy: Lord and Peasant in the Making of the Modern World. Boston: Beacon.

Moran, Richard (1981) Knowing Right from Wrong: The Insanity Defense of Daniel McNaughton. New York: Free Press.

——— (1977) "Awaiting the Crown's pleasure: the case of Daniel M'Naughton," Criminology 15 (May): 7-26.

——— (1974) Political Crime. Ph.D. dissertation, University of Pennsylvania.

Mueller, Claus (1973) The Politics of Communication: A Study in the Political Sociology of Language, Socialization and Legitimation. New York: Oxford University Press.

Murray, Robert K. (1955) Red Scare: A Study in National Hysteria, 1919-1920. New York: McGraw-Hill.

Muse, Benjamin (1969) The American Negro Revolution: From Nonviolence to Black Power, 1963-1967. Bloomington: Indiana University Press.

Myrdal, Gunnar (1944) An American Dilemma: The Negro Problem and Modern Democracy. New York: Harper & Row.

Nagin, Daniel (1978) "General deterrence: a review of the empirical evidence," pp. 95-139 in Alfred Blumstein et al. (eds.) Deterrence and Incapacitation: Estimating the Effects of Criminal Sanctions on Crime Rates. Washington, DC: National Academy of Sciences.

National Advisory Commission on Civil Disorders (1968) Report. New York: Bantam.

National Advisory Committee on Criminal Justice Standards and Goals (1976a) Private Security: Report of the Task Force on Private Security. Washington, DC: Government Printing Office.

——— (1976b) Disorders and Terrorism: Report of the Task Force on Disorders and Terrorism. Washington, DC: Government Printing Office.

Navasky, Victor and Nathan Lewin (1973) "Electronic surveillance," pp. 274-304 in Pat Watters and Stephen Gillers (eds.) Investigating the FBI. New York: Ballantine.

Newman, Graeme (1976) Comparative Deviance: Perception and Law in Six Cultures. New York: Elsevier.

Newman, Peter C. (1975) The Canadian Establishment (Volume 1). Toronto: McClelland and Stewart-Bantam.

Niebuhr, Reinhold (1960) Moral Man and Immoral Society. New York: Scribner. (Original 1932 edition with new preface.)

Nozick, Robert (1974) Anarchy, State, and Utopia. New York: Basic Books.

O'Connor, James (1973) The Fiscal Crisis of the State. New York: St. Martin's.

Oppenheimer, Martin (1978) "The criminalization of political dissent in the Federal Republic of Germany." Contemporary Crises 2 (January): 97-103.

——— (1969) The Urban Guerrilla. Chicago: Quadrangle.

Orlansky, Jesse (1969) "Security investigations," pp. 275-315 in Stanton Wheeler (ed.) On Record: Files and Dossiers in American Life. New York: Russell Sage.

Ortega y Gasset, José (1932) The Revolt of the Masses. New York: Norton. (First published in 1930; authorized translation republished in 1957.)

Ottenberg, Miriam (1965) "Hoover attacks critics of crime rise figures." FBI Law Enforcement Bulletin 34 (May): 22-25.

Paige, Jeffrey M. (1971) "Political orientation and riot participation." American Sociological Review 36 (October): 810-820.

Parsons, Talcott (1951) The Social System. New York: Macmillan.

Pearson, Geoffrey (1978) "Goths and Vandals—crime in history." Contemporary Crises 2 (April): 119-139.

Pelikán, Jiri [ed.] (1971) The Czechoslovak Political Trials, 1950-1954: The Suppressed Report of the Dubcek Government's Commission of Inquiry, 1968. London: Macdonald. (Translation; first published in 1970.)

Pepinsky, Harold (1980) Crime Control Strategies: An Introduction to the Study of Crime. New York: Oxford University Press.

Peterson, Edward N. (1969) The Limits of Hitler's Power. Princeton, NJ: Princeton University Press.

President's Commission on Campus Unrest (1971) Report. New York: Avon.

Pritchett, C. Herman (1958) The Political Offender and the Warren Court. Boston: Boston University Press.

Pye, Lucian W. (1963) "Introduction," pp. 3-23 in Lucian W. Pye (ed.) Communications and Political Development. Princeton, NJ: Princeton University Press.

Quinney, Richard (1975) Criminology: Analysis and Critique of Crime in America. Boston: Little, Brown.

Rapoport, Anatol (1974) Conflict in Man-Made Environment. Markham, Ontario: Penguin.

Redlick, Amy Sands (1979) "The transnational flow of information as a cause of terrorism," pp. 73-95 in Yonah Alexander et al. (eds.) Terrorism: Theory and Practice. Boulder, CO: Westview.

Rule, James B. (1973) Private Lives and Public Surveillance. London: Allen Lane.

Rusche, Georg and Otto Kirchheimer (1968) Punishment and Social Structure. New York: Russell and Russell. (First published in 1939.)

Sachs, Albie (1973) Justice in South Africa. Berkeley: University of California Press.

Sagarin, Edward (1973) "Introduction," in reprint of Louis Proal, Political Crime (first published in 1895). Montclair, NJ: Patterson Smith.

Sampson, Anthony (1974) The Sovereign State of ITT. Greenwich, CT: Fawcett.

——— (1971) The New Anatomy of Britain. London: Hodder and Stoughton.

Sawatsky, John (1980) Men in the Shadows: The RCMP Security Service. Toronto: Doubleday Canada.

Schafer, Stephen (1974) The Political Criminal: The Problem of Morality and Crime. New York: Macmillan.

Scheler, Max (1961) Ressentiment. New York: Macmillan.

Schelling, Thomas C. (1960) The Strategy of Conflict. Cambridge, MA: Harvard University Press.

Schreiber, Jan (1978) The Ultimate Weapon: Terrorists and World Order. New York: William Morrow.

Seeman, Melvin (1972) "The signals of '68: alienation in pre-crisis France." American Sociological Review 37 (August): 385-402.

——— (1959) "On the meaning of alienation." American Sociological Review 24 (December): 783-791.

Sellin, Thorsten (1976) Slavery and the Penal System. New York: Elsevier.

Shearing, Clifford, Margaret B. Farnell, and Philip C. Stenning (1980) Contract Security in Ontario. Toronto, Canada: Centre of Criminology, University of Toronto.

Sherrill, Robert (1973) "The selling of the FBI," pp. 23-48 in Pat Watters and Stephen Gillers (eds.) Investigating the FBI. New York: Ballantine.

Shklar, Judith N. (1964) Legalism. Cambridge, MA: Harvard University Press.

Short, James F., Jr. (1976a) "Gangs, politics, and the social order," pp. 129-163 in James F. Short (ed.) Delinquency, Crime, and Society. Chicago: University of Chicago Press.

——— (1976b) "Politics and youth gangs: a follow-up study." Sociological Quarterly 17 (Spring): 162-179.

——— (1974) "Youth, gangs and society: micro- and macrosociological processes." Sociological Quarterly 15 (Winter): 3-19.

Shtromas, A. Y. (1979) "Dissent and political change in the Soviet Union." Studies in Comparative Communism XII (Summer/Autumn): 212-276.

Sigel, Roberta (1965) "Assumptions about the learning of political values." Annals of the American Academy of Political and Social Science 361 (September): 1-9.

Simmel, Georg (1955) Conflict. New York: Macmillan.

Skolnick, Jerome H. (1969) The Politics of Protest. New York: Ballantine.

Smith, James Morton (1956) Freedom's Fetters: The Alien and Sedition Laws and American Civil Liberties. Ithaca, NY: Cornell University Press.

Smith, Robert B. (1972) "Campus protests and the Vietnam war," pp. 250-277 in James F. Short, Jr., and Marvin E. Wolfgang (eds.) Collective Violence. Chicago: Aldine.

Solicitor General of Canada (1979) Selected Trends in Canadian Criminal Justice. Ottawa, Canada: Research Division, Solicitor General of Canada.

Solzhenitsyn, Aleksandr I. (1974) The Gulag Archipelago (Volumes I-IV). New York: Harper & Row.

Sorel, Georges (1950) Reflections on Violence. New York: Macmillan.

South African Institute of Race Relations [SAIRR] (1979) A Survey of Race Relations in South Africa, 1978. Johannesburg: Author.

——— (1978) A Survey of Race Relations in South Africa, 1977. Johannesburg: Author.

——— (1977) A Survey of Race Relations in South Africa, 1976. Johannesburg: Author.

Spicer, Edward H. [ed.] (1952) Human Problems in Technological Change. New York: Russell Sage.

Spitzer, Steven and Andrew T. Scull (1977) "Privatization and capitalist development: the case of the private police." Social Problems 25 (October): 18-29.

Stark, Rodney (1972) Police Riots: Collective Violence and Law Enforcement. Belmont, CA: Wadsworth.

Stark, Werner (1978) The Social Bond: An Investigation into the Bases of Law-Abidingness. Volume II: Antecedents of the Social Bond—The Ontogeny of Sociality. New York: Fordham University Press.

——— (1976) The Social Bond: An Investigation into the Bases of Law-Abidingness. Volume I: Antecedents of the Social Bond—The Phylogeny of Sociality. New York: Fordham University Press.

Stenning, Philip and Clifford Shearing (1979) "Private security and private justice." British Journal of Law and Society 6 (Winter): 261-271.

Sterling, Claire (1981) The Terror Network: The Secret War of International Terrorism. New York: Holt, Rinehart & Winston.

Stone, Julius (1966) Social Dimensions of Law and Justice. Stanford, CA: Stanford University Press.

Strauss, Harlan J. (1973) "Revolutionary types: Russia in 1905." Journal of Conflict Resolution 17 (June): 297-316.

Szasz, Thomas S. (1965) Psychiatric Justice. New York: Macmillan.

——— (1963) Law, Liberty, and Psychiatry. New York: Macmillan.

Taft, Philip and Philip Ross (1969) "American labor violence: its causes, character, and outcome," pp. 221-301 in Hugh Davis Graham and Ted Robert Gurr (eds.) Violence in America: Historical and Comparative Perspectives (Volume 1). Washington, DC: National Commission on the Causes and Prevention of Violence.

Tapp, June L. and Lawrence Kohlberg (1971) "Developing senses of law and legal justice." Journal of Social Issues 27 (2): 65-91.

Tapp, June L. and Felice J. Levine (1970) "Persuasion to virtue: a preliminary statement." Law and Society Review 4 (May): 565-582.

ten Broek, Jacobus [ed.] (1966) The Law of the Poor. San Francisco: Chandler.

Thaden, Edward C. (1971) Russia Since 1801. New York: John Wiley.

Theoharis, Athan (1971) Seeds of Repression: Harry S Truman and the Origins of McCarthyism. Chicago: Quadrangle.

Thompson, E. P. (1976) Whigs and Hunters: The Origin of the Black Act. New York: Pantheon.

Tifft, Larry and Dennis Sullivan (1980) The Struggle to Be Human: Crime, Criminology, and Anarchism. Over the Water, Sanday, Orkney, England: Cienfuegos.

Tigar, Michael E. (1971) "Socialist law and legal institutions," pp. 327-347 in Robert Lefcourt (ed.) Law Against the People. New York: Vintage.

Tilly, Charles (1978) From Mobilization to Revolution. Reading, MA: Addison-Wesley.

Trible, William E. (1978) "Haymarket Riot: May 4, 1886." FBI Law Enforcement Bulletin 47 (May): 16-22.

Turk, Austin T. (1981a) "Policing in political context," in Rita Donelan (ed.) The Maintenance of Order in Society: Proceedings of an International Symposium. Ottawa, Canada: Canadian Police College.

——— (1981b) "Organizational deviance and political policing." Criminology: An Interdisciplinary Journal 19 (August): 231-250.

——— (1977) "The problem of legal order in the United States and South Africa: substantive and analytical considerations." Sociological Focus 10 (January): 31-41.

——— (1976) "Law as a weapon in social conflict." Social Problems 23 (February): 276-291.

——— (1974) "Political criminality: implications for social change." ET AL 3 (3): 19-25.

——— (1972a) "The limits of coercive legalism in conflict regulation: South Africa," pp. 171-198 in Ernest Q. Campbell (ed.) Racial Tensions and National Identity. Nashville, TN: Vanderbilt University Press.

——— (1972b) Legal Sanctioning and Social Control. DHEW Publication (HSM) 72-9130. Washington, DC: Government Printing Office.

——— (1969) Criminality and Legal Order. Skokie, IL: Rand McNally.

Tygart, Clarence E. and Norman Holt (1972) "Examining the Weinberg and Walker typology of student activists." American Journal of Sociology 77 (March): 957-966.

Unger, Roberto Mangabeira (1976) Law in Modern Society: Toward a Criticism of Social Theory. New York: Macmillan.

United Nations Secretariat (1978) "The prevention of international terrorism," pp. 66-70 in International Review of Criminal Policy, No. 34. New York: United Nations, Department of Economic and Social Affairs.

United States Department of Justice: Law Enforcement Assistance Administration and U.S. Bureau of the Census (1978) Trends in Expenditure and Employment Data for the Criminal Justice System: 1971-1977. Washington, DC: Government Printing Office.

United States Senate (1976) Intelligence Activities and the Rights of Americans, Final Report of the Select Committee to Study Governmental Operations with Respect to Intelligence Activities. Report 94-755. Washington, DC: Government Printing Office.

——— (1972) Abuses of Psychiatry for Political Repression in the Soviet Union. Report of the Subcommittee to Investigate the Administration of the Internal Security Act and Other Internal Security Laws, Committee on the Judiciary. Washington, DC: Government Printing Office.

Useem, Michael (1973) Conscription, Protest, and Social Conflict: The Life and Death of a Draft Resistance Movement. New York: John Wiley.

Vallières, Pierre (1977) The Assassination of Pierre Laporte. Toronto: James Lorimer.

Vandaele, Walter (1978) "Participation in illegitimate activities: Ehrlich revisited," pp. 270-335 in Alfred Blumstein et al. (eds.) Deterrence and Incapacitation: Estimating the Effects of Criminal Sanctions on Crime Rates. Washington, DC: National Academy of Sciences.

van den Berghe, Pierre L. (1975) Man in Society: A Biosocial View. New York: Elsevier.

Walker, Kenneth (1972) "Reply to Tygart and Holt." American Journal of Sociology 77 (March): 966-970.

Walker, Nigel (1968) Crime and Insanity in England. Edinburgh: Edinburgh University Press.

Wall, Robert (1973) "Why I got out of it," pp. 336-350 in Pat Watters and Stephen Gillers (eds.) Investigating the FBI. New York: Ballantine.

Wallerstein, Immanuel (1976) The Modern World-System: Capitalist Agriculture and the Origins of the European World-Economy in the Sixteenth Century. New York: Academic.

Walter, E. V. (1969) Terror and Resistance: A Study of Political Violence. New York: Oxford University Press.

Watters, Pat and Stephen Gillers [eds.] (1973) Investigating the FBI. New York: Ballantine.

Weber, Max (1968) Economy and Society. New York: Bedminster.

——— (1949) The Methodology of the Social Sciences (Edward A. Shils and Henry A. Finch, trans. and eds.). New York: Macmillan.

Weinberg, Ian and Kenneth N. Walker (1969) "Student politics and political systems: toward a typology." American Journal of Sociology 75 (July): 77-96.

Wheeler, Stanton [ed.] (1969) On Record: Files and Dossiers in American Life. New York: Russell Sage.

Wilsnack, Richard W. (1980) "Information control: a conceptual framework for sociological analysis." Urban Life 8 (January): 467-499.

Winslow, Cal (1975) "Sussex smugglers," pp. 119-166 in Douglas Hay et al., Albion's Fatal Tree: Crime and Society in Eighteenth-Century England. New York: Pantheon.

Wolfe, Alan (1973) The Seamy Side of Democracy: Repression in America. New York: David McKay.

Wolff, Robert Paul [ed.] (1971a) The Rule of Law. New York: Simon and Schuster.

——— (1971b) "Afterword," pp. 243-253 in Robert Paul Wolff (ed.) The Rule of Law. New York: Simon and Schuster.

Wolfgang, Marvin E. (1954) "Political crimes and punishments in Renaissance Florence." Journal of Criminal Law, Criminology, and Police Science 44 (January-February): 555-581.

Woods, Donald (1978) Biko. London: Paddington.

Woodward, C. Vann (1957) The Strange Career of Jim Crow. New York: Oxford University Press.

Wright, Erik Olin (1979) Class, Crisis and the State. New York: Schocken.

Yale Law Journal (1955) "Comment: The Communist Control Act of 1954." Yale Law Journal 64 (April): 712-765.

Zimring, Franklin E. and Gordon J. Hawkins (1973) Deterrence: The Legal Threat in Crime Control. Chicago: University of Chicago Press.

AUTHOR INDEX

SUBJECT INDEX

ABOUT THE AUTHOR

AUSTIN T. TURK (B.A., 1956, University of Georgia; M.A., 1959, University of Kentucky; Ph.D., 1962, University of Wisconsin) is Professor of Sociology and Criminology at the University of Toronto, where he is a Senior Fellow of Trinity College. He was formerly Professor of Sociology and Director of the Graduate Training Program in Deviance and Control at Indiana University, and has been a Visiting Professor at the Universities of Natal (1969), Minnesota (1977), and Pennsylvania (1980-1981). He has served as Chair of the Section on Criminology of the American Sociological Association (1975-1976), and as President of the North Central Sociological Association (1976-1977). A Fellow of the American Society of Criminology since 1978, he serves on the Executive Council of that society and on the Board of Directors of the Research Committee for the Sociology of Deviance and Social Control, International Sociological Association. He has been editor or reviewer for numerous social science journals and publishers, and currently serves on the Editorial Board of *Criminology: An Interdisciplinary Journal.* In addition to articles in various research journals and edited volumes, he has authored *Criminality and Legal Order* (1969) and *Legal Sanctioning and Social Control* (1972), and has produced an abridged version of Willem Bonger's *Criminality and Economic Conditions* (1969). His current projects include a volume on conflict theory in sociology and a comparative study of the development, impact, and transformation of legal control structures, focusing upon South Africa and the United States.